Experiential Learning
Rationale, Characteristics, and Assessment

Morris T. Keeton
and Associates

Foreword by Virginia B. Smith

Experiential
Learning

Jossey-Bass Publishers

San Francisco • Washington • London • 1977

The Jossey-Bass Series
in Higher Education

Foreword

Imagine, if you will, a woman in her midsixties presenting herself at your institution, seeking credit for her life experiences. She has never been to college, but she brings with her a list of her experiences, a thick portfolio of reflections written about these experiences, and a collection of commendations on her numerous social contributions. From the list, it becomes evident that she has taught at a private girls' school, helped found a reform school for boys, served as a delegate for her nation to an international organization, aided in the drafting of an important international covenant, spent countless hours visiting wounded servicemen, acted as an official in the ambulance corps, traveled extensively with intensive purpose—visiting the disadvantaged, the ill-housed, and the poor; looking into working conditions in the mines and living conditions in mental hospitals—and then turned her efforts to remedy the conditions she had observed, and delivered over 1000 lectures on a variety of topics. As evidence of her reflection on these activities, she provides you with three published books and copies of several years of syndicated daily columns in newspapers across the nation. As supporting evidence, she offers examples of awards granted her by institutions and organizations throughout the world.

Imagine some possible outcomes for her in assessing her prior experiences at several institutions besides your own. At Metropolitan State University (MSU), assuming she could develop a suitable educational PAC (prior academic credit), she could obtain a bachelor's degree without further educational activities if the assessment team found her experience adequate. But before she would be admitted to MSU, she would have to complete the first two years of college or its equivalent.

At a two-year college in the City University of New York, she could use her prior life experience to earn only about fifteen credits or one semester of work toward the associate of arts degree.

At Empire State College of the State University of New York, assuming appropriate development of educational goals, she could theoretically satisfy all but six months of requirements toward her bachelor's degree; but regardless of experience or educational attainment, Empire State would require six months of residency before awarding the degree.

At a great number of other institutions, her rich life experience would yield only one year of credit. And at still other colleges, no provision would be available for disposing of her request except by denial!

This brief rundown suggests some confusing and perhaps arbitrary forces at work in American higher education. Nevertheless, substantial progress has been made in the past ten years. For when she died, a little more than a decade ago, my mystery woman, whom I am sure you have long since recognized as Eleanor Roosevelt, had received for her social contributions thirty-five honorary doctorates, including one from Oxford, but had never received one earned degree beyond high school. Without an earned degree, she would have been barred from teaching in public schools and disheartened by the classified ads in *The Chronicle of Higher Education,* which demand an earned doctorate as a prerequisite for academic positions in colleges and universities. Despite her thirty-five doctorates, she would have been viewed as taking quite a liberty to refer to herself as Dr. Roosevelt. She would have been unable even now to use much of her life experience toward a doctorate. But today she could at least get a head start on an undergraduate degree.

In the decade following Eleanor Roosevelt's death, the possibility of earning academic credit for learning through experience has grown substantially at most colleges. Four factors have aided this growth:

First, many of us involved in education have begun to realize that we have made too sharp a distinction between life and learning. We were not producing what we had hoped to produce in education, and we began to believe that the way to correct this problem was to provide some work experience within the curriculum. We might not have given Eleanor Roosevelt a degree, but we would have gladly repeated the educational experiences that produced her sense of social responsibility, curiosity, empathy, and analytical skills, had we but known how to do it.

Second, during the past twelve years, the range of subjects taught in college has expanded. Community colleges in large numbers have joined the ranks of higher education, and the curricula of these colleges include occupational and paraprofessional subjects, some of which are taught better through apprenticeship and experiential learning. In addition, concern for affective learning has grown during this period and, here again, learning activities directed toward affective goals usually include experiential elements.

Third, as colleges have become more serious about recruiting and serving adults, it has become clear that some of the precollege activities of these older students look very much like the in-college activities of others. Why should some receive credit and others not?

Fourth, the rhetoric of the day and various external pressures have contributed to the growing demand for credit for life experience. Several commissions have urged greater recognition of learning wherever and whenever it occurs. Civil rights cases, such as *Griggs* v. *Duke* (1971), have questioned the relevance of a degree as a requirement for employment unless the educational activity leading to the degree can be directly related to job performance.

While many factors have aided the increase of credit for experiential learning, there has also been resistance: many faculty within established institutions continue to be reluctant to provide credit for any educational activity not under their supervision. The existence of residence requirements (sometimes state-mandated, sometimes institutional) hampers the full recognition of preenrollment experiential learning. More important than either of these obstacles, we have not yet devised a coherent rationale for crediting experience and for deciding how much credit to give for what experience. For instance, the most important hindrance keeping colleges and universities from incorporating service activities such as the University Year for Action within their programs is the lack of acceptable mechanisms and procedures for granting academic credit for students participating in such activities (Sansbury, 1975, p. IV-1). And the Commission on Non-Traditional Study found that difficulty in assessing nonclassroom learning was almost as important as lack of funds in preventing development of nontraditional programs (Ruyle and Geiselman, 1974, p. 87).

The problem is not just that institutions vary on the amount of credit to grant for similar experiences, but their policies regarding credit seem arbitrary, difficult to explain, and more often than not, based on noneducational reasons. The lack of ability to rationalize credit for experiential learning occurs partly because questions about assessing experience are too often limited to out-of-college experience. The function and role of experience as a part of educational activity wherever it occurs is rarely addressed.

As a matter of fact, the description of much of higher education sounds like some sort of shell game. Ostensibly, students may be spending their time learning about economics or history, but we are told that they are really learning analytical skills. Knowledge of economics or history is only one purpose of the learning: another is the development of analytic ability. For years, many of our educators believed (and some still believe) that learning Latin was an excellent activity—or experience—for learning mental discipline.

Similarly, we rarely question the fact that a chemistry class must include actual student performance of experiments, yet the particular benefits of this type of experiential learning may be attained by most students in the first three or four experiments, while the additional twenty do not constitute new experiential learning but merely repetitions without new learning outcomes. When we look at work resumes, we frequently wonder whether a person has indeed had twenty years of experience or the equivalent of one year of experience twenty times.

What is actually learned in an internship or a year abroad? And why is it that many institutions assume that two years of full-time teaching experience are equivalent to one semester of practice teaching three days a week? Are the learning outcomes so different? Or is it that we are not at all certain what we expect the experience to provide or how to determine that learning has, in fact, occurred? In many experiential components of higher education degrees, we either take a leap of faith, believing that the experience has produced whatever it was that we hoped it would produce, or else we find ourselves, in the absence of adequate assessment of outcomes, using an array of questionable measures of the outcomes of experiential learning.

For example, in college we focus on credits that are related to hours spent in class, and hence the length of an experiential learning activity becomes important to us. Generally we assume that it takes more time to learn on the outside than it does on the inside of a classroom, and thus we usually conclude that it should take much more than a year of accepted experience to equal a year of credit. We forget that if the entire activity of a student is examined, even a full-time student is only attending to his formal studies part-time. If we provide credit for work experience, then why should a student who works full-time not receive as much credit as a full-time student? Experiential learning that takes place in real settings for real reasons may be far more multifaceted than campus-based experiential learning, which is usually less than life-size.

In other instances, we determine credit for an off-campus activity on the basis of its closeness of fit with some existing campus course. But the campus course was presumably designed for quite a different purpose than the experiential activity; if experiential learning has unique benefits, we are not recognizing them by comparing its closeness of fit with nonexperiential classroom activities.

Problems such as these are stimulating educators and researchers to develop more adequate assessment techniques and measures of the outcomes of learning, regardless of whether the learning has been experiential or nonexperiential. The desire to recognize learning wherever and whenever it occurs can no longer be defeated by prejudice against out-of-class and off-campus education. Events of the past decade since the death of Eleanor Roosevelt no longer permit us the luxury of denying academic credit for nonacademic learning. Those colleges and universities that are currently pioneering in the use of better techniques for granting credit for nonacademic learning deserve to be joined by those that even now would deny someone like Eleanor Roosevelt credit toward their regular degrees.

To recognize learning wherever and whenever it occurs, however, requires further advances beyond the current, primitive state of the art of assessing various types of learning outcomes. That art will not progress unless our focus is shifted from the nature and length of the educational activity itself, be it experiential or nonexperiential, to the type of learning outcome desired.

This volume presents the case not only for experiential learning in American higher education but also for its improved assessment. Its case for improvement should not be assumed to apply only, however, to experiential learning. It applies to all learning in all of life.

Washington, D.C.   Virginia B. Smith
January, 1976   Director, Fund for the Improvement
                            of Postsecondary Education

Preface

Virginia Smith's Foreword drives home two observations that state the reasons for the creation of this book—that much learning of great value occurs outside of formal schooling and that people who have achieved such learning should not be handicapped by failure of the credentialing agencies of the society to recognize that learning appropriately.

An adequate response to these two observations is, however, not as easy as might first appear. The reasons for this difficulty are obvious: to recognize such learning properly, there must be accepted standards for credentialing experiential learning. In Eleanor Roosevelt's time, no such standards existed, nor were there recognized bodies whose endorsement of awards of degrees or other credentials would have been given and accepted. Further, to provide such standards of good practice there must be know-how in assessment of experiential learning. To get the know-how, there must have been enough testing and criticism of efforts in credentialing experiential learning that public confidence in the credentialing endeavors will be justified.

By 1973, there had emerged a widespread movement toward the increased use of experiential learning to meet the needs of post–high school learners. The creation in 1971 of the Commission on Non-Traditional Study, headed by Samuel Gould, was testimony to the importance of this movement. In its conclusions, the Commission emphasized the need for development of sound assessment and credentialing practices and standards. The Cooperative Assessment of Experiential Learning (CAEL) was a direct response to this need.

CAEL was broached as an idea in August 1973 to an invitational meeting of individuals and representatives of institutions concerned with the need for action on recommendations of the Commission on Non-Traditional Study. A smaller meeting in November brought together representatives of the Educational Testing Service, some innovating institutions of higher education, and some individuals influential in mainstream institutions of higher education to consider a specific proposal for what turned out to be the CAEL Project. This proposal, after modification, was funded by a grant from the Carnegie Corporation of New York. The organizing meeting for the project took place on March 3–4, 1974.

At the beginning, the project focused on the urgent need to know what was going on in experiential learning in the country, how to evaluate its outcomes, and how to meet the demand for rapid improvement in assessment practices. Because substantial funding was assured for only eighteen months (now extended for at least an additional twenty months), a killing schedule of work was outlined at this very first meeting: a survey of existing practices (published in September, 1974, as the first of the CAEL Working Papers listed in Appendix A), a compendium of assessment methods for the use of CAEL member institutions and others (Working Paper No. 2, September 1974), and a plan for work priorities in the improvement of assessment for staff and institutional activity during the 1974–1975 academic year.

Having set in motion the steps for attending to that work, the CAEL Steering Committee turned to issues of the philosophy,

ownership, and control of the project, the need for a deeper understanding of the nature of experiential learning and its role in postsecondary education, and the conceptual difficulties involved in the
development of good practices and high standards in the assessment
of its outcomes. The committee decided to commission a set of theoretical papers to illuminate, and possibly to guide, the more practical work of CAEL, which was perforce proceeding at breakneck
speed.

This book is a distillation of these commissioned papers. It
may be viewed as a companion piece to the CAEL Working Papers,
the CAEL Resource Book, the CAEL Institutional Reports, the CAEL
Newsletter, and additional materials that to date are of more fugi-
tive form, such as training materials for the CAEL Faculty Development Project and the CAEL Operational Models Project, and a veritable shelf of institutional reports and materials. The Working
Papers are a continuing series of publications on specific problems
in assessment. The Resource Book contains an annotated bibliography of books and other materials relevant to experiential learning
and its assessment, vignettes of the experiential learning programs
of selected institutions, and otherwise unavailable articles of particular utility for this project. The series of Institutional Reports results
from minigrants to CAEL institutions that enabled them to try improvements of assessment of experiential learning and to report their
failures, successes, policy recommendations, and developing assessment tools. The Newsletter is the CAEL house organ, reporting recent events, announcing plans and opportunities, conveying messages
from the committees or staff, and including special features that
may later find their way into the Resource Book.

As the theoretic component in the CAEL library, this book is
a set of independent interpretations rather than a prescriptive credo.
Each contributor has written in his or her own style and in a fashion
that seemed appropriate to the topic. Some of the chapters are detailed while others are general. Some are long; others, short. No
attempt has been made to cause the authors to reach agreement
with one another or even to adopt a univocal language, though on
the latter point the extensive interaction among a number of them
in the CAEL Assemblies and in research on the Working Papers has,
in the sheer interest of mutual understanding, elicited a measure of

common usage. The considerable coherence among the papers results in part because the authors influenced one another, in part because the realities are becoming clear enough to elicit a convergence of findings, and in part because the editors have sought to ferret out needless confusion.

Although theoretical, this book is not meant to be esoteric or unreadable to the laity with special concerns for postsecondary education. Quite the contrary! The book should particularly exercise the minds of those in higher education administration and in faculty and student leadership who are shaping the curricula and quality controls of their institutions and who may be making decisions about whom the institution will serve. It speaks also, however, to those concerned with the priorities and possibilities of our society to whom experiential learning may open up new prospects at advantageous costs in access and dollars. For this reason the book should be of use to legislators, to regulatory and coordinating agencies, and to members of governing boards of institutions of higher education. It bears also upon the need for modes of delivery of educational services other than the traditional institutions of higher education. In all of these respects, of course, the book speaks to students of this time and to that part of the citizenry who are concerned, informed, and capable of thinking through for themselves where the society should be going in these matters and how it should proceed.

To serve these audiences well the book provides three things: In Part One the contributors address first how our society came to its present condition in postsecondary learning options and credentials and what the most important needs are with respect to the role of experiential learning in their improvement. In Part Two the authors provide an analysis of experiential learning: the relationship of experiential learning to information processing, the need to clarify objectives, the potential effect upon higher education of a substantially new priority among objectives (for example, emphasizing the development of maturity) being adopted by many institutions, the effect of new emphases on major arenas of learning upon the conduct of education (for example, a greater emphasis on the use of work sites and environments for deliberately designed learning), and the effect of costs and cost-effectiveness of experiential learning upon the management of higher education enterprises. Finally, in Part Three the writers address the state of the art in the assessment of experiential learning and suggest both approaches to the improvement of assessment practices and standards that should be kept in view as efforts to improve assessment are undertaken.

These three divisions cannot present a comprehensive survey of the varieties of experiential learning nor of the full array of arenas in which it occurs. This fact stems not only from limitations of space but also from CAEL priorities. The Steering Committee decided early in its deliberations that the most useful project results would come from concentrating on certain limited tasks in the improvement of experiential learning assessment. To this end, four priority topics were assigned to four task groups—four elements common to all educational assessment: learning objectives, arenas for learning, instrumentation and methodology of assessment, and the assessors themselves. When the findings of the task groups are combined, they provide four different perspectives on problems of assessment.

We believed that this approach would guarantee better results than would a less diverse attack, yet we recognized that each of these four elements involves an enormous area of inquiry. To bring the assignments of the task groups within bounds, the Steering Committee sought to focus each group on a particular aspect of its domain that might yield the greatest new understanding and practical development for the effort expended. For this purpose, the task group on learning objectives was asked to concentrate on interpersonal skills and personal development—areas in which clearer learning goals are needed and in which the kinds and quantity of learning opportunities are clearly inadequate—in order to encourage institutions to develop offerings responsive to the need by showing how achievement of these skills might be assessed. Similarly, the task group on learning arenas was asked to focus on the sites and setting of work experience, rather than other experiences, and to survey the important features of the landscape of work-education relationships as a model for similar surveys of other types of arena for experiential learning in the future. The task group on instrumentation and methodology was asked to work on the portfolio as a specific tool of assessment. Finally, the task group on assessors gave major attention to the use of expert judgment in assessment. These four priority issues are all addressed in the following chapters.

In the first chapter, I offer a view of our society and its educational and credentialing needs, and examine the directions that experiential learning and credentialing might take in a society where every able-minded adult engages in continuing or recurrent learning. In Chapter Two, Cyril O. Houle offers historical perspective on the roots and earlier uses of experiential learning and on the present need for change in the light of our place in this historical development. In Chapter Three, Alan Gartner analyzes the reasons for the rapid growth of educational credentials and the increasing need for greater educational diversity in recent decades. In Chapter Four, Melvin Tumin warns against the assumption that experiential education can substitute for classroom learning and the belief that changes in educational credentialing can solve economic and employment inequities.

The chapters in Part Two examine, within the perspective provided by Part One, the current state of the art of experiential learning and its management. James S. Coleman, in Chapter Five, opens the part with an analysis of the properties of experiential learning in contrast to those of information assimilation, and provides suggestions about the appropriate mix of these two major modes of learning. Next, stemming from the work of the task group on objectives, Arthur W. Chickering argues the case for adult development as an explicit goal of collegiate learning, based on the use of currently available knowledge of human development in shaping and guiding college education. The next two chapters examine the problems and the possibilities of an enlarged use of the work site as a significant arena for higher learning. Of all the arenas of learning that can and should be used to supplement the resources of the classroom, it has seemed to the CAEL Steering Committee that the most deserving of concerted attention and further exploration are the scenes and setting of employment. In Chapters Seven and Eight, Sheila C. Gordon and Paul Barton depict, from two divergent bases—one closer to higher education and the other to governmental and industrial planning—the important features and problems of work-education relationships: relationships that will be seen as undergoing change, not always necessarily for the better. Finally, in Chapter Nine, George Weathersby and Armand Henault analyze the cost effectiveness of experiential learning and the administrative, political, and economic problems it presents.

Part Three turns to the critical issue of the assessment of experiential learning and to four particular questions about the art of assessment. Robert Kirkwood analyzes the educational and credentialing functions of assessment, with particular emphasis on needed improvements in the assessment of experiential learning as part of current requirements for greater accountability, self-regulation, and consumer protection within higher education. In Chapter Eleven, Aubrey Forrest, Joan Knapp, and Judith Pendergrass examine the portfolio and the narrative transcript as means for improving the instrumentation of assessment and providing reliable and valid information about student learning while at the same time coping with the uniqueness of each student's experiences. In Chapter Twelve, Urban Whitaker asks who are the most appropriate and effective assessors for experiential learning and how their contribution can be brought to bear on the task of good assessment. Finally, in Chapter Thirteen, Warren W. Willingham examines the criteria and standards that assessment of experiential learning must meet if the users of assessment are to have sound evidence at their disposal as an aid to both learning and credentialing.

We attempt in this book, then, both to clarify the conceptual foundations of experiential education and its valid assessment and to depict the current circumstances and conditions that affect the possibilities for improvement. It is our hope that in so doing we contribute to what will be a concerted national effort both to improve postsecondary education and to improve the credentials that it provides.

Acknowledgements

The CAEL project has been marked from the outset by extensive participation from foundations and member and nonmember institutions of higher education throughout the country. To the Carnegie Corporation of New York we are indebted at the outset for both the funding of the initial sixteen months of the CAEL project and for ongoing support of a part of the basic validation studies and

core project for the period ending June 30, 1977. More recently, the
Ford Foundation has made a grant to share with Carnegie the
support of the basic studies and the core project. The Lilly Endow-
ment is supporting the CAEL Faculty Development Project. The
Fund for the Improvement of Postsecondary Education is supporting the CAEL Operational Models Project.

If foundations have been the indispensable financial resource
of CAEL, its member institutions of higher education have been the
indispensable resource for knowledge of experiential education and
for staffing of a critical component of the field research and investi-
gatory effort. The core of this effort has been the task force institutions, initially nine and more recently ten: Antioch College, California State University and Colleges (San Francisco State University),
Community College of Vermont, El Paso Community College, State
University of New York (Empire State College), Florida International University, Massachusetts State College System (Framingham State College), Metropolitan State University, University
of Alabama (New College), and Thomas A. Edison College. The
task force institutions have been complemented by the vast body of
cooperating member and nonmember institutions that have contributed data and other assistance. In the survey of existing practices
in the assessment of experiential education, for example, more than
400 institutions responded to questionnaires; over 40 of these enter-
tained site visits by a combination of faculty members of CAEL institutions and Educational Testing Service staff.

Representatives of member institutions participate in meetings of the CAEL Assembly: the key source of interaction among
participants. One of the basic purposes of CAEL is to share, test, and
coordinate information about assessment, and the Assembly not only
provides this opportunity, it also ensures feedback to the project staff
and committees.

The final critical ingredient to CAEL success has been the
Educational Testing Service, which provided the central management of the project, its unmatched expertise in educational assessment and measurement, and various supporting services from fiscal
management to publications services and conference and workshop
management.

The governance of the CAEL project has been of major import in the conception and development of this book as well as in the whole shaping of the project. The two other members of the CAEL Executive Committee, Jules Pagano of Florida International University and Peter Smith of the Community College of Vermont, acted as an editorial committee responsible for approving the conception of the book and its subject matter and for advising me in the choice of authors and the development of issues to be treated. As Project Director of CAEL and Executive Director for Program Research of Educational Testing Service, Warren W. Willingham also was most active in these areas. When the Executive Committee was enlarged in October 1975 with the addition of George Ayers of Metropolitan State University, Barbara A. Barbato of Webster College, and Sheila C. Gordon of LaGuardia Community College, this expanded body gave the final authorization to publish the book.

Members of the CAEL Steering Committee during the genesis of the volume, listed in Appendix B, received correspondence and offered suggestions that were helpful in raising issues about the choice of essay topics and the argument of the text. Also of assistance were the members of the Implementation Committee listed in Appendix B, who until June 1975 complemented the Steering Committee by serving as field workers on the CAEL Working Papers and "riding herd" on the technical work of the project.

To all of these contributors, and to others who have helped the authors of these chapters with their text—and who are mentioned by the individual authors in their respective chapters—we owe appreciation for helping to make the CAEL project what its name demands: a cooperative endeavor among those seeking to understand the possibilities of experiential education and to aid in the realization of them.

In my office, the preparation of the manuscript has been energetically and generously managed by Vashti Lewis and Inge Hyder, with timely reinforcement from Judith Williams.

Columbia, Maryland   Morris T. Keeton
January 1976

Contents

Contributors

PAUL E. BARTON, *Senior consultant, National Manpower Institute, Washington, D.C.*

ARTHUR W. CHICKERING, *vice president, Empire State College, Saratoga Springs, New York.*

JAMES S. COLEMAN, *professor of sociology, The University of Chicago, Chicago, Illinois.*

AUBREY FORREST, *director, college outcomes measure project, American College Testing, Iowa City, Iowa.*

ALAN P. GARTNER, *professor, Center for the Advanced Study of Education, Graduate School and University Center, City University of New York, and co-director, New Human Services Institute, New York, New York.*

SHEILA C. GORDON, *associate dean, Division of Cooperative Education, LaGuardia Community College, New York.*

ARMAND J. HENAULT, JR., *executive director, Code, Inc., Belmont, Massachusetts.*

CYRIL O. HOULE, *professor of education, The University of Chicago, Illinois.*

MORRIS T. KEETON, *vice president and provost, Antioch College, Yellow Springs, Ohio.*

ROBERT KIRKWOOD, *executive secretary, Commission on Higher Education, Middle States, Philadelphia, Pennsylvania.*

JOAN E. KNAPP, *executive assistant for special projects, Educational Testing Service, Princeton, New Jersey.*

JUDITH PENDERGRASS, *director of admissions and records, Metropolitan State University, St. Paul, Minnesota.*

VIRGINIA B. SMITH, *director, Fund for the Improvement of Postsecondary Education, Washington, D.C.*

MELVIN TUMIN, *professor of sociology and anthropology, Princeton University; consulting senior sociologist, Educational Testing Service, Princeton, New Jersey.*

GEORGE WEATHERSBY, *associate professor, Graduate School of Education, Harvard University, Cambridge, Massachusetts.*

URBAN G. WHITAKER, *dean, undergraduate studies, San Francisco State University, San Francisco, California.*

WARREN W. WILLINGHAM, *executive director, program research, Educational Testing Service, Princeton, New Jersey.*

Experiential Learning
Rationale, Characteristics, and Assessment

Chapter One

Credentials for the
Learning Society

Morris T. Keeton

The amalgam of freedom, justice, and mutual concern is the spiritual capital of American society. As with the preparation of medicines, however, our specific compounding of these potent elements has often involved some very damaging contaminants. Our forebears thought that freedom for male property holders of a certain ethnic makeup was the pure element of genuine liberty. It was, in fact, but the crudest of approximations of the invaluable essence of freedom itself. The meaning of justice in the seventeenth century was devoid of contemporary insights into the consequences of retribution, the injustices entrenched within the content of the law itself, our biases of race and culture, and the further injustices wrought by such causes as unequal access to competent legal services. Our predecessors thought that mutual concern could be adequately implemented through an economic system producing great disparities of income and wealth among the people. The founders of the nation meant to offset a portion of that disparity

1

through charity, first dispensed voluntarily by a few and later mandated in massive amounts by redistribution of means through taxation.

It would be a gross mistake to imagine that we have made an end even of identifying these sources of inequity and inefficiency, much less of extracting them from the chemistry of our culture. Yet it is clear that the educational system of our society has itself reflected, even protected from detection and removal, many of the aspects of cultural lag that limit the ability of society to realize its potential. Among the worst of our sins has been the acceptance of existing limitations as to who should have access to education, what the range of legitimate learning options should be, what degree of respect should be given to different kinds of learning and learners, and how institutions of postsecondary education should be organized and coordinated. These limitations have in turn rested upon limits within our vision of the best available strategies for instruction and learning and of the ways in which the learning that has occurred can be identified and reported.

To the very last of these concerns the Cooperative Assessment of Experiential Learning (CAEL) has addressed itself. Its achievement is and can only be a modest one. But neither the large task of which it is a part, nor the vision which that task can serve is a modest matter. They are, on the contrary, Promethean in their scope and aspiration.

The Rationale for CAEL

Underlying the decision to initiate CAEL was agreement that our present educational practices do not fulfill our needs: they inadequately represent our current understanding of knowledge, the nature of our society, the concept of experiential learning, and the ways in which knowledge and competence can be achieved, recognized, and certified. It has long been recognized that knowledge without experiential content is not truly knowledge. "Concepts without percepts are empty; percepts without concepts are blind," as Kant put it. Plato distinguished between the kind of knowledge that the vision of the Forms provided and opinions that guide action in the everyday world; and the latter, if they were to be true opinions, had to rest upon experience with that world. Similarly, competence in action can only be reliably developed in action, real or simulated; and the greater the reliance upon simulation, the greater the likelihood that some critical and unexpected factor at play in reality may render the preparation inadequate.

There is no question, then, that in some sense experiential content is an essential of genuine empirical knowledge—knowledge of the everyday world of human action. Questions arise when we move from this insight to the task of developing such knowledge and the competency to apply it to achieving our aims in life. Education involves problems of time, cost, risk, and effectiveness. If learning to fly an airplane, for example, is done through simulation, a prospective pilot may learn more safely, more inexpensively, and with adequate effectiveness for at least the first times than at the controls in actual flight under the scrutiny of an experienced pilot. While simulation is not as faithful to the realities of flight as would be a trip up to 35,000 feet altitude with a Boeing 747, it is a kind of experience, and as such is far more likely to produce a competent pilot in short order than would a process of reading books about flying. Reading is also experience; but it is experience of reading, not of flying. The most effective experience in learning is an experience of what is to be learned or of some relatively faithful approximation of the essentials of the learning sought.

Learning through firsthand experience of full-bodied realities or through simulations of high faithfulness to those realities tends to be expensive. It is costly of time, of other resources, of the coinage in which we pay for their use, and sometimes in risks (as would be the piloting by an utterly inexperienced pilot). Therefore, societies arrive at trade-offs between the effectiveness of educational methods and their costs. In Chapter Two, Cyril O. Houle traces a portion of the history of these trade-offs in Western society.

The nature of modern American society is complex, fast moving, interdependent, and highly powered. Such a society can miss its potential by far, or it can rapidly destroy itself, if it is not guided by genuine knowledge prudently and competently applied to critical points of needed effect. Thus in the choices that we must make about trade-offs between effectiveness and various costs we face complex issues in which inadequate knowledge could have disastrous effects—for example, a miscalculation as to the polluting effects of the production and use of nuclear energy—but in which the costs of gaining adequate knowledge may be almost intolerable relative to other human needs. In the example just cited, the experience needed to gain reliable knowledge may be found, not in some readily available work in any of numerous plants, but only in a very expensive and elaborate laboratory designed specifically for nuclear research.

It is not surprising, given the rapidity and scope of contemporary social change, that our educational systems should have come to provide a very poor fit between the mix of experiential and other modes of learning provided and the ideal mixes that would optimize the trade-offs between affordable costs and the needed degrees of reliability of knowledge and competence. As the example of reading has already suggested, the classroom is itself an arena of experience—but only of certain limited kinds of experience relative to those activities of later life or of concurrent extraclassroom life that students must perform. The classroom, because it is economical relative to other places for learning that embody or simulate realities more closely, is a preferred vehicle of education from the perspective of cost. And it once was also the most accessible and convenient vehicle of instruction. But what about effectiveness? And today, when constant reeducation during many varieties of life circumstance may be required, what about accessibility?

The pendulum-swing back toward greater uses of extraclassroom experiential learning antedated CAEL. CAEL arose primarily because of the fact that experience is no guarantor of learning. Just as the memorization of words may carry little or no understanding, so the exposure to many experiences may—contrary to the old proverb —elicit little learning, or not the right kind. One must know what has been learned and what, among various modes of experiential learning, may in the future best be employed as strategies of learning. CAEL, in short, was to contribute to the improvement of policies and methods of assessment of extraclassroom learning in order to assist, in turn, suppliers and consumers of education to do their respective tasks in learning better.

The concept of experiential learning employed in these writings may be defined (except as otherwise indicated) as learning as it occurs outside of classrooms. For a more comprehensive grasp of educational theory and methodology, however, it is important to remember that problems of assessment of learning outcomes are in many respects alike in the two different arenas: the state of the art of assessment of learning outcomes from classroom learning is itself far from satisfactory. There could be more surprising ironies than the possibility that the effect of CAEL upon such assessment might be as worthwhile as its planned effects upon the assessment of extraclassroom learning.

Given these reasons for CAEL, which derive from the nature of knowledge and its development and from the nature of contemporary society and its problems in achieving the desired kind of life for its people, what can be said by way of introduction to the present book about the form that American society of the near future—ten to twenty-five years from 1975—should take in its educational and credentialing systems? What options for learning should be offered? What kinds of credentials should be available? And by what means should they be obtainable?

Learning Options of the Late 1900s

First, what should be, in Houle's phrase, "the nature and shape of modern postsecondary education"? What options should it offer the learner? What systems will deliver the aid one needs for the learning options chosen?

The postsecondary learning of the future will and should differ markedly from that of today in content and meaning, in timing and accessibility to learners, in systems through which instructional services are delivered, in the balance between experiential learning and information processing, and in the ways it is combined with other interests and activities of life. Not, I think, that we will perceive radical discontinuities as these changes come about, but the signs of need for these transitions are already present in current learning systems.

Especially in the social sciences and in the humanities there should be, within the next quarter century, not only an ongoing accumulating of new data, but emerging new intellectual syntheses. These new organizing concepts will begin to do for the study of so-

ciety and of human concerns what such syntheses as those of New-
ton and Einstein did for the grasp of physical sciences data and systems. The recent significant development of new organizing concepts
in the biological sciences are not at an end, and even in the most
developed science—physics—discoveries continue. In the social sciences, a veritable crowd of contending ideas presses for further application and for the pursuit of implications that might transform
still other elements of our view of society. Consider, for example,
perspectives being put forward on norms of family structures, on
forms of deviance that need not be viewed as criminal or as evidence
of mental illness, on the effects of total institutions upon both in-
mates and keepers, on the stages and interplay of different aspects
of human development (treated by Arthur Chickering in Chapter
Six), on the understanding of organizational effectiveness, and even
on the evaluation of the effectiveness of cultures in meeting the
wants and needs of the peoples who populate those cultures.

To return to the first of these examples, Goffman contends
(1961) that present American laws show a bias toward the nuclear
family as normative for all family life, but this family is impossible
or inadvisable for large numbers of parents and children. For them,
the norm either dictates a harmful prescription or condemns them
for something they cannot help. Szasz (1956), in the second example, points out that a considerable proportion of both crime and
mental illness—with their attendant costs and problems—is created
by our attitudes rather than being inherent as consequences of the
deviance itself. On these and other ideas, present knowledge and
knowledge-in-the-making, which need to be widely shared, is inadequately disseminated in our society. As the creation and dissemina-
tion of knowledge proceed, they will generate need for a reconstruction of the whole frame of reference on which we hang the facts and
views with which we organize our lives and try to serve our wants
and needs.

Thus, in the society of the near future, we should have not
just more knowledge to learn, but transformed views of the world
around us. In this sense, the meanings of what we learn should have
changed. Implied in this expectation is the consequence that what
we are learning today will need to be unlearned tomorrow; we

should be preparing to continue updating ourselves if we wish to enjoy and understand the life of which we will be a part.

To be up-to-date in such a world will not permit us to treat new learning as a matter principally of sabbaticals for everyone, whether they be days off or years off. In the world of tomorrow, as Paul Barton recommends in Chapter Eight and as the O'Toole report to the President earlier observed, we should have devised a new structuring of the relationships among work, study, and leisure. Perhaps the concepts of work, study, and leisure will themselves be among those transformed by added knowledge. If by 1980 the right of older adults to have their "twelfth year" of governmentally-assisted learning has been established, then by 2000 this right will surely have advanced to a fourteenth or a sixteenth. But perhaps by then the labeling of education achieved by year levels will also have lost most of its force and meaning.

Such a change in labeling will not happen, however, unless more potent alternatives take hold. One alternative might be some combination of the cumulative personal portfolio and educational passport, which are discussed by Forrest, Knapp, and Pendergrass in Chapter Eleven. Rating and grading will surely not have disappeared, nor do I believe that they should, but at least the bases for recognized ratings and scalings will have grown in diversity and complexity. Warren Willingham in Chapter Thirteen addresses himself to the kinds of criteria that should govern the development of such alternatives.

I do not mean that sabbaticals should be foresworn or discouraged in the America soon to be. They will have to be supplemented increasingly by a combination of daily study to keep abreast in activities from mechanics to medical service and occasional special seminars or workshops for intensive briefing or internship in everything from the new laws governing urban development to the latest techniques of managing group processes. And if an individual's tastes in leisure include bridge, or citizen action for equal rights, or new trends in diet and meditation, there should be readily available opportunities for both improvement of the individual's competence and reconsideration of his or her outlook.

A most notable need in respect to access for learners to appropriate education and to efficient service delivery to them is the need for all-encompassing local or regional systems. These should provide the prospective learner with several things: an overview of his or her options, reliable and pertinent information about the costs and benefits of the various options, practical and flexible means of drawing upon the various resources to create individually tailored learning programs, and assurance that among the various colleges and other enterprises providing services there is an efficient use of community resources. The arrangements should avoid making the learner captive of any of the institutions involved, but should make feasible the use of the best choice among their various offerings.

Imagine, for example, a region with a convenient array of counseling and diagnostic centers. (One is in the making today in Syracuse, New York, through the Regional Learning Service of Central New York.) Such centers should have no pecuniary or other interest in where the student studies or what learning options he or she chooses. They should, however, have comprehensive knowledge and materials about these options and knowledgeable counselors who can assist a student in choosing wisely. Imagine further a region in which all of the libraries and resource banks of intellectual materials are interconnected by one catalog and reference-service system, with membership in that system being a right of citizenship in the region and with daily delivery of wanted materials by wire or by courier to anyone anywhere in that region. Imagine a regional agreement among businesses, agencies of all levels of government, schools, libraries, and other service agencies whereby space available is shared, staff time for upgrading of competence is allocated for learning as part of work, and staff competent to teach are encouraged to devote some of their time each year to the pool of teaching talent deployed among the instructional institutions. Suppose that the right to learn has been interpreted as permitting the learner to spend his or her allotment in any prudent pattern that makes possible a learning plan developed after use of one of the regional diagnostic and counseling centers. Suppose, finally, that state and federal aids to institutions of postsecondary education have been rationalized to foster efficiency in this total system and to foster competition among service deliverers in doing a good job for the resources used.

In such a system for educational services, the student could enter at his or her choice, any of several diagnostic and mentor-service centers (among which competition in quality of service might be fostered). With the aid of the chosen center, the student could gain access to any of the learning options for which he or she qualified and through which he or she could most effectively and conveniently be assisted to learn.

An analogy that might assist in envisaging this future would be to that of a client with a minor health problem and a desire to take precautions to improve his or her health. This person joins a health maintenance insurance plan and turns to the nearest intake office that has diagnostic and patient advisory services. This intake office does not serve a single hospital or a single physician group, but can refer the client to any of these resources as well as to specialized health services of any type. The insurance payments to the health maintenance plan cover most of the costs of the service, wherever obtained. The deliverers of service include both publicly operated clinics and privately managed professional services and clinics. The system combines choice for the client, specialization for the service deliverers, a financing system designed to equalize opportunity and access to the best medical and health services, and choice of institutional contexts for the professionals. No matter what the working hours, health needs, or other circumstances of the client are, a method can be worked out for addressing those needs with reasonable effectiveness and cost. There are, of course, no fully functioning health care systems of this kind today; but there are systems which, in health services, more nearly approximate this model than in education. Enormous problems of management control, democratization of governance and management, cost controls, and quality controls will attend the effort to create such systems.

These are suppositions difficult to imagine working well, but the vision, however far from present realities or from likely achievements of the next quarter century, provides a measuring stick against which to assess the adequacy of our present conceptions and achievements. Seen as a target toward which to aim, this vision could also help us avoid waste motion and unfruitfully divided counsel in getting there. Whether it may be preferable in education to muddle through in a less thoroughly coordinated way is no idle question, but one that raises the critical issue of whether the freedom that is of such great value to all individual and institutional participants may be of greater import than all the rationality and efficiency of a scheme that on paper makes more sense. The testing of this question may be one of the critical agendas of the next quarter century.

In tracing the history of experiential learning, Houle speaks of efforts over past centuries "to move outward from cloistered instruction in basic texts toward direct though supplementary firsthand experience." I believe that academia on the whole remains too radically separated, in its work with a predominantly young clientele, from the experiential inputs essential to the best instruction. As James Coleman's research and analysis suggest (see Chapter Five), there is no one ideal mix of information processing and experiential learning for every learning need. But there are many ways to create a mix that badly misses even a reasonable approximation of the ideal, and we have generally returned too much to the cloister, in mind if not in physical location. Therefore, Houle is quite correct in saying, not only that we may "have to invent as many new structures, concepts, and processes as did our forefathers in the last hundred years," but that "above all we must cultivate a new spirit that accepts the educative value and worth of all experience, not merely that which is devoted to scholarly study or which is guided at every step by professors."

The new infusion of postsecondary education by older students will also constitute an infusion of experiential materials, if recent experiences mixing such students with younger ones are a fair weather vane. As Chickering's survey of research on human development indicates, the immaturity of young students in ego development, conceptual development, and moral development constrains the uses of both ideas and experience. Assuming that he is correct, educators should adjust education for young people to cope with these limitations. Educators should also devise ways to reengage learners in later years, as personal development and enlarging experience prepare them to fulfill their further potential.

It was once thought that the best years of life for learning were over by the time a person had reached intermediate school. But such thoughts sprang from a conception of learning as the assimilation of information, rather than as the transformation of experience into ever more maturing insights and the development of the self into an ever more responsive and responsible participant in a mutually fulfilling society. Now that the larger possibilities of learning begin to be clearer, we must rethink that old limitation, and with it we must reconsider the resulting restrictions which, in that mistaken belief, were put upon the institutions of learning.

Credentials of the Late 1900s

What are the credentials that should be available in the highly credential-conscious society of the future? The need for credentials is a subclass of the need for information. In a highly mobile society composed of very large numbers of people with a complex division of labor and diversity of leisure interests, the number of ways in which a person may want to be credentialed and may, for occupational or leisure purposes, need to be credentialed, are much greater than in a compact, stable, undifferentiated culture.

Even now a person may be a certified swimmer, some kind of master at duplicate bridge, a journeyman in a skilled trade or two, or the holder of a high school equivalency certificate, associate of arts diploma, American passport, credit card, or health plan card. An individual may be tagged as an available and qualified donor of organs in case of death, qualified to drive heavy vehicles as well as passenger vehicles, entitled to bail in case of traffic violation arrests, and so on. We joke about the number of credit cards we carry, and the cards we carry are increasingly those accepted in many places—comprehensive credentials to economize on the number of distinctive credentials we need to carry. Away from home, our credit cards define us. Even in the local community, we are, in this sense, often "away from home."

Is the answer in educational credentials comparable to that in credit credentials—a comprehensive passport? In the case of a citizenship credential, the passport typically expires after a time and must be renewed as a verification that it is still valid. The same is generally true for drivers' licenses. Should educational credential papers carry, like some milk cartons and containers of other perishables, a cutoff date beyond which they cannot be counted upon to be of the quality and potency originally certified? And what about the credentials we do not carry, but which are carried about us— the files in the Internal Revenue Service, the university registrar office, the credit bureaus, perhaps even the Federal Bureau of Investigation or the National Security Agency or the Civil Service? Even as we want privacy, we want an accurate if not always a full record at our disposal.

As is true in the fields of credit, health, and recreation, I believe that there is no one comprehensive and adequate answer to the credentialing needs of educational systems. And separation between fields (for example, between recreational and occupational skills) cannot be fully maintained. It is possible, however, to say some things about credentials that will be of great utility, and to examine some ways in which these credentials can be improved in their validity and reliability.

First, I believe that the credit-hour system, even as it is being pushed to its ultimate limits in some forms of the Continuing Education Unit (CEU), has passed its prime. On the face of the matter, the credit hour appears to be a "time-served" measure. But for both the noncredit CEU and the credit-bearing semester hour or quarter hour (which represents not one-quarter of an hour, but an hour a week for a three-month term or quarter year), there are reservations that take away the standardizing effect of the credential: the hour must have been in a classroom context or its equivalent, it must have been with an appropriately qualified faculty member or in an equivalent kind of effort, and it is accompanied by a further name and number that define the subject matter covered, the level of difficulty, or like information (none of which are sufficiently standardized to make the credentials interchangeable from place to place).

Educational credit is often compared with monetary currencies by those who wish to explain its utility. Insofar as registrars accept credit transcripts in exchange, the system works (at least until faculty members discover the need for makeup work or the repetition that is taking place with some students). But before we become disaffected with the ambiguities of educational credit, we should remember that monetary currencies serve their purpose even when there are many coinages and when no one of them is entirely stable or univocal in its meaning. When currencies fluctuate too rapidly in worth, or when the value of one at home is at too great a variance from its comparative value abroad, problems arise for at least some of the users. Perhaps the problem with the present educational credits is not that their meaning is subject to some variance and ambiguity, but that the number of different currencies has become too large and the degrees of variance and ambiguity too great for the usual functions of exchange and facilitation to work with reasonable convenience and effectiveness. In this circumstance, what can be offered as an alleviation of the ills of the current system?

One of the shortcomings of the present system has been its omissions. Until very recently, learning achieved in the military services generally went unrecognized in higher education circles. The Commission on Educational Credit of the American Council on Education has remedied this difficulty with its *Guide to the Evaluation of Educational Experiences in the Armed Forces* (Miller and Sullivan, 1974). The *Guide* recommends appropriate credit awards on the basis of its study of the relationship between what is learned in the various modes of military instruction and comparable instructional situations within institutions of higher education. This commission is presently at work extending a similar service for the outcomes of instruction provided under the auspices of private corporations and other institutions and associations. This gain in comprehensiveness of coverage is one that should not be lost in whatever systems of credentialing later emerge in postsecondary education.

Another of the shortcomings of educational credentialing is the magnitude and multiplicity of exchange barriers that accompany it. The Servicemen's Opportunity College has been invented to deal with some of these. For example, a person moving frequently by reason of occupational or other shifts not under his control would encounter: maximum allowable amounts of transfer credit accepted, regardless of their merit; minimum residency requirements (amounts of credit to be earned in this new place); exclusions of types of credit regardless of other circumstances; exclusions of credit from certain types of institutions (unaccredited, for example). These limitations hold regardless of how much the student might actually have learned. But why should only former servicemen be helped to overcome such barriers?

None of the recent amendments or remedies for the credit-hour system has attacked its Achilles heel. The Achilles heel is that credit hours do not signify directly what has been learned or achieved, but represent a time-served measure that correlates only roughly and in unknown ways and degrees with what has been learned. This difficulty is easy to name but not so easy to conjure away.

The most cogent and forthright alternative is to state precisely and understandably what has been learned. There are problems with both ends of this program, however: first with stating precisely what has been learned, and then with the receiving party's understanding clearly what the sending party has presumably stated with precision. Before addressing these problems, let me say that the proposal advocated here is that a cooperative effort be made to establish a few reasonably well-defined credentials as models of more useful coinages than are presently available. There ought to be no illusions to the effect that doing so will be easy, that it will remove all variability and ambiguity, or that it will quickly displace the present educational credit system. What is proposed is the beginning of an alternative system that will gain in value as it is refined and extended, but that can only be developed over a long period of time and at considerable cost in intellectual effort as well as in the coin of the realm. The well-defined credentials proposed should meet the following specifications:

With respect to comprehensiveness, two types of credential should be developed: a comprehensive passport, periodically updated both as to new learnings and as to expired competencies; and specialized credentials directed to more restricted purposes.

With respect to source of issuance, no attempt should be made to develop a single central credit bank, as proposed in numerous circles; but one or more national consortia should be formed to take responsibility for consultation and evaluation services with respect to good practices in the issuance of educational credentials. If we may think of all colleges and universities and of some other institutions as credit banks in educational credit, and if we are attentive to the volume and diversity of their crediting tasks, I think it reasonable to aim, not for uniformity and centralization in their work, but for a gradual development of improved practices and mutual understandings among them about terminology, coinages, exchange policies, and the like.

With respect to the overall objective of the educational credentialing system, we should seek for mass delivery of individualized credentials. That is, almost everyone will need his educational passport and his specialized certificates of learning. Unless that need is met, and met in a way that is tailored to the needs of each individual, then our credentials problem is not solved.

As to the question of norm-referenced versus criterion-referenced credentials, I believe that the most practicable system will be one that incorporates both kinds of certification under different circumstances. The point may be briefly grasped if we note that in some endeavors, it does not matter how one's performance compares with that of other people so long as it measures up to a specified level of proficiency (in such cases a criterion-referenced credential is needed); in other endeavors, the employer or the person being certified may need to know where the latter stands relative to alternative employees or alternative competitors (this case calls for a norm-referenced rating). An individual who wished not to enter into competitions might manage to avoid most norm-referenced ratings, but for most people there will be some occasions when they will need and want norm-referenced information about themselves.

As to the most urgent undone tasks, I believe that they include the development of really good models of criterion-referenced standards and credentials. I think it is not unfair to say that until such standards are defined, even the meaning of norm-referenced standards is unclear. And when criterion-referenced standards are in hand, one can often create a usable set of local norms. We manage to have a fuzzy yet practicable grasp of some norms today; without denigrating these, I believe that, rather than enlarging that domain, we must generate well-defined criteria-in-the-concrete that will provide some well-defined credentials.

Within this task, I recommend that the approach taken be one of creating what I have elsewhere called *standards files* and *standards libraries*. A standards file is a combination of three things.

First, it states in abstract terms the objective to be met by an adequate performance at a named level of proficiency. Suppose, for example, that the objective is proficiency in the writing of an essay in standard English. The criteria of literacy (spelling, grammar, punctuation), organization, style, validity of reasoning, and so forth, would be stated in abstract terms. Second, it contains examples of products or performances that meet that abstractly stated level of proficiency on that criterion. On the writing standard, for example, sample student essays with their rating would be in the file. Third, it contains analytic statements by qualified assessors as to the respects in which the products or performances shown do and do not fulfill the terms of the objective. In the writing example, the assessors would state how well or how badly each sample essay fulfilled each of the abstract criteria.

Given only the abstract statement of criterion, different interpreters can read quite different meanings and expectations into the situation. Given only the statement and the products, different interpreters can decide that the products fulfill the statement for quite different reasons. Given all three, differences of interpretation will continue, but the gaps in understanding can be narrowed within reasonable bounds.

With regard to the conduct of credentialing services, there will be a continuing need for their appraisal and improvement. This task might well be the province of regional accrediting bodies. An alternative locus of the responsibility might be state regulatory authorities. The latter might enforce minimum standards (criterion-referenced?) and the former might take on the task of developing improved practices and of improving institutional performance beyond minimum acceptable levels.

With respect to the development of model credentials, both comprehensive and specialized, there will be an ongoing need for new and better credentials. Being as skeptical of monopolies in non-profit as in profit-making endeavors, I believe that the research and development involved in such an ongoing effort should be divided among a number of providers. How many will depend in part on the cost of doing any credential well and in part on the aggregate resources that can be mustered for the work.

As to the modeling of credentialing services, though I have

argued against centralization and uniformity in the issuance of credentials, I believe at the same time that the difficulty of creating good credentials is so severe and the need so great that it would be beneficial if there were a few concerted endeavors to develop substantially better credentials than single institutions of higher education can presently provide. Such endeavors might well take the form of consortial efforts on the part of combinations of educational research institutions, assessment institutions, and teaching institutions. If these efforts were successful, many colleges and universities might contract for the services in the future rather than create their own method of credentials issuance. Such a development would, in my view, be much preferable to an effort to take away the credentialing role from existing credit banks.

In summary, we live in a highly interdependent society in which it is desirable both that individuals and institutions have considerable freedom to make their own choices and pursue their own priorities and that accountability to one another is provided, since the effects of these choices interact upon one another. Often we do not know what the effects of our choices will be until some time after we have had to choose. An example in point is the sluggishness of formal educational systems in providing learning opportunities that are most appropriate to the upcoming needs of their students and of the society. In the United States, for example, colleges throughout the nineteenth century resisted providing options for learning in the sciences—long after it was clear to some people that the culture needed an infusion of understanding that the sciences could best provide. Similarly, the arts were outcast in most academic institutions until the early decades of the twentieth century.

Just as past decades saw lags in the responsiveness of higher education to individual and social needs, so today the options for learning offered by postsecondary institutions are fewer than they should be, sometimes of a kind and in a mix that is less than ideal for societal needs and often coupled with status distinctions that are dysfunctional for social betterment. The university classroom has been greatly enriched in recent years as an arena providing significant aids to learning by the use of audio-visual materials, simulation, games, role-playing, and other methods adding direct or vicarious experience of realities other than those normal to earlier classrooms.

Even so, the classroom cannot bear the economic burden of providing all experiences essential to the most efficient or the highest quality education alone, and our present policies for educational credentials cannot serve the whole range of needs essential to our interdependent and credentialing society.

A further infusion of experiential learning and improvements in its assessment and credentialing within American higher education, in short, will not only enlarge our vision of the aims of education. They will help us meet with limited resources the greatly enlarging demands for postsecondary education that will characterize the learning society of the future.

᠎᠎᠎

Chapter Two

Deep Traditions of Experiential Learning

᠎᠎

Cyril O. Houle

This chapter was commissioned to provide a historical perspective tracing precedents in both philosophical and cultural traditions and in educational practice for the use of experiential learning as an essential strategy, or as a desirable supplemental strategy, for postsecondary education. Within the context of CAEL, special attention was to be given to assessment.

One who tries to fulfill this assignment has few guides to help him. Historians of education have not considered the evaluation of learning outcomes, however achieved, to be a topic worthy of sustained attention. Similarly, specialists in educational evaluation do not seem to care where they have been but only where they are or where they are going. Such are the conclusions of the *Encyclopedia of Educational Research,* of eminent historians and evaluators whom I have consulted, and of a young associate of mine who has a passion for bibliography.* Every promising citation led to frustra-

---

* His name is Richard Yanikoski and I am indebted to him for help on this paper.

tion. Even John S. Brubacher's magisterial volume, *A History of the Problems of Education,* which chronicles seventeen major topics with exquisite care, does not include among them evaluation, assessment, or credentialing.

Yet there is no lack of monographic, literary, or anecdotal material on the basis of which such a history could be written. In the second century before Christ, for example, the Chinese developed their examinations for leadership in the national public service. This system of assessment continued for more than two thousand years until it was abolished in 1905. By the period of the Sung dynasty from 960 to 1279 A.D., when European universities were slowly coalescing into their original primitive structures, the assessment system of China was already highly sophisticated. Edward Kracke (1972), a leading authority, has noted that "candidates were subjected to successive elimination through written tests on three levels, more than a hundred beginning the ordeal for each one who emerged successful; . . . The effort to devise objective and meaningful tests for practical qualities led to long contentions over the subject matter and testing methods . . . examinees were identified by number only and three examiners read each paper."

Furthermore, the distinction between formal instruction and instruction distilled in some fashion from raw experience is far from new. In Plato's *Meno,* an uneducated slave boy is guided by Socrates to rediscover the Pythagorean theorem: the square of the hypotenuse of a right triangle equals the sum of the squares of the other two sides. Where did the slave get the knowledge that could lead him to this complicated conclusion? Socrates said that the slave had been born with it in his soul, but the text shows that even an illiterate could have acquired the basic knowledge from his observation of life. This anecdote illustrates a fundamental question— perhaps *the* fundamental question—of human learning. Can anything worth knowing be taught or must the individual discover it for himself? Socrates educated the slave boy, but only by helping him put in proper form the facts that either God or experience had already given him.

However much we might learn from such episodes and anecdotes, they have not yet been shaped by historians to lead in a direct line to our modern concern with the assessment of experiential learning. In this brief chapter, the traditions of experiential learning will be approached in three ways. First, we shall look as broadly as possible at the whole tapestry of postsecondary education since it emerged from the dark mists of the Middle Ages, trying to see how experiential learning was woven into the overall design. Such a comprehensive view will reveal patterns but only obscure details. Second, we shall focus somewhat more sharply than before on one part of that tapestry, the last third of the nineteenth century, when titanic battles were fought over the inclusion of experiential learning in the postsecondary curriculum. Finally, we shall glance at the immediate past, the part of the tapestry that we ourselves are weaving, not so much to recount its brief history as to show why the modern concern with experiential learning is different from that of a century ago.

Medieval Patterns

As Europeans moved out of the medieval into the modern world, five major conceptions or systems of advanced learning were in operation. Some overlapped one another while others stood sharply separate. Each one either accepted or rejected experiential learning.

The most famous and long-lasting of these systems was that of the universities, which had evolved from cathedral schools and specialized centers of professional training to become places of general study. These universities coalesced very slowly over a period of a century and a half starting at the close of the eleventh century. By 1500, there were still only seventy of them. The general academic pattern was that of a guild of scholars, teaching and studying a broad range of subjects and given an enduring life by a charter of incorporation. This institution, with its first dominant origins in Bologna and Paris, has gradually spread around the world, being constantly adapted in terms of personal leadership and social influence, but still retaining in every time and place at least some vestiges of its original identity.

For seven hundred years, the learning that the university offered was essentially the mastery by the student of content provided by books and lectures. In addition, suppleness of wit was fostered by disputation and debate but always on general theoretical subjects. The purpose of such education was identified by Shakespeare in the first scene of *Love's Labour's Lost* when Berowne asked the King of Navarre: "What is the end of study? let me know." The King responds: "Why that to know what else we should not know." Berowne tries to clarify the point: "Things hid and barr'd, you mean, from common sense?" And the king concludes the passage: "Ay, that is study's god-like recompense."

Experiential learning, like common sense, had no place in the university curriculum. Even medicine was treated deductively in terms of the rules of learned doctors. Occasionally a student had a chance to dissect a cadaver, but he might be severely punished if he was found doing so. Gross anatomy was governed for centuries by theories that could have been refuted by direct observation. Medical schools had been in existence for seven to eight centuries before Harvey demonstrated in 1628 that blood constantly recirculates through the body as the result of the pumping of the heart. But no content field should be singled out for attention. Throughout the university, experiential learning had no part in formal training, though it certainly had a great deal to do with the day-to-day life of the students.

The second form of advanced education was that of apprenticeship training carried out by craft guilds. In this system, a master practitioner accepted learners into his office, workshop, or atelier, and usually into his home as well. The guild, a controlling corporation of masters, might regulate the nature and sequence of instruction but usually the individual master ruled the process, assigning work to his subordinates, reaping the benefits of their labor, and, when he felt that they had the proper competence, knowledge, and appreciation of craftsmanship, attesting to their ability or recommending them for examinations set by the guild. When the tests were passed, the youth became a journeyman, working for the master. Some time later, if he could amass sufficient funds, if an opening occurred in the guild membership, and if the quality of his work had shown steady improvement, the journeyman might set himself up as a master. To prove his worth, he often had to present a masterpiece for judgment by his future peers.

The apprenticeship system was based at every level upon

experiential learning of the most immediate and practical kind and therefore differed very sharply from the teaching of the university. The original word for a guild of any sort had been *universitas,* but when learned scholars gained their charters and established their institutions, they took the term with them. As time went on, the crafts on which the guilds were based often became more complex. The barber evolved into the surgeon and the apothecary into the pharmacist or physician. Thus, theoretical and experiential educational systems eventually existed side by side, the first in the universities and the second in the guilds.

The third pattern of advanced learning was that of chivalry. The wild and ruthless warriors who ruled Europe in early medieval times gradually came under the influence of the Roman church, thereby adding religious devotion and courtly arts to the skills of the fighter. This system of learning was designed for the upper class but sometimes was extended to an unusually brave or strong individual of less exalted birth. The general pattern of education was clear, though far from universal in its application. A boy stayed with the ladies of the court until he was about seven. From then until he was about fourteen, he acted as his father's personal servant within the castle and was taught the rudiments of language and of courtly life. Then he became a squire and his more warlike training began, including service with his father on the battlefield. Finally, at some appropriate time around the age of twenty, when he was judged to have learned the arts of war, to have acquired the graces of a courtier, and to have mastered such manly skills as hunting, jousting, and falconry, he was made a knight in an elaborate and costly ceremony.

The chivalric system of education was almost entirely experiential. The ladies of the court taught the young boy what they would or could; so did the tutors who trained him in at least the rudiments of literacy. But the important skills, knowledge, and attitudes were gained in the courtyard, the tourney-ground, the forest, and the battlefield. Competency-based assessment was stark and clear. The following list of some of the required proficiencies comes from a fifteenth-century manual (I have modernized the language slightly). The squire must be able to: "spring upon a horse while fully armed; to exercise himself in running; to strike for a length of time with the axe or club; to dance and do somersaults entirely armed except for his helmet; to mount on horseback behind one of his comrades, by barely laying his hands on his sleeve; to raise himself betwixt two partition walls to any height, by placing his back against one, and his knees and hands against the other; to mount a ladder, placed against a tower, upon the reverse or under side, soley by the aid of his hands, and without touching the rounds with his feet; to throw the javelin; and to pitch the bar" (Scott, 1824)'.

Chaucer suggests some additional competencies. Of the squire in the Canterbury Tales, he notes that

> *He could make songs and poems and recite,*
> *Knew how to joust, to dance, to draw, to write.*
> *He loved so hotly that when dawn grew pale*
> *He'd slept as little as a nightingale.*
> *Courteous he was, and humble, willing, able;*
> *He carved to serve his father at the table.*

As I said, it was a highly experiential course of study.

The fourth kind of education was well understood but never developed into a single system. It was a sporadic and often unorganized continuation of learning throughout life that occurred in monasteries, courts, and private libraries. In a sense, it was all experiential learning, if that term is defined to include self-directed study. The priests, kings, courtiers, and solitary scholars who studied in adulthood tended to turn away from the rawness of the life about them and to take refuge in literary or abstract study. A few, however, such as Montaigne and Machiavelli, sought direct experience because they wanted to distill principles or policies from it.

The fifth kind of education is hard to understand by anyone pigeonholed in modern behavioral science. Such education centers not upon the active processes of teaching and learning but upon the belief that God or nature can cause a person to be born with wisdom, skill, or sensitiveness or can instill it subsequently with no action or forethought on his or her part. Socrates believed that the soul contained at least the seeds of all knowledge. In the Middle Ages, divine intervention was elevated to a cardinal principle, perhaps because the universities could not educate all the priests the church needed. Even today some religious denominations believe that God can "call" people directly. Upon the proper certification by an established church that an individual has been thus singled out, the state grants him or her the right to perform legally binding sacraments.

Even in the secular realm, either God or genetic selection must give special talents to some individuals. How else explain Joan of Arc's capacity at the age of nineteen to have mastered the arts of warfare and politics and then, at her trial, to confound her learned and subtle judges, or Mozart's ability to compose more than two hundred works by the age of eighteen? It might be argued that results such as these are brought about by self-directed learning, but any such answer is likely to be countered with another question. How do highly talented individuals gain the capacity and drive to learn so much so quickly?

Therefore, in addition to formal instruction and experiential learning, we must add a third way to gain competence, knowledge, or sensitiveness, though we cannot be sure whether that third way is innate or instilled. Unfortunately, neither God nor nature has yet shown me how to cope with it as a learning system.

Nineteenth Century Demands

The basic patterns of formal education and experiential learning underwent constant change throughout the medieval period and in subsequent ages. The city-state gave way to the nation and to the establishment of professionalized armed services that diminished the need for a nobleman to consider his prime obligation to be the waging of war. The industrial society grew up within the feudal way of life and eventually destroyed its essence though retaining some of its rituals. Apprenticeship was no longer based on a craft system but became far more organized and complex than before. The Council of Trent and the seminaries at St. Sulpice and elsewhere established the need for a better-educated clergy and for new ways for creating it. The rise of widespread literacy multiplied the centers for continuing education and gave them countless new forms, such as voluntary associations and public libraries and museums. Other patterns and institutions of schooling arose as the scope of content and clientele broadened.

But universities and colleges flourished, chiefly because they retained their identities while changing their functions and processes. They continue to cling to a few of their medieval customs, but these old forms cannot mask new realities. The university (and the separate college based, in some fashion, upon it) remained fairly constant in purpose, program, and procedure until about 1810 in Germany, about 1850 in England, and about 1870 in the United States. Then suddenly—or so it seemed—important demands began to be made upon campus traditionalists. The essence of this change appeared to be an insistence that the university undertake some of the tasks of providing advanced knowledge that the other systems of education had once offered but could no longer maintain.

The chivalric tradition was dead in all but name, but society still had to have leaders and they had to be educated. How could the masters of the new industrial society be best acculturated? Where were the arts of modern warfare to be taught? The old professions were joined by engineering, agriculture, architecture, dentistry, and other occupations that formerly had been considered crafts. Where were they to be learned? God might still give an initial sense of vocation to a future priest or parson but increasingly sophisticated congregations required religious leaders whose intellects had been disciplined by a close study of theology and who knew how to manage the institutional complexities of a church. Centers of self-guided lifelong learning were no longer adequate. Adults wanted to be taught. Who would teach them? The answer to all these questions seemed to be: the university.

As we have seen, the older systems of education that were being abandoned usually had been based on experiential learning, a form of instruction far different from the traditional way of work of the college or university. But by the 1860s, the need for a combination of systematic instruction and experiential learning was becoming clear on both sides of the Atlantic. Perhaps the most profound enunciation of basic principles on this point was—and still is—that provided by John Stuart Mill in 1867 in his inaugural address as Rector of St. Andrews University in Scotland. Education includes, he said, not only "whatever we do for ourselves, and whatever is done for us by others, for the express purpose of bringing us somewhat nearer to the perfection of our nature; it does more: in its largest acceptation, it comprehends even the indirect effects produced on character and on the human faculties, by things of which the direct purposes are quite different; by laws, by forms of government, by the industrial arts, by modes of social life; nay, even by physical facts not dependent on human will; by climate, soil, and local position. Whatever helps to shape the human being—to make the individual what he is, or hinder him from being what he is not—is part of his education" (1874, p. 333).

Having thus distinguished between formal instruction and experiential learning, Mill went on to describe how they should be harmoniously combined in a liberal arts curriculum. Modern foreign language should not be taught; it is much more readily acquired by living in a country where it is spoken than by recitations in a classroom. Both general literature and history were written to be read by the individual reader; why should they become the subject of courses? Comparative literature and historiography, on the other hand, require the interpretation of sophisticated analysis. Therefore they must be taught. In a systematic and dispassionate fashion, Mill (who had perhaps the best formal education of any man who ever lived) proceeded to make subtle and complex judgments about experiential and didactic instruction. Many will disagree with some of his conclusions today—and his opponents would presumably include professors of modern language, literature, and history —but nobody can deny the rigor with which he distinguished in his address between formal instruction and experiential learning. In surveying his own life, he made an equally profound distinction between the two. One chapter of his *Autobiography* is entitled "Last Stage of Education and First of Self-Education."

In the United States, Jefferson and others had put forth grand schemes of university reform; none of them had come to fruition. The Jacksonians had long tried to change the character of formal education but had been routed by the forces of conservatism. By the 1850s, discussion tended to focus first on whether practical subjects should be included in the curriculum. Francis Wayland, Yale University, the Morrill Act, and Ezra Cornell, in

their separate ways, made it clear that the answer must be yes. Then
the issue became one of content and method. Congressman Morrill
confessed to the Yale faculty that he did not have a firm grasp of
what his own bill meant and said that its "title" (by which he
presumably meant its purpose to "provide colleges for the benefit
of agriculture and the mechanic arts") was not a happy one (True,
1929, pp. 99, 107–108). So far as agriculture was concerned, little
useful content existed. A course that expounded on agricultural
references in the Bible might be admirable in intent but do nothing
to increase the crop yield. And where were the professors to be
found? One of them imported from England by Cornell was a rare
specimen. A nearby farmer told President White that the visitor
from abroad "don't know nothin' about corn and he don't believe
in punkins." As Dr. White went on to say, "to see him come out of
his room at Cascadilla at nine or ten in the morning in an elegant
cutaway coat and yellow kid gloves, walking through the fields
where 'corn and punkins' grew, examining them curiously, at arm's
length, with his elegant rattan cane, did not inspire confidence"
(Lord, 1939, p. 40).

In 1871, the presidents and other officials of some of the
more practical colleges assembled in Chicago in an exploratory ses-
sion to survey the situation. The transcript of that meeting shows
that some of the excesses of experiential learning with which we
are all too familiar today were also practiced by our professional
ancestors. For example, one of their major activities was to pre-
scribe practical work. Young men and women who had lived on
farms all their lives were assigned to three or four hours of labor
a day in fields or kitchens on the assumption that it would educate
them. One worthy president noted that "we are striving to make, as
soon as may be, all the work strictly educational. The student of
pomology, for example, goes into the orchard and vineyard; the
student in stockbreeding has the care of stock; the botanist works
in the garden, and the mechanic in the workshop; and the young
ladies, under a competent superintendent, do nearly all the labor
of the kitchen, the dining room and the bakery" (*An Early View
of the Land-Grant Colleges*, 1967, p. 56–57). But there were
doubters. In Pennsylvania, the work consisted of "picking up thousands of four-horse loads of stone. . . . The question was asked:

'Did the labor required of the student have any connection with their immediate studies.' " The answer was "Not so much as it ought to have" (p. ix–x).

Even while such responses were being given, however, the interaction of theoretical and practical study was already under way. At the 1871 conference, the Illinois representative said: "In the study of natural history and the sciences of observation and experiment, we make a mistake in setting [a student] to learn that from books. When he studies natural history, he studies what cannot be put into a book, but is outside of it. I recollect with what eagerness, when I had been poring over Latin and Greek for so long, I commenced the study of Geology and Botany, and the interest with which I went about it; but this zeal evaporated in nine out of ten [students] before we had been three weeks in the class, simply because we were studying not Botany, but descriptions of Botany" (*An Early View of Land-Grant Colleges*, 1967, p. 67).

During the rest of the nineteenth century and the beginning of the twentieth, the growth of planned experiential learning steadily continued. In previous times, when the curriculum was rigidly uniform, only textbooks were needed, and university libraries were largely irrelevant to formal learning. As the possible areas of content expanded, alternative books and reading lists were required, and supplementary reading was encouraged. The library then became the heart of the university. Formerly, if professors of science used physical material at all, they merely gave demonstrations; but now students began to be required to perform experiments themselves. Unknown compounds were analyzed by budding chemists, and engineering students surveyed areas of the campus that would eventually be surveyed by thousands of their successors.

Then out of the laboratory came the movement toward life. The Johns Hopkins University medical school in 1876 began its emphasis on practical applications of knowledge. William Osler, its first Professor of Medicine, not only required his students to perform autopsies but took them with him to observe his treatment of patients. So unusual was this procedure that when Osler left to become Regius Professor of Medicine at Oxford, he said in his farewell address "I desire no other epitaph—no hurry about it, I may say—than the statement that I taught medical students in the

wards" *(Aequanimitas,* 1906, p. 407). Abraham Flexner used
Johns Hopkins as his model for all medical schools and thereby
revolutionized the training of physicians and surgeons. Eventually,
in profession after profession, the practicum or guided simulation
became essential, though it might be called *practice teaching, moot
court, field work,* or some other similar term.

Since World War II a further step has been taken: to educate the student so that he knows not only how to solve problems
but also how to deal with normal conditions of life. In a medical
school, for example, the beginning student might well be assigned
a three-generational family. It is then his task for the next four
years to understand its needs and to refer all its members who need
help to qualified practitioners. Thus his chief goal becomes the
maintenance of health, not the remediation of disease. Similarly,
though less spectacularly, the year or term abroad, the summer field
trip, the campus museum or art collection, the musical or theatrical
series, and the conducted tour have all become parts of regulated
campus experience.

In the great expansion of American education that began as
universities moved away from a wholly prescribed curriculum, our
predecessors had to invent many new structures, concepts, and processes: the elective system, credits, courses, departments, concentration and distribution of subject matter, majors, minors, departments, honor points, residence requirements, transcripts, and all
the other ways by which faculty, students, and the new platoons
of administrators could make postsecondary education work. Some
of these changes came easily but others could not be adopted without Homeric battles. This expanded system, less than a century old,
grew up at the same time that academicians were finding ways to
incorporate experiential learning into the curriculum. Two hours
of laboratory work is the equivalent of one hour of lecture. Theoretical instruction precedes the practicum. The preclinical and the
clinical years are separated; thus, in medicine, the learner is, in
due succession, a premedical student, a preclinical student, an extern,
an intern, and a resident. Finally, at long last, four of the medieval
conceptions and systems—and, for all I know, five—have been at
least partially consolidated into one modern system that includes
both theoretical and experiential learning.

Current Problems

At least four overlapping kinds of students, however, most of them adults, find that this nineteenth century model of post-secondary education does not yet work very well for them. The first is made up of people who gained their experience before they acquired their theory and who have learned the latter inductively, if at all. The second includes those individuals who prefer to guide their own learning or whose pattern of life requires such self-direction. The third is made up of people who want guided but personalized programs of study, usually including experiential learning. The fourth comprises a vast and heterogeneous collection of people, each of whom wants to compile a record of previous learning (courses, test results, successful work accomplishments, and other forms of assessment) into the basis for further study for a degree, believing that in this synergistic process the whole of his knowledge will become greater than the sum of its parts. The effort to serve these four kinds of learners—and perhaps others—provides the distinctive difference between the innovations in experiential learning of a hundred years ago and those that will be the subject of the other chapters in this book.

The pattern of educational change has been continuous rather than abrupt. Even while the system that was created between 1855 and 1875 was being spread and consolidated during the ensuing century, at least a few institutions were trying to meet the needs of the four kinds of students just identified. A steadily increasing stream of men and women came to college and university counsellors to ask whether, by independent study or by inductively deriving principles from experience, they could reap the same formal awards given to those who had gone through the lockstep of formal education. Cases of this sort began to appear in the nineteenth century and the number increased after World War I, when extension degrees became more common than before. Many a counsellor was generous in responding. It was hard to insist, for example, that a trilingual student must meet the foreign language requirement for a degree by taking twelve semester hours of a fourth language. The counsellor might still require 120 semester hours of credit for a baccalaureate, but the student was given slightly more freedom than before in choosing electives.

As time went on, however, mere substitution did not seem adequate to meet the needs of the sophisticated adults and young people who presented themselves. Perhaps the first significant breakthrough came in the management training programs of major schools of business during World War II. If the experienced middle-level or senior managers who graduated from such programs proved to be more knowledgeable about the intricacies of the business world than recent graduates of the standard curriculum, why should they be denied the M.B.A.? Another thrust toward change came from the secondary school. Results from the General Education Test showed that about 70 percent of those who took it could earn a high school diploma or its equivalent, though they had, on the average, only ten years of schooling, and that those who entered college by passing the test did about as well as those who secured diplomas in the usual way. If the GED worked for high school, why should a similar pattern not be used in postsecondary education? Thus the Advanced Placement Program, the College Level Examination Program, and other systems were initiated.

Among undergraduate institutions, Brooklyn College in 1954 was perhaps the first to award credits directly to adults on the basis of the assessment of previous experience. The University of Oklahoma in 1957 designed the first new baccalaureate degree for adults that wholly abandoned the credit structure, established a new conception of the degree itself, and formulated new ways of meeting its requirements. But other institutions were soon to follow, and histories and descriptions of them, only briefly sketched here, are being carefully recorded (see Houle, 1973; Meyer, 1975; Medsker and others, 1975; and Hall, 1975). These pioneers have their differences but share a belief in the educative power of direct and usually unguided experience, a value that Mill celebrated more than a century ago and that Adlai Stevenson expressed even more strongly in 1963 not long before he died: "What a man knows at sixty that he did not know at twenty may boil down to something like this: The knowledge he has acquired with age is not the knowledge of formulas, or forms of words, but of people, places and actions—a knowledge not gained by words, but by touch, sight, sound, victories, failures, sleeplessness, devotion, love—the human experiences and emotions of this earth and of oneself and of other men; and perhaps, too, a little faith, and a little reverence of things you cannot see" (1963, p. 24).

Future Directions

The chronicles of modern institutional experience and the pioneering work of CAEL will, in time, aid some synthesizing scholar to discern the nature and shape of modern postsecondary education. Macrosociologists call the age in which we live the *postindustrial society* because they cannot yet identify the dominant characteristic by which it will later be known. We refer to *nontraditional learning* because we have not been able to perceive the guiding principles that will give coherence to our new systems of education. The traditions of the modern American university are far from ancient but they are very powerful. Who can say which changes or adaptations of them will eventually prove to be most important, particularly since we have become the heirs of the traditions not only of the university but also of other systems and conceptions, some of which were based on experience, some on scholarship, and some on innate or instilled knowledge?

More than a hundred years ago, universities began to try to deal more creatively than before with experiential and scholarly learning, balancing them in various curricula and institutions. The first effort was to move outward from cloistered instruction in basic texts toward direct though supplementary firsthand experience. Now we are taking another giant step in the effort to discover how guided or unguided experience (often community-based) can provide the skill, knowledge, and sensitiveness that colleges and universities can accept as worthy accomplishments, even, in some cases, for the full satisfaction of degree requirements. To succeed, we may have to invent as many new structures, concepts, and processes as did our forefathers in the last hundred years. Above all we must cultivate a new spirit that accepts the educative value and worth of all experience, not merely that which is devoted to scholarly study or which is guided at every step by professors. Perhaps when our work is permeated by that value, it will provide the synthesizing principle that will describe the educational era that we have already entered but for which we do not yet have a name.

╾╾╾╾╾╾╾╾╾╾╾╾╾╾╾╾╾╾╾╾╾╾╾╾╾╾╾╾╾╾╾╾╾╾╾╾╾╾╾

Chapter Three

Credentialing
the Disenfranchised

╾╾╾╾╾╾╾╾╾╾╾╾╾╾╾╾╾╾╾╾╾╾╾╾╾╾╾╾╾╾╾╾╾╾╾╾╾╾╾

Alan P. Gartner

That schools and colleges fail large numbers of children both literally and figuratively is nothing new. Colin Greer in *The Great School Legend* (1973) documents that this has been characteristic of our society since the inception of public education. In the early 1900s, children of immigrant groups—Jews, Italians, Irish, Swedes —were often labeled uneducable and incorrigible by the schools. This is the same label that has been applied in recent years to blacks and other minority groups.

Since the older immigrant groups succeeded in society despite being denied education, is there any need for special concern now? There is a difference—one that has led to an educational crisis of grave proportions. Schools and colleges now are asked to do a bigger job than ever before, and their failure to do that job is far more visible and has much more serious consequences than in the early 1900s.

Our educational institutions have always been relatively successful with their middle-class clientele. Teachers tend to teach

34

upward or at least to prefer students who are like themselves, with a school culture and a home culture that match. This is often formulated as the home reinforcing the school, but there is no reason why it could not be formulated in exactly the reverse fashion. That is, children from middle-class homes do well in school because the school reinforces the home and all the expectations that exist in the home.

The earlier immigrants who succeeded economically had children who were, indeed, relatively successful in the schools. Here the school in essence rubber-stamped what had occurred economically and culturally in the family. This is as true today among middle-class blacks and other minorities as it was in previous years for Jews, Italians, and the like, and for colleges as well as for schools.

With the rapid expansion of the private sector in the early twentieth century, people who failed in school or left school early still had many opportunities to get ahead in business. This is no longer the case. A major finding of the Jencks study, *Inequality* (1972), that has frequently been overlooked is that at each educational level, the credential was decisive in terms of future income. For example, an individual who has a high school diploma earns a good deal more than one who does not, and college graduates earn more than high school graduates. (Note, however, the continuing reality of racial discrimination with the resulting "color tax" of approximately a degree level: nonwhites at a given degree level earn on the average, the same as whites at the next lower degree level.) More lucrative and prestigious jobs requiring more education and higher credentials are now in the expanding services sector—in government, education, health, research, and the professions—not in factories and small businesses.

It is not so possible now to fail in school and college and still acquire mobility into these occupations and professions. The result is an educational crisis that is considerably more serious than that experienced in the early years of the twentieth century.

Importance of Credentials

In recent years, credentialism, the requirement of academic credentials in order to obtain various positions, has been severely

criticized. Ivar Berg (1970) has cogently argued that large numbers
of positions in this society demand academic qualifications that
have little to do with the job itself and in some cases may even lead
to dissatisfaction in overqualified (that is, overeducated) workers.
Berg suggests that on-the-job training related to job specifications is
more satisfactory and should not be entangled with academic qualifications. Others have noted that some highly skilled positions, such
as Federal Aviation Agency controllers, do not even require a college degree. Large numbers of poor people echo this argument
sharply. Blacks and other minorities, on one hand, have been excluded from various positions because they lack credentials and, on
the other, have been victimized by highly credentialed teachers and
other social service workers who have been less than effective. It appears that many professionals, including teachers and social workers,
have been overeducated and undertrained.

   Another criticism of credentialism comes from state and
federal agencies and their personnel departments. Reflecting the
middle-class taxpayer's bias toward economy and efficiency, they
are balking at paying for academic credentials that are only indi-
rectly related to the job. As a result of various productivity and
manpower studies, these agencies are restructuring tasks previously
done by professionals so that many portions can be done by trained
technicians.

   Other attacks on credentialism have come from the courts
which, in a series of decisions following *Griggs* v. *Duke* (1971),
ruled against the use of aptitude and intelligence tests as well as
formal education prerequisites when these cannot be shown to be
directly related to job performance requirements. A further argument has come from some futurologists and social forecasters who
predict that in the future work will be much more automated and
will therefore require less education.

   In light of these thrusts, one might anticipate that credentialism is dying. But, on the contrary, I think that education and credentials will be more sought after than ever by an increasing percentage of the population. For one thing, now that the minorities
and the poor are beginning to become involved not only in traditional higher education programs but also in new paraprofessional
work-study programs and continuing and recurring education—all

of which are more related to jobs and provide more direct paths to the acquisition of professional and semiprofessional job skills—they are demanding access to the credential. For them, it is a way into the system, and they want the respect and the status it brings. It is, to use S. M. Miller's phrase, a new form of income—not a substitute for cash income, but a desired addition. Now that they are in the ballgame, they do not want to be told that the credential is worthless, something that only a few snobbish academics would want.

The critique of credentialism will likely lead the educational establishment to make the credential more appropriate to job functioning by moving toward various types of performance-based accountability. It is fair to predict the expansion of new routes to higher level professional positions combining various degrees of work experience and education, the inclusion of many more job-related skills and work-oriented education in higher educational training; the expansion of all types of recurrent and continuing education to enhance life in general—both to add to the learner's status and to enhance the capacity to perform well in, and to enjoy, leisure activities. Instead of being debunked and deprecated, the credential will come to reflect actual qualifications and skills. There is already evidence that various professions and institutions of higher education are moving toward performance criteria. The New York State Board of Higher Education has required all teacher-training institutions to establish performance standards. More than half of the states are now involved to some extent in performance requirements for teachers; Washington, Minnesota, Texas, and Florida have been leaders in this effort.

The rapidly proliferating community colleges are much concerned with providing students technical qualifications along with the new (and not always useful) credential, the associate of arts degree. Trade unions, particularly in the public service field, are developing their own colleges (an example is the District Council 37, American Federation of State, County and Municipal Employees campus of the College of New Rochelle) and their own career-oriented programs as ways to allow their members to upgrade themselves through acquiring both skills and credentials. The rapid escalation of various external degree programs, such as the University Without Walls of the Union for Experimenting Colleges and Universities, and of all types of cooperative education programs provide a further illustration of the attempt to combine an academic credential and work-relevant training and experience. The advent of open enrollment should also be seen in this context. And, of course, the work of CAEL itself is further evidence to this point.

Discrimination and Credentials

That education has been an elite activity can hardly be questioned. Defenders of the traditional would have us believe that it was (and is) no more than an elite of ability. Whatever the merits of that argument, and it is one with less merit than at first meets the eye, the discriminatory aspects—by race, class, sex, and age—make clear that it has been (and is) an elite of status. Basically, higher education has been designed for white middle-class children who can attend residential programs. Most everything we do in higher education is in response to or in the context of that ideal model. In this sense, the disenfranchised are the nonyoung, non-white, non-middle- and upper-class, non-full-time, and to a considerable extent, the nonmale students. It is not surprising, therefore, that the education that has been sanctioned has been that most available to the elite; education that was uniquely available to those with the resources and status that allowed for extended periods of uninterrupted withdrawal from the world of work.

It is not only that educational institutions are elite; for, if that were the case, then open admissions would itself be a sufficient solution. Rather, what we are suggesting is that the very type of learning that is sanctioned by these institutions is elite; that is, it can only be differentially available to those in the society who are non-white rather than white, poor rather than rich, older rather than younger, female rather than male, employed rather than with the resources to be unemployed. The failure, then, to provide—and establish as equal in status—modes of learning amenable to these groups insures the continuing elite characteristics of education, a social good that has both instrumental use and use in itself. To state this last point in a different way, the social good itself has been misconceived. It has been envisaged through eyes and minds biased by their own interests that do not include equally legitimate interests of still larger numbers of people. While educational institutions cannot by the mere manipulation of credentials reform a society's biases in its vision of its own good, the institutions and the credentials should at least not add to the barriers against fair treatment to all, and might be of modest help in clarifying the need for change.

We live in a society not only where credentials are of increasing importance, as Morris Keeton has noted in Chapter One, but where the alternatives for people without credentials are increasingly small. The Office of Education has mounted episodic campaigns about careers that can be followed without a college degree, but even the designers of these campaigns might well be asked whether they want their sons and daughters to follow one of those careers. Are not such careers really for other young people rather than our children? Our children ought to get a college degree, a master's degree, a Ph.D., and all the perquisites that they involve, while the people we are trying to convince that degrees are irrelevant and unimportant are disproportionately nonwhite and non-middle- or upper-class.

Experiential learning is a mode of learning more amenable to the realities of the lives of those who have been excluded from the traditional mode. And as the traditional mode requires assessment measures, so, too, does experiential learning. These measures must be recognized as more than "functionally equivalent" achievements, to use Tumin's phrase from the next chapter. Not to do so would amount to continuing to accept the traditional mode of learning as the norm by defining experiential learning as a variant of or substitute for the superior mode of education. It would always be seen as (and thus always be) second-class, and so would those whose learning was experiential.

But it is not only for reasons of equity that the assessment of experiential learning must go beyond functionally equivalent achievements. Although there are areas of commonality between the traditional and the experiential modes of learning, and there should be developed common assessment means or perhaps two-way conversion scales between them, experiential learning may be sufficiently different from the traditional (at least in some important ways) as to require basically different forms of assessment. While we have been willing to open up the game of assessment, we have not really looked at it closely. In a football game, the right standard is "first down and ten yards to go"—but in baseball the same standard does not work, because baseball is a different game. We may need a different set of standards for experiential learning: not better or worse standards, but different.

There are some areas of knowledge that are better approached via an experiential learning mode and others that are better approached via the traditional learning mode. Similarly, there are some learners who find it easier to approach material via an experiential mode and others who favor the traditional. Ultimately what must be attested to is what the individual knows, what he or she can do, and of what use it is to someone else.

The task, then, is clear: to establish standards and procedures of assessing and credentialing experiential learning that have a quality of rigor of their own—separate from but equivalent to those used regarding the traditional mode of learning. Indeed, it is not too much to hope that they will surpass the others.

Chapter Four

Valid and Invalid Rationales

Melvin Tumin

The contrast between nonexperiential and experiential learning is one between more and less abstract, and more and less linguistic, sets of symbols that are employed in the transactions in which learning takes place, whether in the classroom, at the mill bench, or on the golf course. Several points can be made about departures from the more abstract and linguistic methods of traditional school learning.

First, many schools and colleges have been trying experiential methods of learning in one way or another for a long time. For example, John Dewey told of experiential learning eloquently and in a way not yet improved upon, in *The Child and the Curriculum* and *The School and Society*, first published in 1900 and 1902 respectively. Consider his view of experiential learning (1902, pp. 11–12): "No number of object lessons, got up as object lessons for the sake of giving information, can afford even the shadow of a substitute for acquaintance with the plants and animals of the farm and garden acquired through actual living among them and caring for them. . . . Verbal memory can be trained in committing tasks, a certain discipline of the reasoning powers can be acquired through lessons in science and mathematics; but, after all, this is somewhat remote and shadowy compared with the training of attention and of judgment that is acquired in having to do things with a real motive behind and a real outcome ahead."

Dewey cautions us to eliminate the gap that supposedly exists between the child's experience and the subject matter that is the object of study. In this view, the elements present in the child's experience and the elements that operate in developing the subject matter are essentially of the same order. "Abandon the notion of subject matter as something fixed and ready-made in itself, outside the child's experience; cease thinking of the child's experience as also something hard and fast; see it as something fluent, embryonic, vital; and we realize that the child and the curriculum are simply two points which define a single process. Just as two points define a straight line, so the present standpoint of the child and the facts and truths of studies define instruction. It is continuous reconstruction, moving from the child's present experience out into that represented by the organized bodies of truth that we call studies" (1958, p. 11).

Second, Dewey also gave us the sound psychological and sociological basis in theory for these developments in his pioneering and sadly overlooked *Human Nature and Conduct,* first published in 1922. Consider, for instance, the terse brilliance of the following brief paragraph regarding the role of aims or ends in human activity (1957, p. 209):

> *In fact, ends are ends-in-view or aims. They arise out of natural effects or consequences which in the beginning are hit upon, stumbled upon so far as any purpose is concerned. Men like some of the consequences and dislike others. Henceforth (or till attraction and repulsion alter) attaining or averting similar consequences are aims or ends. These consequences constitute the meaning and value of an activity as it comes under deliberation. Meantime of course imagina-*

tion is busy. Old consequences are enhanced, recombined, modified in imagination. Invention operates. Actual consequences, that is effects which have happened in the past, become possible future consequences of acts still to be performed. This operation of imaginative thought complicates the relation of ends to activity, but it does not alter the substantial fact: Ends are foreseen consequences which arise in the course of activity and which are employed to give added meaning and to direct its further course. They are in no sense ends of action. In being ends of deliberation, they are redirecting pivots in action.

Third, numerous educational philosophers have long argued that the important question is not that of classroom learning versus experiential learning, but rather of proper learning versus inadequate and superficial learning, whether in class or out. It follows that we can try to improve the education of all students with a sound concept of experiential learning, as well as try to improve traditional forms of learning for those who seem less able for a variety of reasons to make the grade in the present modalities.

But recently a new rationale has developed for increased emphasis on experiential learning. Our earnest determination to make schools and colleges equally appropriate and fitting for all learners, whatever the differences in their backgrounds and prior training, has raised the question of whether experiences other than traditional classroom exercises will help the less academically inclined (those less attuned to abstraction) become more motivated to learn, feel more comfortable in the learning process, and tap more deeply their reservoirs of talents and abilities. Through various extracurricular and noncurricular experiences, in and out of academic institutions, can some functional equivalents of what is supposedly learned in the traditional curriculum be made more accessible to students who find the traditional academic curriculum unattractive or to others who are alienated from the learning experiences required for some version of normative success in this society?

CAEL emphasis on assessment of experiential learning can be interpreted as focusing precisely on this question of functionally equivalent achievement. Simply put, one rationale for trying experiential learning and assessing its outcomes is provided by the presence in American society of an academically alienated and an academically disadvantaged population in the midst of a largely academically oriented one, and by the fact that certification of academically equivalent achievement is indispensable for access to the middle- and upper-class careers available in our society. If, therefore, we desire success for such people, and want to try to make life more richly available to them, then of course we must try to see what other forms of learning experiences can take the place of traditional forms.

But if we really are concerned with the relative lack of success of some people with the traditional curriculum as compared with the greater success of many, we must face the deeply disturbing question of whether nontraditional experiences can be certified as functionally equivalent substitutes for traditional academic achievements. This effort at changing certification is substantially different from the attempt either to improve the learning of all through experiential involvements or to improve the traditional learning of the disadvantaged through nontraditional means.

If one does not seek for functionally equivalent learnings, but rather for functionally equivalent certification processes, it may not matter much whether the learning has taken place. If we set up alternative forms or criteria of certification, and if those alternative criteria are accepted as functionally equivalent for occupational location and placement, then we might become increasingly indifferent to what has been learned in the process. But I believe that this outcome is most improbable. The certification process is far more complex than the concept of functionally equivalent learning suggests. Even if we knew that we could obtain such learning outside the traditional modalities, a very large gap would remain between the number and percentage of people who are certified for better positions and life styles in this society and those who actually attain them.

To pose the issue another way, functionally equivalent learning achieved experientially may be a necessary but not a sufficient condition for the total process of certification as it is traditionally practiced. However many people who are trained in new ways in various new behavioral skills are admitted into the occupational system by fulfilling new criteria of qualification and placement, their number will be infinitesimally small compared to all their counterparts who are not so admitted. Moreover, any attempt to introduce larger numbers into established occupational slots by the use of new criteria of eligibility will simply result, as it has already, in a perceivable, steady deterioration of the estimated value of the occupation and, in turn, of the payoff of the occupation. Thus I think we can safely assume that whatever new room the established order makes for a handful of differently trained and equipped people, it is not likely to make room for many, nor be willing, without fundamental social change not yet in sight, to redefine the nature of our class-structured society.

Our enduring commitment to greater equality in the face of persisting inequality makes us seek almost desperately for ways to break the self-reinforcing circle of inequality. We no longer are content to characterize American society as an open society or to applaud our types and rates of socioeconomic mobility. Compensatory educational programs and all forms of so-called affirmative action, including poorly disguised quota systems, are now rationalized (and perhaps properly, depending on one's values) as worth the while. They represent the overspill of our common guilt about long-standing inequality and our common determination to do something of some consequence about that inequality. And we are prodded by the quite understandable and, from their point of view, quite justifiable indignation of the traditionally disadvantaged for whom the rest of society cannot change fast or deeply enough.

But we shall make terrible and bitter mistakes here if we do not distinguish, first, between learning and certification; and second, just as important, among three quite different aspects of the world of equality and inequality: equality of opportunity, equality of situation, and equity.

The first, equality of opportunity, exists when nothing except the differences in native talents appropriate to valued tasks and achievements determine the relative success and failure of competitors. Children get the same chance to have their relevant talents identified, trained, and recruited, so that only their genetic makeup matters in the outcome.

Assuming that there is competitive selection and commensurate rewarding of the most talented, then, of course, total equality of opportunity fits hand in glove with total inequality of situation. In that regard, Jencks was quite right, and his critics quite wrong, when Jencks argued that no matter how equalitarian the schools are they can make no difference in the unequal distribution of the good things of life except to circulate and rotate the elites, so long as that distribution is predicated on differential rewarding for competitive success and failure.

By contrast, equality of situation represents a portion of the socialist view—"to each according to his needs"; and, if we are concerned with motivation and are conscientious, represents also "from each according to his ability." In this instance, we reward equally regardless of differences in talent and achievement, and, if need be, regardless of differences in equality of opportunity. It is possible, then, to have maximum inequality of opportunity and maximum equality of situation simply by revolutionizing the system of differential rewards.

By contrast with both the former states, equity exists when, whatever the rules of the system, at the least they are known to all, they are considered mostly fair, and it is believed that the system operates largely according to these fair rules. Thus, we may have equity either with equality or inequality of situation or of opportunity.

I see the interest in experiential learning as arising mostly from the determination to get more equity into the social system and to mildly adjust the situation of unequal opportunity. The intent and rationale is to open up different lines of access to valued and well-rewarded occupations, on the assumption that traditional lines of access are blocked, or unfriendly, or not in tune with the life orientations of large numbers of people of all ages. This aspiration may be noble and indeed justified according to the requirements of equity; but that is very different from saying that because it is morally justified it will work.

I, for one, doubt seriously that it will work except for a trivial few. Our system can well stand this trivial few, and probably a lot more, without suffering an overload of inefficiency. But that rescue mission will still affect only a small number. Larger numbers will result in a crisis of confidence in equity from people who have been unfairly displaced.

Simple sociological analysis shows us, too, that you cannot significantly alter the educational certification system of society without large-scale social change in other institutional arrangements, and in the preceding values and supporting resources. Consequently, however morally justified and however much the demand for equity cries out for innovations and experiments with experiential learning, let us not be misled into thinking that, short of basic fundamental changes in social structure, we are going to do very much about changing the traditional academic learning and certification system. Affirmative action may hasten the process for a select few. Experiential learning may alter the process for still others. Redefinition of tasks and of traditional assumptions of appropriate rewards may benefit still another small number. But I will give odds—and substantial ones—that newly rising populations are going to have to take their slow (often bitterly and despairingly slow) turns at getting into the system of opportunity and then into the system of differential rewards.

At the same time, it makes a good deal of sense to say that it is worthwhile to develop alternative modes of experience called education, on the chance that they may work for some. Nothing we do in the schools and colleges is so beautiful and precious that it ought not be tinkered with, at least experimentally. But the question remains: how much of our limited resources should be given or taken away from other ongoing educational ventures to do so?

One needs to issue loud words of caution about faddish demands for large-scale educational change in the absence of any evidence whatsoever that one thing will work better than another. Moreover, traditional education obviously makes a great difference in the lives of the people of our society and of the society taken as a system at large. Contrary to all the misinterpretations of James Coleman's work on desegregation and inequality, schooling makes an enormous difference. Where elso do people learn anything of value so far as basic literacy is concerned? Where else do they get certified? And where else does the extraordinary elite of 20 percent who perform the most complex tasks learn basic skills? Twenty years of running gambling casinos may make some card sharps better probability experts than the statisticians, but John Scarne, in his extraordinary book, *Complete Guide to Gambling* (1961)', says that even that is not the case, for numerous owners of casinos run their establishments on the basis of computed probabilities that are wrong as measured by sound probability theory. Curiously, errors consist mostly in underestimating the likelihood that bettors will win when making certain kinds of bets. Scarne's case is persuasive, not simply because he has himself been a successful professional gambler, but because he has used the best methods for calculating probability.

In sum, is experiential learning worth the effort and the resources? Is there a substantial moral and political justification for it and for using life experiences as functionally equivalent substitutes for traditional certification criteria? The answer, I think, is no, if experiential learning is seen as a major instrument of educational and social change. I think it will fail when so conceived. But the answer is decidedly yes if we realize, first, that many important things are not learned well in traditional schools and, second, that many important things are not learned at all. These two deficiencies in our traditional educational system affect virtually all students.

One can think of six groups of people for whom some version of experiential learning might therefore provide an opportunity to learn things not learned and to learn things well that might otherwise be learned poorly: all those who succeed relatively well in school by traditional criteria; those who fail, relatively speaking; those who drop out early for one reason or another; those who are bored even if successful; those who are not in school but want to continue growing; and those who are not now in school but want to return. It does not take much acuity to see that these six groups embrace large numbers of our people. Surely, then, there is a solid rationale for experiential learning if it is designed to improve and augment the learning and the lives of so many people. All other things being equal, any part of that complex task is worth trying.

Chapter Five

ⓘⓘⓘⓘⓘⓘⓘⓘⓘⓘⓘⓘⓘⓘⓘⓘⓘⓘⓘⓘⓘⓘⓘⓘⓘⓘⓘⓘⓘⓘⓘⓘⓘⓘⓘ

Differences Between Experiential and Classroom Learning

ⓘⓘⓘⓘⓘⓘⓘⓘⓘⓘⓘⓘⓘⓘⓘⓘⓘⓘⓘⓘⓘⓘⓘⓘⓘⓘⓘⓘⓘⓘⓘⓘⓘⓘⓘ

James S. Coleman

There is a body of work in educational theory that goes under the general heading *theory of instruction*. This body of work is distinct from learning theory, for, as Bruner notes (1966, p. 40), it is normative, not descriptive. While learning theory attempts to explain the psychological and physiological processes that take place when learning takes place, theories of instruction attempt to specify the optimal set of activities on the part of an outside agent (an instructor) for bringing about learning. For example, Bruner's theory of instruction includes the following elements (1966, pp. 40-41): "(1) specify how to implant a predisposition toward learning; (2) specify the optimal structuring of the body of knowledge to be learned; (3) specify the most effective sequencing of materials; (4) specify the nature and pacing of rewards and punishments."

* A portion of this paper has appeared previously in modified form in Coleman and others (1973). I am indebted to Steven Kidder for discussions that clarified several of the points in the paper.

49

Such theories of instruction contain implicit assumptions about the learning processes that take place within the individual, and they contain implicit assumptions as well about the nature of what is being learned. It is the latter that I want to explore, because unless these assumptions are made explicit, some curious variations in ways that things are learned remain unexplained. These variations can best be exemplified by contrasting the kind of learning that takes place in the classroom and the kind that takes place in much of life outside it. Much of the learning that takes place in class proceeds through instruction, in which information or knowledge is transmitted from an instructor to the learner, while much of the learning that takes place outside class proceeds through acting (or in some cases, seeing another person act), and then experiencing or observing the consequences of action. In everyday parlance, the latter learning is often contrasted to instructor-induced learning by describing it as learning through trial and error, or learning in the school of hard knocks.

Such a distinction between these two different patterns, which I will call *information assimilation* and *experiential learning* respectively, so evident to everyone from having attended school, has important implications for determining how persons can best learn certain things; yet little attention has been given to it. I want in this chapter to point out some differences between the two patterns, and to suggest their implications for learning. As will be apparent, both processes have their virtues and faults, and neither is sufficient as the sole process for human learning. But the processes are partially substitutable, and one may reasonably ask, for particular things to be learned, which process is better.

Steps in Learning

The information assimilation process, the one by which much of academic learning takes place, occurs through a series of steps. The first step is receiving information. Information is transmitted through a symbolic medium. An example is a lecture or a book, where words are the symbolic medium. Information is transmitted concerning a general principle or specific examples as illustrations of the general principle. In classical learning experiments, the procedure that corresponds most closely to this step is the learning of nonsense syllables, in which the information is visually transmitted, and the learning process consists of committing this information to memory.

The second step is assimilating and organizing information so that the general principle is understood. At this point one can be said to have learned the meaning of the information, to have assimilated this information as knowledge. In most things to be learned, the information is intended to be processed so as to lead to understanding a generalization, rather than mere commitment to memory.

The third step is being able to infer a particular application from the general principle. This implies some cognitive abilities, a general intelligence that allows one to see how a general principle applies in a particular instance, or what general principle applies to the particular instance.

The last step is moving from the cognitive and symbol-processing sphere to the sphere of action. This step involves all of the previous three but here the knowledge gained is actually applied. Only when this step has been completed can the person be said to have completed the learning so that the information initially received is useful to him in his everyday action.

The experiential learning process proceeds in almost a reverse sequence. It does not use a symbolic medium for transmitting information, and information is in fact generated only through the sequence of steps themselves. In the first step, one carries out an action in a particular instance and sees the effects of that action. This is like the classical experimental animal learning, in which an animal carries out an action and experiences the consequences, ordinarily termed a reward or a punishment. In the case of human experiential learning, however, the observation of effects of the action is somewhat more general because the effects may be neither rewarding nor punishing, yet provide information about a sequence of cause and effect.

Following the action and the observance of its effects, the second step is understanding these effects in a particular instance, so that if exactly the same set of circumstances reappeared, one could anticipate what would follow from the action. At this point it can be said that the person has learned the consequences of the action, and thus has learned how to act to obtain his goals in this particular circumstance.

The third step is understanding the general principle under which the particular instance falls. Generalizing may involve actions over a range of circumstances to gain experience beyond the particular instance and suggest the general principle. Understanding the general principle does not imply, in this sequence, an ability to express the principle in a symbolic medium, that is, the ability to put it into words. It implies only the ability to see a connection between the actions and effects over a range of circumstances.

When the general principle is understood, the last step is its application through action in a new circumstance within the range of generalization. Here the distinction from the action of the first step is only that the circumstance in which the action takes place is different, and that the actor anticipates the effect of the action. At this point, the person can be said to have completed the learning so that the experience he has undergone is useful to him in future actions.

It might appear that these two processes are applicable to learning of different things. This is suggested, for example, by the fact that the prototypes of the two cases in classical learning experiments do involve learning different things. The prototype for the information assimilation process is learning experiments with human subjects, involving symbolic material, most often words. The prototype for the experiential learning process is animal experimentation, in which the animal first acts and then experiences the consequences of that action, leading to modification of the action in the future. Despite the apparent differences, however, the two patterns are directly applicable to, and are used in, learning the same things. For example, there are two different extremes in ways of bringing about learning the operations of arithmetic with real numbers. One, corresponding to the first process, is to learn first, as general principles, the laws obeyed by the operations of addition and multiplication (commutativity and associativity), the identity under addition (zero) and the identity under multiplication (one), and the fact that the real number system is closed under addition and multiplication. Next, one is shown through examples the applicability of these general principles to specific numbers. Finally, the student is expected to be able to apply the general principles to specific numbers.

At the other extreme, corresponding to the second process, a child is given materials, such as Cuisenaire rods, that involve a physical isomorphism to particular numbers. With guidance, he learns the relationships between these physical objects through using them. Though the fact that this relationship holds for a variety of sizes of rods, he learns to generalize the behavior he experiences. A correspondence is then learned between abstract symbols, numbers, and the physical objects, so that he can manipulate the abstract symbols as he would the objects. At a higher level of learning, when familiarity with these symbols can be assumed, the process is exemplified by the game of Equations. Equations involves placing wooden cubes with particular numbers or operations ($+$, $-$, $\times$, $\div$) in a sequence to create equality to a predetermined number. The game is carried out in a competitive context. The assumption is that after intensive and extensive experience with these particular cubes, the player will come to understand the general principles involved, and will be able to use these operations in everyday activities with real numbers. Note that for both the Cuisenaire rods and the game of Equations, there is no dependence on language—that is, on symbols not an intrinsic part of the system to be learned—except in the guidance that facilitates the actions of the learner. In the first process, however, language is essential in transmitting the general principles with which the whole learning process begins.

Now I am not arguing that schools use only the information assimilation process in teaching arithmetic. Particularly in early years when a child cannot be assumed to be adept with linguistic skills, most schools use a mixture of these two processes in teaching arithmetic. But both in learning arithmetic and in learning other things, schools depend increasingly upon the first process as the child proceeds through school. The question of what the appropriate mix of the two processes is for a given child at a given age is seldom raised.

Properties of the Two Processes

The two processes have their own characteristic properties. First, learning through information assimilation with a symbolic medium can enormously reduce the time and effort necessary to learn something new. It is the embodiment, in a symbolic medium, of the experiences of others, and thus the crystallization of inferences from a broad range of experience. Without it, each generation would have to traverse the whole path of civilization, and in truth ontogeny would recapitulate phylogeny. School is the institution, more than any other, designed to transmit this crystallization from experience, and it is not surprising that this is the main process of learning used by the school.

The process used at its best is described by Bruner in a summary of a chapter on the importance of structure (1961, pp. 31–32): "Teaching specific topics or skills without making clear their context in the broader fundamental structure of a field of knowledge is uneconomical in several deep senses. In the first place, such teaching makes it exceedingly difficult for the student to generalize from what he has learned to what he will encounter later. In the second place, learning that has fallen short of a grasp of general principles has little reward in terms of intellectual excitement. The best way to create interest in a subject is to render it worth knowing, which means to make the knowledge gained usable in one's thinking beyond the situation in which the learning has occurred. Third, knowledge one has acquired without sufficient structure to tie it together is knowledge that is likely to be forgotten."

One can fully agree with Bruner on the importance of structure to tie together otherwise disparate facts without agreeing that the process he describes is the only, or even the best, way to create that structure. In experiential learning, in which the general principle follows action rather than preceding it, the resulting structure that is embedded in memory involves not only principles and ideas from which facts may be inferred, but also sequences of action and consequence, from which new actions may be created through generalization and analogy. Indeed, the quick rate of loss of human memory seems to be better inhibited by the memory of an action taken and the environmental response (as, for example, in the use of a sentence of a foreign language in a goal-directed action toward someone who speaks that language) than by the organization of principles and ideas from which the facts may be inferred. Bruner's assumption, in this passage, seems to be that all knowledge is stored in memory by use of the symbolic representation of language. While this is probably efficient, as suggested above, much knowledge is very likely stored through a structure involving remembered sequences of action and response, which may involve no symbolic medium at all.

A second property of the information assimilation process, implied in the above discussion, is that it depends very heavily upon a symbolic medium, ordinarily language. The first step requires the ability to understand the language, to assimilate information that uses that language as a medium. The second and third steps require processing of information that still lies in the form of words and whatever associations they bring. Thus there is a cost to the compression of experience through language, a cost that lies in incompletely understood language, defects in chains of associations that words may bring, defects in processing of information stored in the form of words and their associations. Indeed, this process of learning depends on prior learning of a complex system of symbols. When this set of symbols, and the skills of manipulating it, are learned poorly, then learning through information assimilation with a symbolic medium must itself be poor. For young children, one finds that even in the classroom this process of learning plays a much smaller role than it does for older children, while experiences with toys, games, and a variety of other activities play a larger role. This is normal, for young children have learned only incompletely the symbolic skills necessary for this process of learning. But for any person who has learned poorly the symbolic media through which information is transmitted, the process of learning must be defective. This would be particularly true for children characterized as culturally disadvantaged, for such disadvantage lies largely in linguistic and verbal skills.

Apart from the critical dependence of learning through information assimilation on the symbolic medium of language, the weak points in the chain, even for those who use this symbolic medium well, are the third and fourth steps: particularizing and acting. For example, academic tests of what is learned are, typically, paper and pencil tests that ask the student to show, in words, his understanding of the general principle, or in some cases his verbal description of applicability. A typical complaint about students is that although they can perform well on such tests, they cannot apply what they have learned: they can understand something, but they cannot act upon the understanding. What this means is that the learning is incomplete: it has proceeded through the second, or possibly, the third step, but not to the final step where they can use the information they have received. Apparently the major hurdle in this process of learning (assuming that the symbolic media are well learned and capable of carrying one through the first two or three steps) is the translation from a symbolic framework of understanding and thinking to a framework involving concrete sequences of action.

Still another property of the information assimilation mode of learning is that it must depend on artificial or extrinsic motivation. Because the action comes at the end, rather than the beginning, there is no incentive for learning until the connection between the information and the action becomes clear—which may be not until the third step in the sequence. Thus motivation must be extrinsically supplied, as, for example, by grades in school.

The properties of the experiential process of learning are, of course, very different. It is time-consuming, for it involves actions sufficiently repeated and in enough circumstances to allow the development of a generalization from experience. In its ideal form, this process does not use a symbolic medium at all, but only action and observation of concrete events following the action. It is not at all effective when the consequence of the action is separated in time or space from the action itself. For example, some phenomena are exceedingly difficult to learn in this way, because of a time lag between actions and consequence. Anthropologists report that some primitive tribes do not make the connection between sexual intercourse and birth because of the lapse of time; and even today some persons hold false notions about the point in the menstrual cycle at which a woman is fertile.

However, when consequence is perceptibly connected to action, then such experiential learning provides a direct guide to future action. There is no hurdle from a symbolic medium to action, only modifications of the action to fit the circumstance. A typical observation of someone who has learned something through this process is that he cannot verbalize it, but he can do it. Some of the most remarkable examples are found in experienced gamblers. An experienced gambler may have various rules of thumb, various generalizations about what actions to take in particular circumstances. The gambler can beat a probability theorist who knows how to calculate the probabilities of various combinations but cannot do so in time; yet the gambler cannot begin to verbalize his or her actions in terms of probabilities. Such an individual can verbalize probabilities only in terms of what action to take in what circumstances, or which odds to accept and which to decline when the crapshooter has a particular point to make. The gambler has embedded these rules of thumb in memory through use of structure involving sequences of action, with less dependence than the probability theorist on general principles carried by a symbolic medium. There may be several additional calculations or symbol manipulations to carry out in order to be able to verbalize the general principle by which the gambler is acting. These are manipulations that are intrinsic to the information assimilation mode of learning. But for the experiential mode, the individual need not learn them, since they are not necessary to his or her use of the learning.

It is likely that this bypassing of symbolic media is responsible for the frequent observation in experiential learning that the student does not perform well on paper and pencil tests, although observation of the student's behavior indicates that he or she appears to have learned the phenomenon well. In learning through games, a form of experiential learning, for example, it is a common observation that some players are able to pursue a strategy of play very well, but when asked to describe the strategy they used, cannot begin to do so, or state a strategy that they clearly did not use.

Another property of the experiential mode of learning that contrasts to the information assimilation mode is that motivation is intrinsic. Since action occurs at the beginning of the sequence rather than at the end, the subjective need for learning exists from the outset. If learners are to gain their ends through the action, they must learn whatever is necessary to guide action. For this reason, motivation is seldom a problem with experiential learning, while teachers often see it as the major problem of learning in the classroom.

The weakest link in the experiential process of learning appears to lie in the third step, in generalizing from particular experiences to a general principle applicable in other circumstances. Persons seem to differ considerably in their quickness to infer a general principle from a set of experiences. Thus some persons can engage in the same action repeatedly without extending the principle to other cases, while others perceive the principle immediately.

It is probably because this step is the weakest link in experiential learning that postgame discussions appear to be very important in the experiential learning that takes place in simulation games. In such discussions, some players will be able to infer general principles from their experience in the game, while others will not. The statement of these principles, taken together with the experience from the game, seems for most players to be sufficient to bring about learning of the general principle, while play of the game is sufficient only for a much smaller fraction of persons.

A final property of experiential learning is that it appears to be less easily forgotten than learning through information assimilation. The reason may be that the associations that embed it in memory are with concrete actions and events to which affect was attached, and are not merely associations with abstract symbols or general principles expressed in abstract symbols.

Although this discussion gives a glimpse of the differences between these two modes of learning, it also shows the primitive state of knowledge in this area. These comments can be regarded as merely a starting point for a more general investigation into these two modes of learning. But even now it is clear from some of the properties of experiential learning that academic learning can be made considerably more effective by the appropriate mix of experiential and information assimilation modes of learning.

The Mix of Learning Modes in Formal Education

The present mix of learning modes in schools and colleges appears to follow a particular pattern. In the very early grades, a high proportion of experiential learning is employed through the use of play, games, individual performances, and many related activities. This proportion sharply diminishes in elementary school and beyond, being replaced by lectures, classroom discussions, and other modes of information assimilation. For some persons toward the end of formal education whether in high school (for vocational training) or in college or graduate school (for professional training), the proportion of experiential learning again increases. At this level it takes the form of vocation performance, in an apprenticeship or other form that involves little instruction but much observation and performance. For many persons, however, who do not have vocational, technical, or professional training, the later years of schooling do not involve an increase in experiential learning, but merely a continuation of the information assimilation mode to the end of formal schooling.

Apart from this pattern, there is a general belief that experiential learning is good for disadvantaged children and youth, while information assimilation is better for those who are educationally advantaged. I believe there are several assumptions underlying these uses of the two modes. It is assumed that young children require an experiential mode because they do not have good symbolic skills (with words and numbers), and because they can be better motivated in the experiential mode. Once these symbolic skills are learned, however, the more cumbersome and time-consuming experiential mode can be replaced with information assimilation by use of language. But preparation for actual performance or functioning in an activity, as will be necessary in jobs after formal education ends, requires some practice and experience in the activity. Unmotivated or slow-learning children require experiential learning for the same two reasons that young children do.

These assumptions generally appear sound, but I believe they fail to recognize certain characteristics of experiential learning that make this mode beneficial at certain points in the process of learning any knowledge or skill, throughout the whole period of formal education. I will mention two of these that appear to me especially important.

The first is the motivation that action provides, as distinct from passive receptivity. Action involves an investment of the self, which induces a certain tension that is only relieved when the activity is successfully performed. This is particularly true when the action involves other persons in some way. For example, when one attempts to make oneself understood to persons speaking only a foreign language, a tension is initiated that makes one want to learn enough to be understood. With this tension, and without the extrinsic inducement of grades, an immigrant or traveler becomes highly motivated to learn the language. Similarly, in a game, the necessity to act, whether the game is an intellectual one like chess, an athletic game, or an educational game that requires knowledge of certain facts, is inherent in the drive to win. The importance of the other persons in the action setting provides an additional affect or emotional involvement that arises in an interpersonal setting. This both increases the motivation and provides an associative structure of events in memory that helps insure that whatever has been learned is not lost.

Because of this general principle, experiential modes of learning involving interpersonal interaction, whether in real-life settings, in game settings, or in some form of simulated environment, are important at the beginning of a learning activity. Though these modes may well be followed by information assimilation, their use at the beginning can reduce sharply the need for an importance of extrinsic rewards that grades provide in formal schooling.

The second characteristic of experiential learning that I want to point to is the obverse of the first: it is the self-assurance and sense of accomplishment and mastery that successful action provides. Again, this intrinsic reward of accomplishment is stronger if the successful actions are in the context of other persons: either actions toward the other persons or in some other direct relation to them, in a realistic setting. To continue the example of learning a foreign language, the reinforcement effect of successfully using a foreign language to get what one wants is an especially strong one, and the resulting sense of accomplishment is also especially strong. This second characteristic of experiential learning suggests that it is particularly valuable in the later stages of learning an activity, both for the reinforcement effect it provides and for its functions in strengthening self-esteem and a sense of personal mastery.

These comments on the appropriate mix of experiential learning and information assimilation are far from definitive, and are intended primarily to raise issues for serious examination rather than to provide conclusive prescriptions. The investigation of these matters has a long way to go; what is important to recognize at this point is that careful and intensive examination of experiential learning will lead to it becoming far more fully embedded in the curricula of schools and colleges, and not relegated to peripheral tasks or limited to very young children, disadvantaged youth, and preprofessionals.

Chapter Six

Developmental Change as a Major Outcome

Arthur W. Chickering

It is a tale better told by poets than by scientists how human beings develop competency, living styles, and maturity and, if they live long enough, suffer decline. What Shakespeare lacked in controlled data in describing his seven ages of man—from mewling infant, whining school boy, and sighing lover through quarrelsome soldier and caponed justice to shrunken and beslippered elder on to second childhood sans teeth and all—he made up in concreteness and perspective upon the whole. In order to learn how better to educate, we must cut up, pick apart, and chew over this apple of human experience to know its causes and possible cultivation. That is the agenda of this chapter: to sort out current understanding of individual development, styles, competency, and character; and to show how this new knowledge may be used to improve the content of higher education, the conduct of its institutions, and the focus of assessment activities in measuring its outcomes. As we do so, however, we must not forget that only art and actual lives show the fruit whole, richly colored, singly shaped and textured.

In this chapter the term *experiential learning* means the learning that occurs when changes in judgments, feelings, knowledge, or skills result for a particular person from living through an event or events. It is not confined, as some usages have it, to such events as encounter groups, field trips, and work experiences. Within our usage, experiential learning may result from attending a lecture, but the learning would be that resulting from living through the event with its attendant joy or suffering, and not simply from the content of the lecture, though that is clearly part of the event. Experiential learning may also result from an encounter group or an exam, discussion or demonstration, work or play, travel or sitting on a stump.

A key problem for educators is to develop conceptual clarity concerning students' motives and learning styles, and the major outcomes of various educational programs and teaching activities. When such concepts are clear, learning settings pertinent to particular purposes can be identified or created, activities to foster desired outcomes can be specified, and evidences of progress can be recognized. With a conceptual framework in hand, theories concerning experiential learning, which posit relationships among institutional settings, teaching activities, and evidence of student progress, can be formulated and systematically examined. And the capacities of learners, teachers, and educational institutions may increase, so that lifelong learning and the learning society can move from rhetoric to reality.

The most solid basis for understanding the motives and learning styles of college students lies in research and theory concerning adult development and cognitive styles. This information has clear and powerful implications about educational motives, orientations toward knowledge, teaching practices, approaches to evaluation, and student-faculty relationships. Systematic organization of this information can provide a conceptual map or matrix useful to administrators in decisions concerning staffing, facilities, educational resources, and academic processes; to faculty members as they try to improve their teaching effectiveness; and to students themselves as they plan and carry out their own education.

This chapter addresses that task in two parts. The first part describes major dimensions of adult development. If much of this section seems like common sense elaborated, we must ask why education has been designed in apparent indifference or defiance to the needs of natural development as research unfolds them. That question leads us, in the second part, to indicate some of the implications for education.

Adult Development

Most theorists take age sixteen or eighteen as the beginning of adulthood. During those years many young persons legally and functionally assume several major adult responsibilities and obligations, and while doing so disengage themselves from family and home. Some theorists seek to discover developmental *ages*—relationships between age and general orientations, problems, dilemmas, developmental tasks, personal concerns, or other adult characteristics. They have identified periods of stability and of transition, and describe some of the characteristics associated with them. Other theorists seek to discover the *stages* of development in a defined area such as intellectual development, moral development, or ego development. The brief summaries of developmental ages and stages that follow do not claim to be comprehensive. The literature is already too large for that to be practical here, and my current knowledge is too scanty for it to be possible. But most of the major theorists are recognized. Furthermore, any brief synthesis oversimplifies, and like Procrustes, cuts or stretches to fit the bed. Frequent subvocal repetition of "yes, but" and "it's more complicated than that" is called for.

In terms of developmental ages, Levinson and others (1974), Gould (1972), and Sheehy (1974) describe a general pattern of adult development that begins with the transition from adolescence to adulthood during the late teens and early twenties. During the midtwenties—a period of provisional adulthood—first commitments to work, to marriage and family, and to other adult responsibilities are lived out. Then another transitional period occurs during the late twenties and early thirties where these initial commitments are reexamined and their meaning questioned. The long-range implications of continuing with the current work, spouse, community, life style, have become apparent and one or more of these may look less challenging or satisfying than they did earlier. In some cases, changes must be made. In others, reaffirmation and renewed commitment occur on a more solid basis, sometimes after trial flirtations with one or more alternatives.

The thirties are a time for settling down, for achievement, for becoming one's own person. But as the forties approach, time becomes more finite. Responsibility for one's parents begins to be assumed while responsibilities for adolescent or college-age children continue. The likely limits of success and achievement become more apparent, and midlife transition is at hand. Major questions concerning priorities and values are examined. Unless a change in work is made now, the die is cast. Affirmation of the present career most frequently occurs, but with moderated expectations and drives. A long-standing marriage may be temporarily or permanently upset. Friends, relatives, and spouse become increasingly important as restabilization occurs during the late forties and fifties. Interests foregone in the service of work receive more attention. Mellowing and increasing investment in personal relationships characterize the fifties.

Bernice Neugarten's work (1963, 1971) builds on Erik Erikson's seminal formulations (1950, 1959) concerning the life cycle. Neugarten, more than any other theorist, elaborates the role of age and timing in adult development. The shift in the midforties from a period where the future seems to stretch forth (and death is an abstract)' to a period when time is finite (and death is personalized) sets boundaries for other major changes: from a sense of self-determination to a sense of the inevitability of the life cycle, from mastery of the outer world, through reexamination, to withdrawal and preoccupation with the inner self and sponsoring others; from achievement to self-satisfaction. Neugarten found that when normal events were "on time"—children leaving home, menopause, death of a spouse, even one's own death—they were not experienced as crises. Departure and death of loved ones cause grief and sadness, as does the prospect of one's own leaving, but when these events occur at times and in ways consistent with the normal expected life cycle, most persons manage the event or the prospect without major upset.

These various studies tell us much about the outcomes of experiential learning that occurs through the life cycle. They identify major motives—dilemmas, interests, aspirations, circumstances —that lead students to pursue further education. In addition, they suggest some fundamental concerns and developmental tasks that lie behind the desire for a degree, the pursuit of a better or different job, and the wish to read more widely and experience more deeply, to meet new persons and new ideas, to explore dimly seen horizons.

Turning from developmental ages to stages, theorists define the term *developmental stages* with varying degrees of rigor. For example, Kohlberg's stages of moral development must be evidenced by behavior change that is "irreversible, general over a field of responses, sequential, and hierarchical" (Kohlberg and Mayer 1972, p. 486). Robert White talks of growth trends characterized by both direction and processes: "Growth in a given direction takes place under certain conditions and through certain types of experience. It is not something that happens just because we grow older" (1966, pp. 373, 374). In general, theorists see development as a series of hierarchical stages, each of which builds on and includes the earlier stage. Movement from one stage to the next occurs not simply through instinctual unfolding, but through person-environment interactions influenced by genetic predispositions and limitations.

Ego Development. Several theorists (Table 1) have conceptualized comprehensive statements of the stages of human development. Loevinger describes the general similarities among concepts as follows (p. 3): "All of the conceptions project an abstract continuum that is both a normal developmental sequence and a dimension of individual differences in any age cohort. All represent holistic views of personality, and all see behavior in terms of meaning or purposes. . . All are more or less concerned with impulse control and character development, with interpersonal relations, and with cognitive preoccupations, including self-concept. . . Finally, although the sequence of stages is not identical from author to author, there are many recurring similarities" (Loevinger and Wessler, 1970, p. 3).

After summarizing the presocial, symbiotic, impulsive, and self-protective stages of childhood (Table 2), Loevinger describes the conformity stage (p. 4): "Here the child identifies himself with

Table 1.

Author	Ego or Character Types					
	Amoral	Fearful-dependent	Opportunistic	Conforming to persons	Conforming to rule	Principled autonomous
Peck and Havighurst (1960)	1. Amoral		2. Expedient	3. Conforming	4. Irrational-conscientious	5. Rational-altruistic
Sullivan, Grant, and Grant (1957)	1_1 Presocial	1_2 Passive-demanding	1_3 Conformist (exploitative)	1_3 Conformist (cooperative)	1_4 Authoritarian Guilty	1_6 Self-consistent 1_7 Integrative
Harvey, Hunt, and Schroeder (1961)	Sub-1	1. Absolutistic-evaluative	2. Self-differentiating	3. Empathic		4. Integrated-independent
Loevinger (1970)	1. Presocial Symbiotic	2. Impulse-ridden, fearful	3. Self-protective	4. Conformist	5. Conscientious	6. Autonomous 7. Integrated
Vanden Daele (1968)	1. Excitation-oriented	3. Conflict-avoidant	5. Peer and reciprocity oriented	6. Social conformist	7. Duty and responsibility	8. Independent agent orientation 9. Self-social integration

Source: Adapted from Kohlberg (1973), p. 46.

Table 2. STAGES OF DEVELOPMENT

Stage	Impulse Control, Character Development	Interpersonal Style	Conscious Preoccupations	Cognitive Style
Presocial		Autistic	Self versus non-self	
Symbiotic		Symbiotic		
Impulsive	Impulsive, fear of retaliation	Receiving, dependent, exploitive	Bodily feelings, especially sexual and aggressive	Stereotypy, conceptual confusion
Self-protective	Fear of being caught, externalizing blame, opportunistic	Wary, manipulative, exploitive	Self-protection wishes, things, advantage, control	
Conformist	Conformity to external rules, shame, guilt for breaking rules	Belonging, helping, superficial niceness	Appearance, social acceptability, banal feelings, behavior	Conceptual simplicity; stereotypes and cliches
Conscientious	Self-evaluated standards, self-criticism, guilt for consequences	Intensive, responsible, mutual concern for communications	Differentiated feelings, motives for behavior, self respect, achievements, traits, expression	Conceptual complexity, idea of patterning
Autonomous	Add: Coping with conflicting inner needs, toleration	Add: Respect for autonomy	Vividly conveyed feelings, integration of physiological and psychological causation of behavior, development, role conception, self-fulfillment, self in social context	Increased conceptual complexity, complex patterns; toleration for ambiguity, broad scope, objectivity
Integrated	Add: Reconciling inner conflicts, renunciation of unattainable	Add: Cherishing of individuality	Add: Identity	

Note: "Add" means in addition to the description applying to the previous level.

Source: Loevinger and others (1970)

authority, his parents at first, later other adults, then his peers. This is the period of greatest cognitive simplicity. There is a right way and a wrong way, and it is the same for everyone all the time, or for broad classes of people. . . . What is conventional and socially approved is right. . . . Rules are accepted because they are socially accepted." She reports that the transition between the conformist stage and the next stage, the conscientious stage, which appears to be modal for students during the first two years of college, is marked by heightened consciousness of self and of inner feelings and the perception of multiple possibilities in situations (p. 5): "Rules are seen to have exceptions or to hold only in certain contingencies. Inner states and individual differences are described in vivid and differential terms. One feels guilty not primarily when one has broken a rule, but when one has hurt another person. Motives and consequences are more important than rules per se. Long term goals and ideals are characteristic; ought is clearly different from is. . . . Achievement is important, and it is measured by one's own inner standards rather than being primarily a matter of competition or social approval."

According to Loevinger and her colleagues, the stage immediately following the conscientious is the autonomous stage. The transition from one stage to the other is characterized by a sense of individuality and emotional independence. While problems of dependence are present in all ego development stages, this transitional stage particularly stresses the awareness that one is emotionally dependent even when physically and financially independent of others.

In the autonomous stage, the individual recognizes other people's need for autonomy, and is freed from the overwhelming sense of responsibility characteristic of the conscientious stage. "Moral dichotomies are no longer characteristic. They are replaced by a feeling for the complexity and multifaceted character of real people and real situations. There is a deepened respect for other people. . . . We do not believe that inner conflict is more characteristic of the autonomous stage than of lower stages. Rather, the autonomous person has the courage to acknowledge and to cope with conflict rather than blotting it out or projecting it onto the environment. The autonomous person is concerned with social problems beyond his own immediate experience. He tries to be realistic about himself and others" (p. 6).

The final stage in this model is the integrated stage, in which one reconciles inner conflicts, renounces the unattainable, cherishes one's individuality, and finds one's identity.

Loevinger cautions against the "temptation to see the successive stages of ego development as problems to be solved and to assume that the best adjusted people are those at the highest stages. This is a distortion. There are probably well adjusted people at all stages. . . Probably those who remain below the conformist level beyond childhood can be called maladjusted. . . . Some self-protective, opportunistic persons, on the other hand, become very successful. . . Certainly it is a conformist's world, and many conformists are very happy with it, though they are not all immune to mental illness. Probably to be faithful to the realities of the case one should see the sequence as one of coping with increasingly deeper problems rather than as the successful negotiation of solutions" (p. 7).

The extracts from *Measuring Ego Development* quoted above give a general sense of the major stages of adult development. That study describes the general stages in terms of four major dimensions: impulse control and character development, interpersonal style, conscious preoccupations, and cognitive style. Changes in developmental stages requires changes in these four major areas. Change need not necessarily occur simultaneously or in precise one-to-one fashion; but if there is little development in one dimension, further development in the others is restricted. Living by self-evaluated standards is difficult if one is still powerfully preoccupied with appearance and social acceptability. Differentiated feelings and motives, or respect for the autonomy of others, cannot be readily achieved if one is still in the grips of stereotypes and cliches. While theorists differ in terminology and in significant details, the level of agreement among them is sufficiently strong and broadly based to provide one set of solid information that has implications for experiential learning.

Moral and Ethical Development. These major dimensions posited by Loevinger identify areas that have been pursued in more detail by others: moral and ethical development, intellectual development, and the development of interpersonal relationships.

Table 3 indicates correspondences between Loevinger, Kohlberg, and Perry.

Kohlberg (1973) emphasizes shifting orientations toward authority, others, and self, such that self-chosen principles replace those given by authority or defined by peers, group identification, or the general culture. Perry, in a complementary analysis, describes complex ways of knowing and thinking about moral issues and increasingly complex ways of defining and maintaining values and commitments, while recognizing pluralism and accepting contrasting values and commitments of others.

The systems of both Perry and Kohlberg express very general human values: pluralism, respect for human dignity and integrity, dissent, individual self-determination and development. Yet on other dimensions of valuing, they are relatively content free. Thus educational activities designed to enable change from one stage to the next can be carried on in relation to a wide range of moral and ethical values or issues. Commitment to either a conservative or a liberal sociopolitical view, or to a theistic or an atheistic religious belief can be carried to the highest stages, although the particular belief or commitment will be held very differently.

Intellectual Development. Bridges can be built between ego theorists who postulate moral and ethical stages, and theorists who focus on cognitive development. Kohlberg has done this for the relationship between his stages and Piaget's (Kohlberg, 1973, p. 45)'. Table 4 summarizes the general stages of ego development, Kohlberg, Perry, and Loevinger's cognitive styles, and intellectual development described by Piaget and Bloom and others (1956). In cognitive development, there is a general sequence from concrete memorization, through recognition of relationships among events, instances, and classes, to cognitive processes that construct combinations of relationships, isolate variables or create new combinations or groupings, and culminate in the ability to apply principles or concepts to new situations and evaluate the results.

Development of Interpersonal Styles. Thus far we have seen that there is considerable consensus among students of human development about modal patterns of stages of ego development, cognitive development, and moral development. This picture is complicated, however, by the fact that people differ markedly in their

Table 3. PHASES OF EGO DEVELOPMENT ASSOCIATED WITH MORAL AND ETHICAL DEVELOPMENT

			Ego Development Stages			
Loevinger	Presocial Symbiotic	Impulse-ridden, fearful	Self-protective	Conformist	Conscientious	Autonomous Integrated
			Moral and Ethical Development			
Kohlberg	Egocentric	Obedience-punishment oriented	Instrumental egoism and exchange	Good-boy, approval oriented	Authority, rule, and social order oriented	Social contracts, legalistic oriented Moral principle orientation
Perry	Basic duality	Multiplicity prelegitimate	Multiplicity subordinate, multiplicity correlate, or relativism subordinate	Relativism correlate, competing or diffuse	Commitment foreseen	Initial commitment, implications of commitments, developing commitments

Source: Adapted from Kohlberg (1973), p. 46.

Ego Development	Moral and Ethical Development			Intellectual Development	
	(Kohlberg)	(Perry)	(Loevinger)	(Piaget)	(Bloom)
Amoral	Egocentric	Basic duality	Stereotypy, conceptual confusion	Symbolic, intuitive thought	
Fearful-dependent	Obedience-punishment oriented	Multiplicity prelegitimate		Concrete operations: 1. Categorical classification	Memorization
Opportunistic	Instrumental egoism and exchange	Multiplicity subordinate		Concrete operations: 2. Reversible concrete thought	Application
Conforming to persons	Good-boy, approval oriented	Multiplicity correlate or relativism subordinate	Conceptual simplicity; stereotypes and cliches		
Conforming to rule	Authority, rule, and social order oriented	Relativism correlate, competing or diffuse	Conceptual complexity, idea of patterning	Formal operations: 1. Relations involving the inverse of the reciprocal	Analysis
				Formal operations: 2. Relations involving triads	
Principled autonomous	Social contracts, legalistic oriented	Commitment foreseen	Increased conceptual complexity, complex patterns; toleration for ambiguity, broad scope, objectivity	Formal operations: 3. Construction of all possible relations	Synthesis
				Systematic isolation of variables	
	Moral principle orientation	Initial commitment, implications of commitments, developing commitments		Deductive hypothesis testing	Evaluation

interpersonal style and in their competence in interpersonal relationships.

Loevinger articulates several different levels of interpersonal *style*. Others, notably Argyris and Schon (1974), Fine (1970), Foote and Cottrell (1955), and White (1963) examine interpersonal *competence*. White (1966) also posits the *freeing of personal relationships* as a general area of adult growth.

Style and competence clearly have different implications. The first implies distinctive or characteristic modes of relating to others; the second implies a more limited domain pertinent to certain professional settings or more generally necessary for an adequate existence. But the two are inseparable. As White observes (1963, p. 73), "Every interaction with another person can be said to have an aspect of competence. Acts directed toward another are intended consciously or unconsciously, to have an effect of some kind; and the extent to which they produce this effect can be taken as the measure of competence. When interactions are casual, when we are merely 'passing the time of day,' the element of competence may be minimal, although even in such cases we are surprised if we produce no effect at all, not even an acknowledging grunt. When matters of importance are at stake, the aspect of competence is bound to be larger. If we are seeking help or offering it, trying to evoke love or giving it, warding off aggression or expressing it, resisting influence by others or trying to exert influence, the effectiveness of our behavior is a point of vital concern."

One way to conceive of the problem of interpersonal competence is to recognize that personal styles acquired during childhood and adolescence may be singularly inappropriate for certain adult relationships at work, at home, and in the community. Therefore a key problem in achieving competence is to gain greater control over those imprinted interpersonal reflexes. There does seem to be a general direction of change by which this greater personal control and flexibility is achieved.

There are strong similarities among theorists concerning the direction of change for interpersonal relationships. White describes it this way (1966, pp. 385–386): "In general . . . social interaction in adolescence is apt to be marked by impulsive inconsiderateness and egocentricity, even when it is not burdened by anxiety and neurotic inhibitions. The youngster tends to be so immersed in his own behavior, so intent on the impression he is making or the point he is trying to put across, that he fails to perceive clearly the people around him. During young adulthood there usually proves to be still a good deal to learn before one truly interacts with others in their own right as individuals. As a person moves in this direction he develops a greater range and flexibility of responses. He notices more things in the people with whom he interacts and becomes more ready to make allowance for their characteristics in his own behavior. Human relations become less anxious, less defensive, less burdened by inappropriate past reactions. They become more friendly, warm, and respectful. There may even be greater room for assertiveness and criticism. In short, the person moves in the direction of increased capacity to live in real relationship with the people immediately around him."

Loevinger's developmental stages of interpersonal style, given in Table 2, are consistent with White's description. Each stage of interpersonal style is linked closely to other basic elements of development. Thus movement along the continuum of interpersonal style influences and is influenced by development in impulse control, conscious preoccupations, and cognitive styles.

Two models for professional practice and interpersonal relationships recently elaborated by Argyris and Schon (1974, pp. 68, 69, 87) are outlined in Table 5. The second and third columns, action strategies and consequences for the behavioral world, describe the interpersonal orientations and behaviors that characterize the two models. The formulations are consistent with, and carry forward, the general work of other major theorists who have addressed the areas of professional competence and organizational behavior, such as Fritz Rothlisberger, Douglas McGregor, Rensis Likert, and Warren Bennis.

In Model One, interpersonal relationships are goal-oriented toward maximizing winning and minimizing losing, with strong emphasis on rationality and minimal open expression of negative feelings. Relationships tend to be characterized by persuasion, stereotyping, intellectualizing, suppression of feelings and information, competition, manipulation, and outward conformity with limited internal commitment. In Model Two, the emphasis is on creating

Table 5. Models of Professional Practice and Interpersonal Relationships

Governing variables	Action strategies	Consequences for the behavioral world	Consequences for learning	Effectiveness
MODEL ONE				
1. Define goals and try to achieve them	1. *Design and manage the environment* unilaterally (be persuasive, appeal to larger goals)	1. Actor seen as defensive, inconsistent, incongruent, competitive, controlling, fearful of being vulnerable, manipulative, withholding of feelings, overly concerned about self and others or underconcerned about others	1. Self-sealing	Decreased effectiveness
2. Maximize winning and minimize losing	2. *Own and control the task* (claim ownership of the task, be guardian of definition and execution of task)	2. Defensive interpersonal and group relationship (dependence upon actor, little additivity, little helping others)	2. Single-loop learning	
3. Minimize generating or expressing negative feelings	3. *Unilaterally protect yourself* (speak with inferred categories accompanied by little or no directly observable behavior, be blind to impact on others and to the incongruity between rhetoric and behavior, reduce incongruity by defensive actions such as blaming, stereotyping, suppressing feelings, intellectualizing)	3. Defensive norms (mistrust, lack of risk-taking conformity, external commitment, emphasis on diplomacy, power-centered competition, and rivalry)	3. Little testing of theories publicly. Much testing of theories privately	
4. Be rational	4. *Unilaterally protect others from being hurt* (withhold information, create rules to censor information and behavior, hold private meetings)	4. Low freedom of choice, internal commitment, and risk-taking		

Table 5. Models of Professional Practice and Interpersonal Relationships *(Cont.)*

Governing variables	Action strategies	Consequences for the behavioral world	Consequences for learning	Consequences for quality of life	Effectiveness
MODEL TWO					
1. Valid information	1. Design situations or environments where participants can be origins and can experience high personal causation (psychological success, confirmation, essentiality)	1. Actor experienced as minimally defensive (facilitator, collaborator, choice creator)	1. Disconfirmable processes	1. Quality of life will be more positive than negative (high authenticity and high freedom of choice)	
2. Free and informed choice	2. Tasks are controlled jointly	2. Minimally defensive interpersonal relations and group dynamics	2. Double-loop learning	2. Effectiveness of problem solving and decision making will be great, especially for difficult problems	Increased long-run effectiveness
3. Internal commitment to the choice and constant monitoring of its implementation	3. Protection of self is a joint enterprise and oriented toward growth (speak in directly observable categories, seek to reduce blindness about own inconsistency and incongruity)	3. Learning-oriented norms (trust, individuality, open confrontation on difficult issues)	3. Public testing of theories		
	4. Bilateral protection of others				

Source: Adapted from Argyris and Schon (1974), pp. 68, 69, 87.

valid information so that internal commitment to free and informed choices can occur, and so that actions can be openly and continuously monitored. Interpersonal relationships call for initiative, collaboration, direct observations, attention to one's own biases and inconsistencies, minimal defensiveness, trust and respect for individuality, and open confrontation on difficult issues.

A professional or an organization can be more or less skillful in either model. There is a rich array of educational materials, courses, training programs, and the like, which aim to foster competence for one model or the other; but Model One is by far the dominant mode. Sidney Fine, for example, posits the hierarchy of interpersonal skills given in Table 6. It is worth noting that even the highest level, mentoring, is formulated in Model One terms. If Argyris and Schon, and other professionals who share their view, are right in asserting that Model Two represents a higher level of professional competence and organizational effectiveness, then Fine's system needs reconceptualization and reformulation, especially from level four on, for consulting, instructing, treating, supervising, negotiating and mentoring. Indeed the uncertainty, turmoil, and ferment in the health professions, law, community services, and education, which recognize a much stronger role for the client in determining the nature of treatment and service, can be seen as attempts to shift from Model One to Model Two in professional practices and in the new kinds of interpersonal relationships required.

Increasing interpersonal competence is extremely difficult to achieve because it requires a fundamental change in what White (1963, pp. 74–75) calls a sense of competence: "sense of competence has been widely recognized in negative forms: feelings of helplessness, inhibition of initiative, the inferiority complex. The positive side has perhaps been poisoned for many of us by that hastily conceived dream-figure of perfect mental health who has attained invulnerable self-confidence and serene self-esteem—obviously a conceited fool. But the extreme cases, real or fictional, should not draw attention away from sense of competence at the daily operating level. Our best insight comes from the ordinary phenomenon of confidence, which is an aspect of virtually every act. . . . We can detect the influence of sense of competence in the judgments we

Table 6. HIERARCHY OF INTERPERSONAL SKILLS LEVEL

Level	Definition
1A	*Taking Instructions—Helping* Attends to the work assignment, instructions, or orders of supervisor. No immediate response or verbal exchange is required unless clarification of instruction is needed
1B	*Serving* Attends to the needs or requests of people or animals, or to the expressed or implicit wishes of people. Immediate response is involved
2	*Exchanging Information* Talks to, converses with, and/or signals people to convey or obtain information, or to clarify and work out details of an assignment, within the framework of well-established procedures
3A	*Coaching* Befriends and encourages individuals on a personal, caring basis by approximating a peer or family-type relationship either in a one-to-one or small group situation, and gives instruction, advice, and personal assistance concerning activities of daily living, the use of various institutional services, and participation in groups
3B	*Persuading* Influences others in favor of a product, service, or point of view by talks or demonstrations
3C	*Diverting* Amuses others
4A	*Consulting* Serves as a source of technical information and gives such information or provides ideas to define, clarify, enlarge upon, or sharpen procedures, capabilities, or product specifications
4B	*Instructing* Teaches subject matter to others, or trains others, including animals, through explanation, demonstration, practice, and test
4C	*Treating* Acts on or interacts with individuals or small groups of people or animals who need help (as in sickness) to carry out specialized therapeutic or adjustment procedures. Systematically observes results of treatment within the framework of total personal behavior because unique individual reactions to prescriptions (chemical, physician's, behavioral) may not fall within the range of prediction. Motivates, sup-

Table 6.   Continued

Level	Definition
	ports, and instructs individuals to accept or cooperate with therapeutic adjustment procedures, when necessary
5	*Supervising* Determines and/or interprets work procedure for a group of workers, assigns specific duties to them (particularly those which are prescribed), maintains harmonious relations among them, evaluates performance (both prescribed and discretionary), and promotes efficiency and other organizational values. Makes decisions on procedural and technical levels
6	*Negotiating* Exchanges ideas, information, and opinions with others on a formal basis to formulate policies and programs on an initiating basis (e.g., contracts) and/or arrives at resolutions of problems growing out of administration of existing policies and programs, usually after a bargaining process
7	*Mentoring* Deals with individuals in terms of their overall life adjustment behavior in order to advise, counsel, and/or guide them with regard to problems that may be resolved by legal, scientific, clinical, spiritual and/or other professional principles. Advises clients on implications of diagnostic or similar categories, courses of action open to deal with a problem, and merits of one strategy over another

Source: Fine (1973).

are constantly making, often half-consciously, about what we can and cannot do. . . . Past actions, successful and unsuccessful, have taught us the range of our effectiveness. Sense of competence is the result of cumulative learning, and it is ever at work influencing the next thrust of behavior."

Of course, one's sense of competence depends to some degree on the reality of one's competency. Self-confidence depends upon the ability to cope with life's problems and to maintain equilibrium under diverse circumstances. Yet self-confidence and absolute ability operate across a wide range with substantial independence from one another. Interpersonal competence, as well as the concrete productivity and effectiveness achieved with a given level of ability,

varies greatly with one's sense of competence. Competence in interpersonal relationships is difficult to develop not only because self-
confidence plays such an important role, but also because long-
standing personal styles developed during childhood and adolescence
have become heavily ingrained. And these styles are related to other
personality structures not easily modified.

It is also difficult to change interpersonal competence because
usually we cannot attend to it directly. "Responding to people in
their own right . . . is not easy even for the most socially seasoned
adult. . . . To some extent this lag results from the inherent difficulties that attend learning in a social situation. . . . Social interactions have a content as well as an emotional undertone. We are
apt to be doing something with the other person, or talking about
something, so that our learning is by no means confined to the
process of interaction. . . . Most of our social interacting is learned
under conditions of high distraction. We do not fully perceive either
the other person or ourselves, and this circumstance tends to favor
the persistence of old attitudes rather than the learning of new ones"
(White, 1966, pp. 382, 383).

The conditions White describes for social situations are am-
plified in most work situations where the stakes are often even
higher, where differences and conflict are more prevalent, and
where the number of different things to be attended to at the same
time may be great indeed. It is not surprising that changing professional and organizational behaviors from Model One to Model
Two is time consuming, difficult, and fraught with failure.

Model One conforms well to the interpersonal styles of Loevinger's impulsive stage, marked by characteristics such as receiving,
dependent, exploitive, wary, and manipulative, and to her conformist stage, marked by characteristics such as belonging, helping, and
superficial niceness. Model Two, on the other hand, conforms to
interpersonal styles associated with Loevinger's conscientious, autonomous, and integrated stages, which exhibit, respectively, characteristics of intensive, responsible, mutual concern for communica-
tions; respect for autonomy; and cherishing of individuality.

Argyris (Hersey and Blanchard, 1972, p. 51) has posited an
immaturity-maturity continuum that contains elements highly consistent with Loevinger's elements of ego development (Table 7).

Table 7. Immaturity-Maturity Continuum

Immaturity	Maturity
Passive	Active
Dependence	Independence
Behave in a few ways	Capable of behaving in many ways
Erratic shallow interests	Deeper and stronger interests
Short time perspective	Long time perspective (past and future)
Subordinate position	Equal or superordinate position
Lack of awareness of self	Awareness and control over self

Source: Hersey and Blanchard (1972), p. 51.

The close correspondence between Loevinger's developmental stages and the models posited by Argyris and Schon is frightening because most of our schools and colleges, businesses, legislatures, social agencies, and community organizations operate in Model One fashion. Argyris argues that in doing so they keep individuals from maturing, as employees and students are given minimal control over their environment and are encouraged to be passive, dependent, and subordinate. Thus the pattern of keeping people immature is built into the fundamental management practices of most organizations.

This self-perpetuating condition argues powerfully for systematic attention to interpersonal competence by educational institutions so that the circle of limited personal development accompanied by limited prefessional competence and organizational effectiveness can be broken. Then both individuals and institutions can move toward more complex, satisfying, and productive behaviors.

The relationships between Loevinger's developmental stages and the Argyris and Schon models have powerful implications for education and for assessing experiential learning. Educational activities designed to foster Model One competence will be very different from those designed to foster Model Two competence. Indeed, there are well-developed institutions, seminars, workshops, and training materials that are oriented specifically toward one or the other pure type, as well as many undiscriminating mixtures of both. For an educational institution, clarity about which model is being addressed, and how, is imperative lest self-canceling and contradictory activities and values be unwittingly built into the same program.

It is an interesting question whether Model Two professional development activities can be pursued with a person at the self-protective or conformist stage of development, where interpersonal style is manipulative, exploitive, or superficially nice. Conversely, what happens when an autonomous, integrated person encounters a Model One professional development program? Although the empirical evidence is not in, a reasonable match between the developmental stage and the activities designed to foster increased professional competence or to modify interpersonal style would seem to be required.

Experiential learning can be especially helpful in achieving increased interpersonal and professional competence and in modifying interpersonal style. Experiential learning permits students to live through various work settings and social situations, and then to enlarge their perspectives on those situations by systematic observations, reading, discussion, reflection, and self-observation. This approach to learning can contribute significantly to interpersonal competence in ways that businesses, agencies, and organizations in which students are directly involved otherwise cannot. In addition, educational institutions can help students unlearn old behaviors and devise and practice new ones, so that professional and personal development can proceed in this key area.

Interpersonal competence has been considered at some length because of its general significance, because of its extreme pertinence to college students of all ages for both social and occupational reasons, and because experiential learning provides powerful opportunities for students in this area. But there are two other developmental areas yet to be recognized: the development of purpose and generativity, or the expansion of caring.

Clarifying purposes. "Lewis Carroll observed that no good fish goes anywhere without a porpoise, and many personality theorists agree. Adler emphasized the role of fictional goals (Ansbacher and Ansbacher, 1956). Erikson (1964) says 'Purpose, then, is the courage to envisage and pursue valued goals uninhibited by the defeat of infantile fantasies by guilt, and by the foiling fear of punishment (p. 122).' Allport (1961)' asserts, 'The core of the identity problem for the adolescent is the selection of an occupation or other life goal. The future, he knows, must follow a plan, and in this respect his sense of selfhood takes on a dimension entirely lacking in childhood . . . long-range purposes and distant goals add a new dimension to the sense of selfhood (p. 126). And later (p. 391) he observes that it is the pursuit of major goals that 'configurates a life' " (Miller, Galanter, and Pribram, 1960).

Miller and his colleagues have elaborated in detail how plans and purposes guide behavior. They point out that knowledge, action, and evaluation are essentially connected; knowledge guides action and action is rooted in evaluation, for without comparative values, deliberate action is pointless. They ask, "Does a plan supply the pattern for that essential connection of knowledge, evaluation and action?" (p. 61). The rest of their book answers yes.

Interests can play a role similar to that of purposes. "Interest" suggests that a course of action or an occupation engages an individual thoroughly. Activities do not exist in a vacuum. They require material, subject-matter, and educational conditions for implementation. They also require certain kinds of knowledge, competence, and values on the part of the self. Genuine interest brings these two areas together so that the individual finds his or her well-being identified with the outcomes.

White calls this growth trend "deepening of interests," "a movement toward fuller engagement with objects of interest so that 'their own issue,' their inherent nature and possibilities for development, increasingly guide the person's activity and become a part of the satisfaction. . . . Interests often enough grow broader as well as deeper, but our concern here is with one particular quality rather than with quantity or extensiveness. We are also not referring to the amount of time a person devotes to his interests; a trend toward deepening does not imply that he spends more and more of his hours in a state of absorption until at last everything else is excluded. The trend we have in mind is away from a state in which interests are casual, quickly dropped, pursued only from motives that do not become identified with advancement of the object. It is toward a state in which the sense of reward comes from doing something for its own sake" (1966, pp. 391, 393).

Persons with the most diverse, rich, and meaningful interests often seem to have difficulty in settling on future plans and in developing clear purposes that provide motivational power. For it is difficult to recognize, and more difficult to accept, that every affirmation is 90 percent renunciation, that every choice to do one thing is a choice not to do ten others. It is hard to give up becoming an expert skier, an accomplished musician, and a successful entrepreneur, in order to pursue a profession. It is likewise hard to give up reading contemporary literature, dabbling with mobiles, lying in the sun, building with wood, gambling. All interests provide satisfaction and stimulation. Who wants to surrender them for the abstract, hazy, and unexperienced rewards that may reside down some vocational path? Small wonder that many secure, able, and creative persons put off such decisions and spend prodigious ingenuity and energy keeping as many options open as they can.

Whatever the outcome of research on particular groups of people, it appears that development of purpose requires formulating plans and priorities that integrate avocational and recreational interests, vocational plans, marriage, family, and life-style considerations. As the research on developmental ages suggest, the emphasis given to one or another of these focal areas varies. The research also documents the continued concern for these areas as each person works through shifting personal priorities in response to changing external circumstances and internal needs.

Expansion of caring. The development of maturity is affected both by the clarifying of purposes and by the expansion of caring. *Expansion of caring* is Robert White's term, which he introduces thus (1966, p. 395): "The idea is by no means new. Something of the sort was suggested in Adler's descriptions of *social interest,* the natural tendency which he believed flowered in all of us to the extent that we outgrew egotism and the urge to be superior. Adler indicated his meaning in phrases such as 'sense of human solidarity' and 'fellowship in the human community' (1927, p. 23). Angyal offered the concept of a trend toward homonomy. The individual longs, he maintained, 'to become an organic part of something that he conceives as greater than himself . . . to be in harmony with superindividual units, the social world, nature, God, ethical world order, or whatever the person's formulation of it may be' (1941, p. 172)."

These ideas imply transcendence of the egocentrism that is natural in childhood and often prominent, and not entirely inappropriate, in adolescence. Allport's concept of extension of the sense of self is similar. The sense of self is extended when the welfare of another person, a group enterprise, or some other valued object becomes as important as (or identical with) one's own welfare: "Maturity advances in proportion as lives are decentered from the clamorous immediacy of the body and of egocenteredness. Self-love is a prominent and inescapable factor in every life, but it need not dominate. Everyone has self-love, but only self-extension is the earmark of maturity (1961, pp. 283, 285)."

The point will be missed if the term *caring* is understood in a superficial sense. It does not imply mere participation in the affairs of family, neighborhood, or larger community. Such activity can serve as an escape from loneliness and boredom or can simply offer pleasure in company and conversation; it does not necessarily signify real affective involvement in the welfare of others. Neither is the expansion of caring necessarily signified by having children or by being in an occupation like teaching or nursing where the welfare of others is the stated professional goal. Children can be produced but their interests neglected. Jobs can be taken simply because they provide security and a comfortable income. Nor is caring necessarily involved when a person expresses interest in bettering the condition of the disadvantaged. Such interests may serve needs to rebel against the established order, or to secure political power. As White says, "Caring refers only to the things one really has at heart. It cannot be safely inferred from externals. The true hallmark is in the sphere of feeling: how much the person suffers when the object of his caring suffers, how much he rejoices when the object rejoices, how naturally and spontaneously he does the things that are required to promote the object's well-being" (White, 1966, p. 402).

Erikson's concept of generativity is closely allied with White's term. In *Childhood and Society,* he defines this concept as "primarily the concern in establishing and guiding the next generation, although there are individuals who, through misfortune or because of special and genuine gifts in other directions, do not apply this drive to their own offspring. And indeed, the concept generativity is meant to include such more popular synonyms as productivity and creativity, which, however, cannot replace it" (1963, pp. 266–267).

Ages and stages. Our discussion thus far has described some of the principal dimensions of adult development: ego development, moral and ethical development, intellectual development, interpersonal style and interpersonal competence, development of purpose, and expansion of caring. Work in some of these areas is much more advanced than in others, and certainly the relationships suggested across areas and stages are still largely hypothetical. But these solid bodies of research and theory tell us much we need to know about students seeking postsecondary education.

The research on developmental ages is in a formative state. Major phases—pulling up roots, provisional adulthood, age-thirty transition, rooting, midlife transition, restabilization—are beginning to be identified. The impacts of critical life events—leaving home, falling in love, getting married, having a child, taking a job, getting fired, quitting, facing career limitations, death of a parent, changing a career, retirement—are becoming clearer than before.

Taken as a whole, current knowledge concerning ages and stages has powerful implications for higher education. But before turning to those we must recognize that the research and theory referred to here were generated almost entirely during the past thirty to forty years, in the United States. Therefore the results are limited by the historical conditions of those times, especially as they were influenced by special cultural forces operating in the United States during those years. The individualism, capitalism, materialism, affluence, and democratic idealism; the depression of the 1930s, World War II, and the postwar boom; the youth movements of the 1960s —all have influenced the lives of the researchers and the researched. To be sure, cross-cultural studies and earlier research and theory support much of what has been said, but we are far from any time-free and culture-free picture of the human condition.

Nevertheless, we do face challenges to education here in the United States, now. Despite the larger limitations of current knowledge, enough is known, on sufficient evidence, to be taken seriously.

This knowledge provides a solid foundation on which to build the conditions for lifelong learning and the learning society.

Implications for Education

The data early in this chapter concerning aging and the life cycle help us think more soundly about educational content and process. They clarify the larger motives behind the investments of time, money, and energy made by many students. Such data show us the more fundamental purposes behind significant desires, from the desire to earn a degree or change careers to the desire to meet new persons, read more widely, and explore new ideas and interests. This research reminds us that the existential questions of meaning, vocation, social responsibility, and human relationships, which so many adolescents face with difficulty, are reconfronted by many when they are thirty or forty or sixty years old.

With such information in our working knowledge we can more effectively distinguish between individuals whose aim is simply professional training and those for whom professional concerns are aimed toward clarifying the major expectations of a job and the career patterns associated with it. We can better recognize that the thirty-five-year-old who comes for clearly specified professional knowledge or competence because he desires a promotion or a new opportunity will define a program and approach it very differently from the forty-five-year-old who wonders whether all those long hours, family sacrifices, short-changed human relationships, and atrophied interests were really worth it. Both of these students will be different from the twenty-five-year-old eagerly exploring the potentials of a first career choice. The thirty-year-old housewife pressured by a husband who thinks that she should become more sophisticated, develop broader interests, get out more and define her own career, will be very different from the twenty-five-year-old just settling into the challenges and satisfactions of new babies and a new home, and from the fifty-year-old who is building a richer existence with a devoted spouse. These data also help each student and faculty member anticipate the problems and changes that may come in the future. Educational purposes and plans for study can then take account of these predictions.

By recognizing these general patterns and responding to individual differences within them, our ability to help students identify their own motives and educational needs will be enhanced substantially. When both students and faculty take account of such research and theory, educational activities more often will be on target, programs can be more effectively planned, and more general issues concerning staffing, resources for learning, and evaluation can be soundly settled.

Beyond this information about age differences, the research and theory concerning developmental stages has more fundamental implications for colleges and universities. It suggests some of the major changes necessary for more effective higher education. Table 8 takes the levels of ego, moral, and intellectual development and posits relationships among them, and motives for education, orientations toward knowledge, learning processes, institutional function, and educational practices. The table draws on materials developed by Harold Lasker and his associates for use with and by adults at the Harvard Graduate School of Education, on observations by Jack Noonan at Virginia Commonwealth University, and on my own research and experience (1969, 1973, 1974). The relationships also are consistent with other substantial bodies of research and theory. The varied studies of cognitive styles, despite their diverse formulations and points of departure, find relationships similar to those indicated. Witkin's (1972) studies of field-dependent and field-independent students, for example, support the suggested relationships with different stages of ego development, moral development, and intellectual development. So do Stern's (1970) studies of authoritarians, antiauthoritarians, and rationals, and of relationships between student needs and educational environments. The work of Feldman and Newcomb (1969), Heath (1968), Katz (1968), and others concerning college impacts on student development also supports many of the postulated relationships.

The basic point made by Table 8 is that motives for learning, learning styles, and orientations toward knowledge are linked to levels of ego development, moral development, and intellectual development. These motives and orientations, backed by the broader reinforcements of developmental levels, in turn define appropriate institutional functions or roles. If learning processes, and educational

Table 8. Individual Differences and Educational Practice

Ego Development	Moral Development	Intellectual Development	Motive for Education	What is Knowledge?	What Use is Knowledge?
Self-protective Opportunistic	Obedience-punishment oriented	Knowledge (simple recall)	Instrumental; satisfy immediate needs	A *possession* which helps one get desired ends; ritualistic actions which yield solutions	Education to get: means to concrete ends; used by self to obtain effects in world
Conformist	Instrumental egoism and exchange; good-boy, approval oriented	Comprehension Application	Impress significant others; gain social acceptance; obtain credentials and recognition	*General information* required for social roles; objective truth given by authority	Education to be: social approval, appearance, status used by self to achieve according to expectations and standards of significant others
Conscientious	Authority, rule and social-order oriented	Analysis Synthesis	Achieve competence re competitive or normative standards. Increase capacity to meet social responsibilities	*Know how:* Personal skills in problem solving; divergent views resolved by rational processes	Education to do: competence in work and social role; used to achieve internalized standards of excellence and to serve society
Autonomous	Social contracts, legalistic orientation Moral principle orientation	Evaluation	Deepen understanding of self, world, and life cycle; develop increasing capacity to manage own destiny	Personally generated *insight* about self and nature of life; subjective and dialectical; paradox appreciated	Education to become: self-knowledge; self-development; used to transform self and the world

Where Does Knowledge Come From?	Learning Processes	Institutional Function	Teaching Practice	Student-Teacher Relationships	Evaluation
From external authority; from asking how to get things	*Imitation;* acquire information, competence, as given by authority	Arouse attention and maintain interest; to show how things should be done	Lecture-exam	Teacher is authority, transmitter, judge; student is receiver, judged	By teacher only
From external authority; from asking what others expect and how to do it		Provide predetermined information and training programs; certify skills and knowledge	Teacher led; dialogue or discussion		By teacher only
			Open "leaderless" "learner centered" discussion	Teacher is a "model" for student identification	By teacher and peers
Personal integration of information based on rational inquiry; from setting goals; from asking what is needed, how things work, and why	*Discover* correct answers through scientific method and logical analyses; multiple views are recognized but congruence and simplicity are sought	Provide structured programs which offer concrete skills and information, opportunities for rational analysis, and practice, which can be evaluated and certified	Programed learning; correspondence study; televised instruction	"Teacher" is an abstraction behind system. Student a recipient	By system
Personal experience and reflection; personally generated paradigms, insights, judgments	*Seek new experiences;* reorganize past conception on the basic of new experiences; develop new paradigms; create new dialectics	Ask key questions; pose key dilemmas; confront significant discontinuities and paradoxes; foster personal experience and personally generated insights	Contract learning: 1. Time, objectives, activities, evaluation negotiated between student and teacher at the outset and held throughout	Student defines purposes in collegial relationship with teacher; teacher is resource, contributes to planning and evaluation	By teacher, peers, system, self; teacher final judge
			Contract learning: 2. Time, objectives, activities, evaluation defined generally by student, modifiable with experience		By teacher, peers, system, self; self final judge

Note: Just as each developmental stage incorporates and transforms earlier stages, so also each subsequent learning process and institutional function incorporates and transforms earlier levels.

Source: Personal communication; adapted from materials developed by Harold Lasker, Harvard Graduate School of Education.

practices consistent with them, are developed to carry out these institutional functions, a systematic institutional response can be created that best serves students at particular levels of development.

The problem is that most institutions only pitch to one or two developmental levels, although their students span the full range. Most institutions are oriented toward the opportunistic, conforming-to-persons, or conforming-to-rule levels of ego development and to the memorizing, applying, and analyzing levels of intellectual development. They treat education as though it were a commodity, a collection of discreet items, packaged in a few standard-sized boxes, sold by the Carnegie unit. It is not by chance that the supermarket has been an appealing metaphor for some educators, and that curriculum committees and departments, like merchandizers, primarily talk about offerings of this year or next year in the light of shifting student interests.

The metaphor may be hackneyed and overstated. But it is more truth than poetry for many institutions. Take any ten at random. How many curricula, courses, classes, seminars, and examinations help students build knowledge from personal experiences and personally generated syntheses and paradigms? How many teachers in the natural sciences, the humanities, and the social and behavioral sciences help students not only to acquire basic concepts, competency, and knowledge, but also help them to use those learnings to make some sense of life and of themselves, to generate personal insights through subjective and dialectical processes? Certainly many students are not prepared, or motivated, for that level of work. But of those who are, how many are recognized and responded to accordingly? And how often are explicit efforts made to help those not ready to become so?

Most institutions treat truth as objectively real, modeled, given by authority, or "discovered" by logical or scientific analyses. Conceptions concerning the nature of knowledge, where it comes from, and how it is to be used emphasize acquiring information or competence in order to satisfy immediate needs, to obtain immediate benefits, to do a particular job, or to fill a particular role. Current changes toward competency-based programs create closer correspondence between objectives, educational activities, and outcomes, and specify more apposite criteria for evaluation. Greater "truth in packaging" and more effective education for some students may result. But most competency-based programs address the same developmental levels as the typical system.

The relationships between motives and orientations become more apparent when explicit teaching practices, student-faculty relationships, and orientations toward evaluation are addressed. The lecture-examination system as typically practiced best suits the fearful-dependent, opportunistic, and conforming-to-persons levels of ego development and the obedience-punishment, instrumental egoism and exchange, and good-boy orientations of moral development. The key dynamic here is the comfortable fit between, on the one hand, the student's disposition to identify with persons in authority, to accept their definitions of right and wrong, and to avoid punishment by referring to their power, and, on the other, the teacher's assertion of authority, emphasis on dispensing information for students to memorize, and use of exams to punish wrong answers and reward right ones. When the lecture-examination approach goes beyond the personal authority of the teacher and makes use of more abstract authority, as often is the case, then the approach moves to a level oriented toward authority, rule, and the social order. Here it is the system that defines right and wrong. The same authoritarian dynamic occurs except that it is more generalized. Socratic dialogue or teacher-led discussions best fit the opportunistic, instrumental egoism and exchange level; they provide rich information about the teacher's views and permit the student to shape his own responses accordingly, receiving immediate rewards through the satisfying exchanges that result. Open, leaderless, learner-centered discussions best fit the approval orientation where sensitivity, pleasing and helping others, and acceptance of group decisions are called for. Programed learning, correspondence study, and most other forms of mediated instruction currently used best fit the authority, rule, and social order orientation.

Contract learning can take two forms. In one form, the objectives are set by the student but the time, activities, and criteria for evaluation result from negotiations between the student and teacher. The contract is a commitment to the plan developed, and the plan is held throughout unless major events call for renegotiation. This approach to contract learning best fits the principled autonomous stages of ego development, and the social contract, legalistic orientation of moral development. In the second form of contract learning, the student, with or without help from the teacher and others, defines the objectives, time, activities, and criteria for evaluation. The contract may be quite specific or very general. In either case it is held flexibly and modified in the light of experience as it is pursued. This approach to contract learning best fits the principled autonomous stage and the moral principle orientation.

Of course, contract learning can be highly teacher-controlled and authoritarian, not only in terms of learning activities and evaluation, but also in the purposes judged acceptable. Furthermore, skilled teachers can use lectures and exams, seminars, and group discussions in ways that challenge autonomous students and also serve opportunistic, conformist, and conscientious ones. The assertions made above rest on studies of students' responses to typical teaching practices. There are exceptional teachers, courses, classes, seminars, and discussion groups. Most of us have experienced them, but they are exceptions to the general fare.

Different teaching practices also are expressions of different approaches to student-teacher relationships and evaluation. The teacher as an authority, transmitter, and judge, who carries sole responsibility for evaluation, best fits the obedience-punishment and the opportunistic-instrumental egoism stages. Where the teacher is a model, known well enough to permit student identification, and where evaluation includes fellow students as well as the teacher, the fit is with the conforming-to-persons, approval-oriented stage. In programed learning and other forms of mediated instruction, the teacher is an abstraction behind the system. Criteria for evaluation are specified by the system and responses are usually mechanically scored, often by machines. In contract learning, the teacher is a resource person who contributes to planning and evaluation. The relationship may be more or less collegial; and the student may carry more or less responsibility for defining the program and for evaluation, depending upon the approach used. The patterns of relationship and the approaches to learning and evaluation in contract learning best fit the principled autonomous stages of ego development and moral development.

The relationships set forth in Table 8 suggest a way of thinking about and planning postsecondary education for lifelong learning. But they are only a beginning. Any institution serving a diverse range of adults will have students at different developmental ages and different developmental stages. They will range from opportunistic to principled autonomous levels of ego development, from obedience-punishment orientation to moral principle orientation in moral development, and from concrete operations and memorization to complex formal operations, application and evaluation in intellectual development. There will be Model One students and those at or striving toward Model Two; students with deep interests and clear purposes and others uncertain, diffuse, or in transition from one job, life style, or marriage to another.

Because of this diversity, an institution cannot simply pitch its educational program at a particular stage or limit it to a particular area. Many opportunistic and conformist students come to higher education with important purposes that deserve to be met. These purposes should not be ignored; those students should not be turned away or turned off. But neither will their needs be fully served if they are not helped to see more clearly the dynamics of age and stage by which they are more generally governed. Alternatives need to be developed that more effectively serve students at more complex levels of development, but an institution serving diverse adults cannot limit itself simply to those more complex levels.

Colleges and universities must be responsive to the major dimensions of adult development and to the ages and stages of the students served. How can we accomplish such a complex task? How can we get hold of it in a productive way? Table 9 summarizes the major areas and levels of development described in this chapter and the relationships among them. It can be seen as a crude map that defines a course of development for postsecondary education, lifelong learning, experiential learning, and its assessment. This map probably contains fully as much error and misconception as those that guided Leif Ericson, Christopher Columbus, and Vasco de Gama. But with courage, ingenuity, and persistence, they found new worlds and created more accurate maps in the process. There is no reason why higher education cannot do likewise in the future.

Work is already underway in several key areas. Lawrence Kohlberg and his associates have developed materials and teaching

Table 9. Relationships Among Areas and Stages of Human Development

Ego Development	Moral and Ethical Development			Intellectual Development		Developing Purposes	Expansion of Caring	Interpersonal Style	
	(Kohlberg)	(Perry)	(Loevinger)	(Piaget)	(Bloom)			(Loevinger)	(Argyris and Schon)
Amoral	Egocentric	Basic duality	Stereotypy, conceptual confusion	Symbolic, intuitive thought		Play		Autistic Symbiotic	Model One
Fearful-dependent	Obedience-punishment oriented	Multiplicity prelegitimate	Conceptual simplicity	Concrete operations: 1. Categorical classification	Memorization	Sex/social	Close friendships	Receiving, dependent, exploitive	Defensive, inconsistent, competitive, controlling, fearful of being vulnerable, withholding feelings, overly concerned about self and others, or underconcerned about others
Opportunistic	Instrumental egoism and exchange	Multiplicity subordinate	Stereotypes and cliches	Concrete operations: 2. Reversible concrete thought	Application			Wary, manipulative exploitive	
Conforming to persons	Good boy-good girl, approval oriented	Multiplicity correlate, or relativism subordinate						Belonging, helping, superficial niceness	Defensive interpersonal and group relationships Defensive norms Low freedom of choice, internal commitment and risk-taking

Conforming to rule	Authority, rule, and social order oriented	Relativism correlate, competing or diffuse	Conceptual complexity, idea of patterning	Formal Operations: 1. Relations involving the inverse of the reciprocal	Analysis	Marriage, family	Wife, children	Intensive, responsible, mutual concern for communications	Model Two Minimally defensive
Principled autonomous	Social contracts, legalistic oriented	Commitment foreseen	Increased conceptual complexity, complex patterns	Formal operations: 2. Relations involving triads		Vocational, professional	Institution, organization, avocation	Respect for autonomy	Minimally defensive interpersonal relations and group dynamics.
	Moral principle orientation	Initial commitment; implications of commitments; developing commitments	Toleration for ambiguity; broad scope; objectivity	Formal operations: 3. Construction of all possible relations	Synthesis	Life style	Commitments in intimacy	Cherishing of individuality	Learning-oriented norms.
				Systematic isolation of variables		Social service	Devotion to human welfare and dignity; social responsibility		
				Deductive hypothesis testing	Evaluation				

approaches that explicitly aim to help a person move from one level of moral development to the next, and have used these in secondary schools, colleges, and prison settings. Harold Lasker is tackling Loevinger's stages of ego development and is trying various approaches to achieve change from one stage to the next with Shell Corporation employees and adult students at Harvard. Chris Argyris and others are helping corporation presidents, educational administrators, and graduate students increase professional and interpersonal competence, pushing ahead both conceptually and practically. The CAEL project has begun work in this critical domain.

But higher education need not, and indeed cannot, leave all the work to professional specialists or to externally funded consortia, for the most important job is to reexamine current classes, courses, majors, general education programs, and degree requirements in the light of this knowledge. The disciplinary and interdisciplinary subject matters, the areas of vocational and professional preparation, and the programs oriented toward social problems and social concerns will remain the practical focus of most students, and the bread and butter of higher education. Although it is useful to develop specific programs, resources, and activities that explicitly address one or another area of development, aiming to help students move from one stage to the next, it is much more important to begin modifying and amplifying current programs so that students can pursue them at their optimum level of development, and progress developmentally while meeting their more immediate and practical purposes.

Students, faculty members, and administrators all can contribute to and profit from such a reexamination. A college president or provost can sit down with Table 9 and ask questions like these: How do current students distribute themselves among the areas and levels? Which areas and levels of development are best served by the major educational alternatives we provide, and by the facilities, faculty characteristics, and employment expectations that support those alternatives? A curriculum committee or the faculty of a department can ask which cells are addressed by current courses, external programs, seminars, honors courses, and major sequences. They can ask that courses and sequences specify relationships between teaching methods, field experiences, areas of student responsibility, readings, writings, examination questions, and the developmental areas and stages for which they are most appropriate.

Participation by faculty members in reexamining their own fields is critical, because they know most about the diverse possibilities available in textbooks and primary sources, in audio-visual materials, programed learning and other forms of mediated instruction. They know what kinds of field observations, work experiences, or volunteer activities may have most power. They know the areas of controversy, where the value issues reside, what kinds of career patterns may be possible. In short, the professionals who are directly involved can be the richest sources of creative suggestions for redesigning current courses, majors, and general education programs in ways that more adequately cover the ages, areas, and stages that characterize current college students.

Table 5 also can be a conceptual framework that students themselves use for self-evaluation and educational planning. With appropriate supplementary materials each student can decide first, whether to pursue one or another area directly, and second, how to pursue more immediate educational or vocational purposes in ways that also enable stage changes in one or more valued areas of development. On the basis of such reflections each student can make more powerful, efficient, and economical use of educational alternatives available, can help create others not yet considered, and can take more effective charge of his or her learning and personal development.

The importance of concrete contributions by individual students and faculty members, by departments and curriculum committees, and by individual administrators cannot be overestimated. They will provide the wide array of concrete examples that are critically needed. More basic research and theory is necessary and will be undertaken by the professional specialists whose business it is. But the basic need now is to demystify the affective domain, to demonstrate that colleges and universities can contribute to human development in ways that go beyond simple marketing of skills, information, and credentials.

For instance, experiential learning in academic disciplines such as philosophy, literature, drama, history, and science can contribute powerfully to several major dimensions of adult development, including moral and ethical development. We are most accustomed to thinking about the contribution of these academic disciplines to intellectual development, although we could become more explicit about ways in which the intellectual skills of application, analysis, synthesis, and evaluation can be fostered by various disciplinary and interdisciplinary studies. We are less accustomed to thinking about ways in which these disciplines contribute to moral and ethical development, interpersonal competence and style, and the development of social interest and clarity of purpose.

Often, professional and vocational studies are considered the key areas for these outcomes, but the disciplines themselves can be equally effective. Focusing on moral and ethical development in the following five fields may suggest possibilities for all fields that could be realized with further thought and energy. These particular examples (which draw heavily on Collier, Wilson, and Tomlinson, 1974) are simply illustrations, and by using them I do not mean to ignore or minimize the importance of other dimensions of development or other areas of study.

Philosophy. Philosophy does not contribute to moral and ethical development by explicitly, surreptitiously, or unconsciously instilling a particular set of metaphysical assumptions or beliefs through indoctrination and less obvious forms of persuasion. Nor does philosophy contribute most effectively by teaching about particular belief systems or philosophic orientations. Philosophy contributes direction through its root purpose, the search for truth through logical reasoning, and through its basic method of analyzing the grounds on which fundamental beliefs are held and by examining the concepts for expressing them. Socrates gave us a model, driving home the power of dialogue and dialectic.

The requirements of philosophy speak directly to moral and ethical development: take truth seriously; set aside yourself; penetrate your prejudices; distinguish between what is right and what you like; use care with language; define your terms; abide by publicly stated rules; subject your views to public criticism. These requirements express general values, but they do not state particular beliefs nor do they assert a metaphysical assumption. In this sense, the study of philosophy is free of authoritarian and even authoritative dynamics. There are no answers like those created by mathematical systems or scientific research. Indeed, answers shrivel in significance compared with the importance of the doing. It is by helping each student to learn the doing, to develop the skills and habits required in relation to whatever content is significant for that person, that makes philosophy powerful.

In terms of the definition of experiential learning used in this chapter, most teachers would probably agree that lecturing to students is less likely to stimulate such learning than experiences involving dialogue: dialogue between teacher and individual student, among several students, between students and other adults. The location can be the classroom, but could be as well the departmental office, the coffee shop in the union, the professor's home after supper, the dormitory lounge, or any site where the student can discuss values, ideals, and beliefs with someone else and ponder the implications afterwards. Conversations with the student's parents and with other older adults whom the student emulates may be the most valuable of such events.

When the requirements for doing philosophy are brought to bear on concrete issues and experiences encountered at work, in the home, or in the community, increased potential for moral and ethical development results. To what extent is a corporate or institutional decision made on its merits and to what extent does it serve special individual interests? Are the political issues squarely faced or are substantive issues really a smoke screen for underlying personal interests? Do parental standards concerning behavior really rest on judgments concerning the child's well being and development? Or do they basically aim to meet parents' needs for comfort, quiet, order, peace of mind? Are the arguments and data from younger family members recognized and evaluated for soundness and accuracy, or are they patronized and passed over? How much philosophical rigor characterizes the writing, debates, open discussions of community issues concerning zoning, busing, taxes? How much rigor characterizes the individual student's position on such issues? "Doing philosophy" in relation to such experiential contexts as these not only enriches understanding of the content and implications of various philosophic systems, it also helps each student move ahead in the ways his or her particular beliefs and values are held.

Literature. Literature, of course, involves characters. Characters display motives and emotions; they reveal values, attitudes, and belief systems with the reasoning processes, prides, and prejudices that lie behind them. Literature gives us these persons in a context, and provides insights concerning the pressures and sequences of experience that lead to change in characters and consequent outcomes.

What levels of moral and ethical development characterize the key persons in best sellers like *What Makes Sammy Run* and *The Fountainhead,* or in classics like *The Red and the Black* or *The Grapes of Wrath?* What are the pressures which force these persons toward one level or another? What internal strengths, from what sources, provide leverage against those external forces?

In literature we find persons who have acted out our most private fantasies, who have pushed our most cherished assumptions to the utmost, who exemplify *in extremis* our most fundamental predispositions. By examining those characters and by putting ourselves and our experiences against them, we gain insight and nourish our moral and ethical development.

Literature provides the plot, the issue, and the flaw that gives the dramatic fulcrum. O'Neill's and Pinter's characters struggle with dominance and submission, mastery and mastered. Shakespeare uses mistaken identity to continually contrast role and self. Conflicts between self-interest and commitment run rampant. Dostoyevsky, Kafka, and Malraux portray the inexorable connection between morality and identity with protagonists whose values are so challenged that sense of self and equilibrium are upset. Moral ambivalence is a dominant theme in contemporary literature. An entire culture understands the term *Catch 22.*

Most significantly, perhaps, literature takes us beyond vague generalities about goodness, truth, justice, integrity, and responsibility. Commitment to personal, social, and educational values, which assert concern for responsible citizenship, tolerance of others, and autonomy and interdependence is easy in the abstract, but literature, by being descriptively specific, shows what those values can really mean. It protects us against easy labeling and facile self-deception.

The typical emphasis on critical analysis of character, plot, imagery, and the like, need not be displaced. It can be enlarged and more powerfully driven when explicit links to moral issues are forged. An awareness of these factors, accompanied by the individual's personal reflection, evaluation, and analysis can lead to more informed and intentional behavior. Thus the study of literature can become the catalyst for increased self-awareness, and can be made an encounter that forms a kinetic link between literature, the student, and his or her moral and ethical development.

Although reading is a solitary experience that can change attitudes and knowledge, it is through discussion that most of us are stimulated to prove these issues. Group discussions, such as those exemplified by many classes and Great Books meeting groups, provide such opportunities when they move beyond the technical consideration of the writer's craft to a consideration of the issues raised by the characters, plots, and social contexts. Beyond reading and discussion, writing itself stimulates further thought. Character sketches, metaphors, autobiographical vignettes, imaginative narrative—all can aim to capture different levels of moral and ethical development, thereby changing and enlarging one's perspective.

Putting literature against personal experiences and current contexts not only enriches the understanding of the literature, it also provides insights useful for personal development. Who are the Sammy Glicks and Willie Lomans where I work or live? What is their social context? What plot are they playing out? And what is the novel I have lived so far and continue to create? Which character and conditions match my own? What forces operated for them and with what result? What is the likely climax and denouement when my play has been staged?

Drama. Sophocles, Shakespeare, Shaw, Synge—drama long has been the art form that most commonly confronts the citizenry with matters of moral concern. That is why there are pervasive and persistent problems of censorship in film, television, radio, and theater. Although the empirical evidence concerning effects on viewers is limited and mixed, except perhaps with regard to violence, our subjective experience is often profound. But the concern here is not with the experience of watching drama but with learning it through performance. Study of plays is similar to study of other literary forms and therefore has the same potentials as those mentioned for literature. Consider, however, the variety of learning experience possible in creating, producing, directing and performing in a drama.

Drama is representation. Actors assume roles. The director and the cast, individually and collectively, must first reconstruct for themselves the historical condition, the situation, the issues, the persons, and the dynamics of relationships among them. Then, drawing on these experiences, each person must assume a particular role in order to present the play. This process requires that participants make the author's work their own: the author's situation, dilemma, persons and reactions, values, opinions, actions, and consequences have to be owned. Those elements can be analyzed for understanding but they cannot be judged. They must be responded to personally if powerful representation is to occur; they cannot be dismissed or distorted to conform to personal biases or beliefs. Paradoxically therefore, drama requires both dissociation from self and use of self: it requires stepping outside oneself to be someone else while drawing on self to understand that being.

Note also that dynamic directors often see interpretation and rehearsal not as working from a text but toward it. Improvisations and rehearsal texts differ from performance texts; they demand action and experiences in real life situations prior to onstage representations in order to build toward a coherent, powerful, and entertaining representation. Drama need not always proceed from an author's text. Both professional and amateur theater create plays by working directly from personal experiences, original documents, or both. Improvisations are sharpened, issues and dynamics are clarified. Public audiences are admitted as the creation evolves.

Of course, creating theater does not automatically lead to moral and ethical development. There is no empirical evidence that demonstrates consistent differences between theater people and others, and individual cases seem to span the full range. That would not be unexpected for professionals where dissociation from self is built into daily existence. Students likewise can create those compartments and must do so to realize the play. But the play creates an experiential context that supplies rich capital for postplay self-confrontation and self-examination. Activities that analyze the dissociation and exploit its capital have powerful potential for moral and ethical development.

History. History, perhaps more than any other academic discipline, speaks directly to the core problem of moral and ethical development as that development is conceptualized by Kohlberg and Perry. History is a record of persons who must make absolute decisions in the face of pluralistic values, with relativistic and contingent information. History confronts us with that essential human condition, with ways particular situations have been met, and with the consequences of the decisions and actions taken. If history is a record of human consciousness and human decisions, it is also a record of human morality in action.

History also records the remorselessness of sequence. It makes apparent the fact that each act is a moral statement, that each individual is both constrained and freed by the actions of others and by the sequence he or she creates through living. Consider the issues of the past and those before us: the Crusades, the Inquisition, the American, French, and Russian Revolutions, the American Civil War, Nazi Germany, Hiroshima, Vietnam, the Arab-Israeli conflict, Watergate, busing, New York City, the United Nations. Consider the persons: Moses, Nero, the English kings and queens, Napoleon, Catherine the Great, Lincoln, Hitler, Churchill, Roosevelt, Truman, Kennedy, Johnson, Nixon. What levels of moral and ethical development were implicit—or explicit—in these events and times? At what level of ethical and intellectual development did these persons act?

The basic objectives for the study of history need not be supplanted by activities that speak to moral and ethical development. Historiography, historical methods, and historical understanding can be pursued in ways that foster moral development while achieving disciplinary aims. The eventful experiences for this development can range from the analysis of primary documents and field trips to important sites to analyses of one's own background and actions and interviews of parents, other relatives, friends, and acquaintances regarding major turning points in their lives and their own views of life and responsibility.

Science. Like philosophy, the practice and methodology of science and the principles on which these rest have direct implications for moral and ethical development. Rules of evidence and methodological constraints exist to screen out subjectivity and to control for biases introduced by special interests or conditions. Issues are to be settled on the basis of evidence, not through coercion, personal argument, or appeal to authority. Yet scientists cannot fully control their biases and will delude themselves and others if they claim objectivity. These principles and problems take us a long way down the Perry-Kohlberg continua for moral and ethical development.

In addition, the content of the sciences has moral and ethical implications: evolution, environment, limits to growth, genetics and geriatrics, biofeedback and behavior modification, fission and fusion. And there are the scientists: Darwin, Copernicus, Galileo, Nobel, Bacon, Oppenheimer, Watson, Skinner, Coleman. How have they coped with the ethical implications of their work? What are the sociocultural, familial, and personal roots of the values they hold? How are those values held? Innocence is no longer adequate preparation for the social role of scientist. For the first time, scientists are foreclosing certain avenues of research because the ethical implications look unmanageable. Is that decision morally sound? On what grounds?

Basically, then, the method and content of science and the social role of scientists offer significant opportunities for moral and ethical development. Given the pressures to cover increasingly complex and comprehensive information, activities to address these objectives will probably be most readily introduced as science for the nonscientist. But perhaps the need is more urgent for the budding professional. In a world where professional expertise has become institutionalized and where the fruits of science and technology have become increasingly dominant, extension of professional training to include explicit attention to moral and ethical concerns may be critical.

Laboratory experience has long been accepted in science education, both in learning scientific methodology and in replicating critical past experiments. Actual participation in new experiments can be even more eventful, particularly if the participation involves discussion of methodological responsibility and the substantive implications of findings. Vicarious participation, through reading such books as Watson's *The Double Helix,* can prove useful if similarly combined with discussion. And participating as the subject rather than the experimenter, for example, in a psychological or sociological experiment can lead to consideration of responsibility for other subjects, both human and nonhuman, of research.

These examples could be extended into other disciplines and other areas of development. But they may be sufficient to illustrate that for higher education to go beyond its traditional concern for information, cognitive skills, and credentials into other critical areas of adult development, teachers need not become psychotherapists and courses need not become sensitivity training sessions. The best approach lies in relatively simple modifications of activities and areas of study already underway that can trigger changes in judgments and feelings as well as knowledge through significant events and experiences.

Chapter Seven

Campus and Workplace as Arenas

Sheila C. Gordon

If the educational goal of most colleges and universities continues to be broad preparation for life, and if the postcollegiate life and work of their alumni offer the ultimate test of the effectiveness of their learning (the ability to transfer, apply, and use knowledge), then many institutions must consider whether their programs and methods are geared toward producing graduates who not only speak and write as educated people but also function, perform, and make decisions as educated people. As James S. Coleman has pointed out in Chapter Five, people learn in at least two different ways: through information assimilation and through experiential learning. Some few institutions may be able to emphasize only the first of these learning modes, but most must incorporate multiple learning strategies in their programs.

Students, together with their families, share the expectation that their college experience will help them achieve more informed, enlightened lives after college. A central aspect of their lives will be

108

work; upon graduation, students face the job market and the workplace with hopes that their college experiences have prepared them to negotiate and take maximum advantage of this new milieu.

The workplace, in turn, expects such preparation of college graduates. It expects them to have gained a considerable level of sophistication through knowledge of the arts and sciences, history, and literature. Beyond any technical skills graduates may have mastered in their own fields of study, they are expected to be able to identify, investigate, analyze, and solve problems, and to relate general skills to the objectives and style of the employing agency.

New employees need to have an understanding of their own values and incentives. Conflicts of status, autonomy, degree of interpersonal contact, economic incentives, and physical surroundings are some of the typical and not infrequently competing values that form eddies around the experienced worker. The Watergate debacle and the agonies of a John Dean and a Jeb Magruder cast into relief the problems, temptations, and confusions that a young person may face in work.

Were value confusion not enough to make beginning work experience a trial, recent graduates are often saddled with another difficulty. They may feel ill-prepared to set objectives for themselves, to measure their own learning, growth, or work performance in the work setting. The pristine educational world has preset objectives for them and has oriented them to the measurement tools of tests and papers. Employers, however, find that the workplace uses different measures, typically ones such as time, cost, and impact.

Time, for example, is a negligible factor in a world where study schedules are individualized and "incomplete" grades negate deadlines. In the highly interdependent world of work, deadlines are harder to defer and five o'clock may often provide a seemingly arbitrary (but real) cutoff to daily activities. Time and productivity commingle in the workplace in a way that is foreign to academe —and recent graduates often feel frustration and confusion. A graduate may feel equally disconcerted when he or she has drafted a report with elegant language and detailed citations, which would have merited an A in school but which the boss dismisses as irrelevant, too late to respond to the problem, or both. Similarly, the young engineer or secretary may be confused to find well-developed technical skills considered to be secondary to general skills of judgment and interpretation.

In summary, the college graduate entering the workplace has multiple needs. He or she needs to have a broad understanding of the dynamics of the workplace and to be able to transfer to those settings the general theories and approaches learned in liberal arts and other courses; to be able to sort out the distinctive values, operating styles, and politics of the workplace; to be prepared to understand his or her own values and incentives within the context of that setting; to be able to measure his or her own learning, growth, and performance in the experiential setting; and to be able to recognize the need to modify or upgrade technical skills learned in the classroom.

In short, the well-educated person ought to be one capable and confident of the relationships between what he or she has studied and how he or she can apply that knowledge beyond college—for example, in the workplace—so that instead of being controlled by the environment and by a job, he or she can master it.

Such preparation should not be interpreted as vocational education. It is, instead, preparation for life. And it is not enough to assume that conventional classroom preparation in a specific academic discipline leading to advanced study in that field is the best route to this solid, general preparation. Colleges must ask how and if their curricula help prepare their graduates to move toward positions of leadership, if their students themselves understand the roles they may play and how they will bring their education to bear on these roles, and if their students have gained skills pertinent to the changing requirements of life and work.

In short, after many years of neglect, the question of the relationship of education to life and work is drawing considerable attention. Until recently, trends in postwar higher education contained an inherent contradiction. On the one hand, the values and style of the university—those of promoting research and inquiry within academic disciplines—increasingly drew a wedge between undergraduate education and later life and eclipsed the collegiate values of general education and preparation for life. Yet, in an irony of history, this trend paralleled that of the growth of mass—almost compulsory—higher education, with the college degree becoming the standard credential for employment. Thus, new or nontraditional students typically find their need to go to college (to get a better job) confounded by the institutional emphasis on scholarly research. In many cases, they find not only that their general skills and understandings relating to work are poorly developed but also that the technical skills learned in the classroom are inappropriate, insufficiently adaptable, or obsolete.

The junior computer programer may find no demand for her skills; the young accountant may find himself helpless without sophisticated knowledge of data processing; and the B.A. or M.A. in a liberal arts field such as history, philosophy, or language, may experience the greatest discontinuity: his or her highly developed skills are directly adapted to only one career path, research and teaching in that discipline. Since only a tiny fraction of graduates can expect to follow that option, the vast majority join the frustrated computer programers and elementary education majors, directionless, frequently jobless, and at a loss as to how and where to seek other opportunities. Moreover, the growing population of mature, adult students returning to college raises questions about how higher education relates to prior work experience and to the specific and often sophisticated needs of adult students for career improvement and change.

Supplements to the Classroom

Many institutions have assumed that their extracurricular programs will fulfill objectives of personal development. Others have considered the extracurriculum a popular frill and have had no particular expectations for it. In many cases, it is primarily through student government, the campus newspaper, and other student activities that students come to recognize and develop the skills that will prove central to their later success—for example, judgment, decision making, interpersonal competence, self-confidence, problem solving, and understanding and effecting change.

The limits of the extracurriculum are obvious, however. Its activities do not reach all students—in fact, they typically reach only a few; the activities receive little input from experienced individuals, including faculty; and they are seldom structured learning situations.

There are learning opportunities in the extracurriculum that faculty could more effectively explore, although such activities cannot be expected to substitute for major gaps in classroom offerings. In short, with recognition of its limits, the extracurriculum could be woven effectively into institutional program objectives.

Many institutions contend that their placement offices and counseling staffs provide the needed links to work and future careers. But, typically, inadequate attention is given to the connections between their efforts and the formal curriculum as well as to the degree of impact that such services have. In fact, in many institutions, only a minority of students have any contact with career counseling services, and placement and counseling services often seem to be unrelated to academic advising.

Institutions considering an expansion of their curricular relationships to life and work ought to do more than rely on the extracurriculum or these student service offices. One approach is to reinforce or directly complement existing fields of study with non-classroom experience. An example of a reinforcement approach is field research in which a student applies concepts, generally from a liberal arts discipline, in a faculty-supervised project, such as participating in an archeological dig or collecting statistical data for a sociological research project. Other illustrations include preprofessional experiences, well-established in a number of fields, including practice teaching, social work field assignments, and clinical practica in the health fields. Here the student is specifically assigned to observe and apply course objectives learned in the classroom. In addition, cooperative education programs have frequently emphasized the student's involvement in a work placement directly related to his or her field of study. A student in a cooperative education program majoring in mechanical engineering thus expects to gain experience related to that field, as does a computer science student through work in a data processing installation.

In contrast to the reinforcement approach, institutions may choose other approaches designed to supplement existing curricular offerings and foster general education outcomes, such as personal development, community participation, career awareness, and individual responsibility. Thus a number of colleges require freshmen to participate in personal growth and development experiences through

such activities as survival training in the wilderness through affilia-
tion with the Outward Bound program, interpersonal workshops,
and special freshman seminars. In other cases, colleges participate in
service-learning internships and social-political action programs that
place specific emphasis on direct public, social, or community service
—best illustrated by the extensive program of learning opportunities
coordinated by the North Carolina Internship Office in Raleigh,
under the direction of Robert Sigmon. Equally, cross-cultural experiences stress student exposure to different cultures and societies,
either within the United States or abroad, through such activities as
living and working with an Appalachian family or in a Bolivian
community, keeping a journal, and preparing a careful analysis and
report of knowledge gained. Similarly, the month-long intersession
under the 4-1-4 calendar permits a structured, temporary opportunity for career exploration or less structured time to travel or
simply to live in a community.

Finally, a college may choose to provide generalized exposure
to work and work values through its own operations. A unique
illustration of this approach is the labor program of Berea College
in Kentucky, which for over a century has relied on student work to
staff the institution. All students, as part of both a financial aid and
a philosophical approach, are required to participate in this program by staffing the cafeteria, the maintenance department, the
laboratories and offices; and they are expected to analyze what
they have learned from these experiences as well as to develop a
fundamental appreciation of the worth and dignity of labor.

The reinforcement approach typically emphasizes frequent
and consistent relationships between classroom-learned skills and
out-of-class practice. In contrast, the supplemental approach involves less coordination. Similarly, the reinforcement approach requires a high degree of faculty involvement—perhaps one faculty
supervisor per ten or fifteen students—and close student-faculty interaction, while most supplemental programs depend on the workplace or on-site supervisor for instruction and may have faculty-stu-
dent ratios ranging from one to fifty to one to two hundred during
any one term. In addition, the reinforcement approach tends to
require participation for graduation and allot academic credit for
it, while the supplemental approach involves more optional programs

on a purely volunteer basis, utilizing the summer or intersession periods, with no academic credit or graduation requirements attached.

Each institution must develop its own strategy for these varieties of experiential learning. This will vary in its purposes, location, student body, and other factors. A rural institution, for instance, may require work or field experience far from the campus, while an urban institution may incorporate part-time, off-campus work into a structured curriculum. A college serving an affluent student body may emphasize volunteer work experiences, conceivably abroad, while a less affluent institution may need to seek paying jobs for its students. A liberal arts college may encourage general and exploratory experiences not firmly related to one career, while another institution with a specialized, technically oriented curriculum may stress work placements that clearly reinforce classroom skills.

In addition, institutions must respond to a whole range of specific issues that are intimately related to their other programs: cost factors of various approaches; desirability of adding specially trained staff to run programs as compared to training existing faculty for this task; organization of a separate office or department to administer the work program and credit its learning as compared to decentralization to existing departments and individual faculty members; the number of credits awarded for off-campus experience (some institutions offer as few as three credits for three months of work experience while others offer up to fifteen credits for a semester of work). Answers to these issues may, of course, vary enormously, but one thing is clear: if institutions are to ensure that their offerings meet their goals, they must face these issues and respond creatively.

Problems of Integration

Clearly, students can both perform work and learn at the same time, as the experience of more and more colleges demonstrates. Yet problems exist in the relation between work and education that are likely to be important in determining the effectiveness of the workplace as an arena for student learning.

Among the most important of these problems are the diverse priorities of purpose that educators and employers bring to their interaction. For example, it is widely known that success in college correlates weakly with success in employment after college. This finding likely results in part from the fact that colleges generally have different priorities than employers, and these priorities are rooted, in turn, not simply in a division of labor between colleges and institutions of economic production but in different visions of what life and society ought to be.

When we put students under college supervision in work sites under employer supervision with the dual purpose of being work-productive and learning-productive, and when, in doing so, we avoid the issue of whether these different visions and immediate purposes can be accommodated in some mutually agreeable manner, we dim at once the prospects of a productive ongoing relationship. And added to this fundamental tension is the more specific need of both college and employer to set up mechanisms for supervision and evaluation of the student's performance. To meet each need requires expenditure in time and other resources, and these may be more than routine.

A second problem when work and learning are combined is the frequent outcome that either the work objective suffers or the learning objective does. More often than not, if work is paid for and is also meant to be the site of learning, the learning suffers when any potential conflict arises between getting the work done and doing the learning. If the work is not paid for or is poorly paid, the learning objective is more likely to be stressed by most learners in the event of a conflict of priorities between the two.

In some work situations, employers may themselves give priority to certain kinds of learning objectives over certain kinds of work or productivity objectives. For example, a beginning law clerk may be seen as a potential partner in the law firm or at least as an attorney in charge of major legal tasks. During the clerk's first year with the firm, it may put higher priority on learning more sophisticated tasks than on immediate work output of value to the firm. Similarly, when a manufacturing firm employs a craftsperson or when an insurance company employs a salesperson, the first few weeks of work may be devoted primarily to learning certain skills, learning company policies and practices, or applying past experience to the particular tasks the worker will be performing for the employer. Such an investment in learning is thought to pay off more handsomely for the employer than would a higher priority on output of the kinds of work product of which the worker is immediately capable. This type of investment, however, is often less possible for the temporary or part-time college student who is only a potential candidate for full-time employment. Compromises between the learning expectations of the college and the work expectations of the employer may require periodic adjustment as a result.

Alternately, a student may put different priority on work and learning objectives in different work situations. For example, one student may view a cooperative job as merely a source of bread and butter while he or she studies outside of the work situation to qualify for another job, while another student may view the same job as one in which he or she can both learn the necessary skills and demonstrate the necessary qualifications to qualify for more responsible and possibly more personally rewarding work with the same firm.

A third and key issue is the fact that most faculty members have backgrounds that are almost exclusively academic, with little exposure to other work settings. It is not surprising that they thus tend to support curricula that are effectively geared to preparation for academic careers. In order to have the institutional program relate more directly to other forms of work, serious attention may need to be given to selecting different kinds of faculty or to developing training programs and off-campus experiences for faculty that will facilitate their own development and the modification of their curricula. Probably some blend of these two approaches is most appropriate. Carefully selected individuals from work backgrounds outside academia can be brought to campus and can become effective teachers. At the same time, many faculty will be open to change in their responsibilities, provided such change is proposed sensitively and flexibly. However an institution proceeds to strengthen its staff by either means, it will want faculty who are skilled in helping students understand the learning that they can obtain in the work setting. Such faculty will be able to exploit the resources of the workplace, help students learn standard subject matter from that ex-

periential laboratory, and recruit persons with whom students interact at work as additional instructors. The difficulty of developing
such faculty should not be underestimated, nor should its importance in aiding the institution to forge links to the world of work.

The Role of Government

In some societies, the government takes an interest in the
priorities with which both employers and workers approach work
and learning. In the Civilian Conservation Corps (ccc), the Peace
Corps, and the Job Corps, for example, the United States government had a vested interest in what the enrollees learned as well as
in what they produced. In the ccc and the Job Corps, it had a
particular interest in putting income in the hands of otherwise unemployed people, in keeping young people out of crime, and in performing socially useful services that private enterprise could not
afford and would not pay. Here the work output and the learning
output were probably both subordinate to other priorities of social
policy, which nevertheless permitted a stress on learning and productivity with little interference. Effective implementation of the
foreign policy mission of the Peace Corps (however well or poorly
conceived) required some learning about cultural differences and
societal functioning.

In contemporary China a still different kind of social purpose is at work in which work sites are thought to be the only or the
most effective places where certain critically important things can
be learned. To indoctrinate its intellectuals in the correct value system for the realization of the good society, and to avert a chasm
of values and communication between intellectuals and peasants, the
government has required university students and professors to perform, with peasants, the agricultural labor essential to the national
economy. While there is an immediate loss of efficiency in the performance of these tasks by some students and professors, there is
thought to be an enormous long-term gain in effectiveness and efficiency in achieving the societal purposes and priorities as defined
by the government.

A theory of the role of government in the relationship between work and education can address both what these relationships

have been and currently are, and what they ought to be. In a society such as that of the United States, whose ethics are pluralistic and whose politics are civil libertarian, this theory might best describe what would be entailed by different philosophical and ideological commitments, ranging from the purposes of Jacques Barzun and Leonard Woodcock to George Wallace and David Rockefeller. Probably few people in the United States would support a compulsory program of government service by all young Americans as a part of their education, except in a military emergency; but many educators and employers would approve federal support that encouraged interaction between education and work, including cooperative education, career exploration, service-learning internships, and volunteer social service.

In attempting to increase their own effectiveness in relating their programs to postcollegiate life and work, colleges and universities inevitably will find themselves changing their teaching techniques and reassessing their own values and mission, as well as becoming increasingly involved both with employers on the one hand and government agencies on the other. This process will be difficult and often tension-producing, but it will offer an important challenge to higher education and, especially in the current social context, much promise of increased educational vitality.

‫മ

Learning Through
Work and Education

‫മ

Paul E. Barton

Too many Americans find themselves at two times in their lives in situations that almost perversely mirror each other. In the first, a young person just out of school or college pounds the pavement looking for a job, carrying the diploma by which the educational system certifies that one is prepared for adulthood. The first several employers that the graduate approaches quickly dismiss that particular meaning of a diploma. They say that one must have experience in order to get a job. How does one get the experience? They do not say.

In the second situation, an adult already well-experienced at work but without advanced education wants further educational opportunity or an educational credential. But the currency of ex-

The knowledge and views expressed here emerge from work on the development of an education-work policy, the results of which appear in W. W. Wirtz, *The Boundless Resource* (Washington, D.C.: New Republic Book Company, 1975).

perience, in such short supply during youth, is not legal tender in the educational community; and the educational system requirements, schedules, and financing provisions seem forbiddingly out of step with the reality of adult life. It is widely said that experience is the best teacher. Scholars have even said it too, although, of course, in many more words. But few give credit for its teaching.

People seem to be able to move smoothly within the system of education, and within the system of experience, but not between them. For three quarters of a century, the linking mechanisms enabling one to move from high school to college and from one college to another have been honed through College Board scores, semester credit hours, standardized grading systems, and comparable transcripts. At the same time, employers generally have recognized the preparation given by other employers; and if there was any doubt about how well the prospective employee performed before, the answer was there for the asking. But connections remain inadequate at the crossovers between education and employment, and between employment and education. It is not clear exactly how the situation got this way, but we do know some of the elements. Consider first the young person's situation and then the adult's.

The Inexperienced Graduate

The biggest reason that employers want to hire young workers who already have experience is that American industry does not offer a great deal of formal training, particularly for entry-level positions. The system it uses is on-the-job training, and is so inseparable from the production system that the Bureau of Labor Statistics has had great difficulty in finding a way to measure it. This informal training is really nothing but experience in the job, making mistakes, learning—somehow—from another worker who knows the task. This being the case, it makes a lot of sense, from the employer's perspective, to hire someone who is already experienced.

Employers however, are looking for more than job skills: they see prior work experience as increasing the chances that a person will be punctual, responsible, and stable—indeed, will possess a whole set of qualities that they associate with productive employees, although no one has objectively determined which qualities contribute the most to performance. Some employers use experience as a substitute for explicit age requirements. Several recent studies have found, however, that about three fourths of employers do not want to hire young people until they are age twenty or twenty-one whether or not they have a high school diploma, except for women wanting to become secretaries. Some employers will not hire young people under age twenty or twenty-one because they rightly suspect that not enough experience has been gained until that age, but others apparently presume that people are not punctual, responsible, and stable until they have aged a bit. Such employers seem to believe that seventeen- and eighteen-year-old high school graduates lack the maturity desired, except for casual jobs at hamburger stands and car washes.

Yet youth are capable, if provided experience and training, of being as productive as other entry-level employees. Since, however, the American labor market seldom gets so tight that older entry-level labor is unavailable, employers have had little need to change their traditional screening devices or to participate in education and training. If they are to do so, they need assurance that the youth they hire can do the work.

Just as most employers have not participated in education, most schools have not concerned themselves with employment. Schools pride themselves on how many of their graduates go on to college. Only a few keep tabs on how many of the others succeed in the employment world. Those who do not go to college go from the classroom, where no one knows about work, to that segment of the labor market specializing in low-cost, youth labor, and then to an entry job in regular employment three or four years later. Four years to get a high school diploma; four more just to become four years older; then a real job. That is roughly the relationship between education and work for teenagers.

There are, of course, exceptions. Some employers do train systematically, preferring to teach new graduates their own way. Some vocational schools turn out graduates with the kind of training employers want; and where employers recruit from the ranks of young people trained in these schools, the connection is pretty good. A growing number of technical occupations involve so much training that preparation takes place in two-year private and public schools. And there are models where education and work overlap: for example, the work experience or cooperative education programs of high schools and colleges. In quantity, however, such programs do not represent a widely available option for students. In terms of variety, they offer several interesting possibilities, although at the high school level they are concentrated in service and retail trade industries, and much less available in the manufacturing and finance sectors. But the central tendency of on-the-job experience remains.

Where education and work overlap on a planned basis, as in work experience programs, so many of the puzzling pieces of the youth situation fall into place that one wonders why the growth of such opportunities has been so gradual. The need for them is not a new discovery. John Dewey, writing near the turn of the century, warned us that "as formal teaching and training grow in extent, there is the danger of creating an undesirable split between the experience gained in more direct association, and what is required in school" (1961, p. 9). In good cooperative programs, the school and employer are engaged in a joint venture, first to educate and second to provide a smooth transition to regular employment. An opportunity is created for a dialogue to take place between the school and the employer concerning one individual, with the employer spotting practical deficiencies in the person's ability or preparation, and the school official spotting work situations that offer little stimulus to human growth or future opportunity.

This desirable dovetailing of schooling and experience is catching on slowly. One of the earliest missions of education was that of removing children from work that they should not have been doing. School attendance laws function not only to keep youth in school but also to keep them out of employment. Separation has been reinforced by the simple fact of bureaucratic life; school systems, like other bureaucracies, go about their business within the confines of their system. Vocational education, federally assisted since 1917, might have been expected to create those needed linkages between education and work, but its effort has been limited, and training has been largely a classroom affair. The net impact of classroom vocational education has been to perpetuate the dichotomy between formal education and experience, rather than to bring about a closer relationship.

Government (excluding the school system itself) has played a very modest role in the situation. The federal government erected modest restrictions on youth work in the Fair Labor Standards Act of the 1930s. Only recently the major barrier to youth work experience—the prohibition on fourteen- and fifteen-year-olds working during the school day—was relaxed experimentally by the Labor Department, and the minimum wage legislation contains a learner rate exception, not widely used or, for that matter, widely known. The support of the National Institute of Education for Experience Based Career Education may develop a greater intermixture of work and education, depending on how it is ultimately defined at the local level.

While secondary education has so far proven remarkably resistant to such change, the number of postsecondary institutions with cooperative education plans is growing. As college education—and especially liberal arts education—becomes less and less an assured route to employment, closer linkages between college and work are necessary. This does not mean that higher education must have greater occupational content, but that the intermixing of education and work experience can be a way to bridge the gap between education and work for the college student. More and more, high school graduates and college graduates with nonoccupational educations are going to share the problem of gaining access to the best jobs; a gradual entry that starts during the schooling period may be the best approach available.

It is here posited that, except for those receiving specialized occupational certifications in the school, experience is a primary basis for employment; that education and work can be better connected if they overlap; and that the whole of this will improve education, the transition to employment, and work performance. A number of matters will require attention if we are to facilitate growth of those opportunities:

Employers will want to see some evidence that engaging in educational ventures will not increase the cost of manning their establishments. Because of the access to schools that a new relationship would provide, employers will be looking for some combination of a better-quality workforce, lower turnover, and better education. They will want some order in the system by which they are solicited for experience opportunities.

Schools will want to know that experience can be arranged without exploitation of youth, and that needed classroom work will not be eliminated.

Unions will want assurance that student labor will not affect job opportunities for adults or depress wages of adults—matters not to be taken lightly.

Young people will have to see that experience opportunities work for them, that they provide something that leads somewhere in the adult world.

And what of the role of assessment of experience at this stage of youth's transition to work? At least four objectives and possibilities can be suggested for exploration:

First, assessment of work experience may give educators a better understanding of what happens in personal development outside the classroom. A consensus is slowly developing among educators and scholars that experience is important, and that consensus already exists among employers. Some record keeping of the changes that experience produces may bring about a greater understanding of the learning process, and may make clearer the place of experience in education.

Second, assessment may give us tools with which to improve the quality of education-experience programs. In the best programs, the employer's agent and the school coordinator are in touch concerning the progress and the needs of the student. What they are finding out, if it can be systematically measured, can help us identify the elusive outlines of quality in such programs.

Third, assessment may improve opportunities for youth under age twenty or twenty-one to be hired for regular adult jobs. The great majority of employers hiring for regular-entry jobs do not want to hire youth, even when they have high school diplomas. To the extent that these hiring policies are based on stereotypes of youth as immature and irresponsible, they can be counteracted by formal records of work experience accomplishments.

Fourth, assessment may enable work experiences to be better analyzed. Some employment experiences offer more than others by way of development of the human potential. Record keeping should provide some basis for understanding the quality of work and for identifying the best *educational work,* a term used by Willard Wirtz as the logical counterpart to the term *worker education.*

These possible outcomes of experience assessment need to be tempered with an appreciation of the unique character of experience. Without any attempt to enter the kind of discussion of different kinds of learning explored by James S. Coleman and Melvin Tumin earlier in this volume, one can observe that classroom education is highly structured and experience is not. In American employment, the learning is whatever is involved in a person's immersion in the work process and in conversation with more experienced people. Educators will be tempted to alter experience to make the learning aspect seem more rational or to make it easier to measure. This may be a mistake. Employers may be wrong in handling training in a casual, seemingly unstructured fashion, but educators are prone to come quickly to strongly—if temporarily —held beliefs about the correct procedure of learning. The integrative ability of the teenage mind, put in a real life situation, may be considerable. The employment community will have to be deeply involved in developing useful assessment tools for measuring learning in school as well as at work. That will be the beginning of improving the work-education situation for young people.

The Experienced Adult

Although the connection between education and work in the early period of life is a faulty one, a connection does exist. People expect that a transition will take place. Once adults begin work, however, work tends to define life itself. There are exceptions— millions of them—but they remain exceptions in American practice and thought. For example, the latest Office of Education survey of adult education, fielded in 1972, defined *adults* as those beyond compulsory school age and engaging in part-time educational activities. The underlying assumption is that adults work, and that education is a side venture. (Of course, there are adults in school full time; they just were not counted.)

As measured, then, adult education in this country today

is for those who already have the most education, those who have the highest income, and those who have most recently been to school. Such education is strongly connected with work: six out of ten of the part-time students are enrolled in order to improve and advance in the current job or to get a new job. This close relationship of current adult education to job advancement is not surprising. Employers pay for the educational activities of four million adults and public money finances another 2.8 million, mostly to encourage skill improvements in such professions as health, social service, law enforcement, and education. Much of the self-financed education is in response to professional requirements for salary increases or continued certification.

These observations are not meant to downgrade the value of part-time education or of education for job advancement. They simply underscore the fact that adult life is set aside for work, and only for work. What people go to the classroom for now reflects what others are willing to pay for and not necessarily what they would like to do if more resources to pay for learning and if more options to learn were available.

My premise is that education does belong in adult life, that everything one needs to know cannot be absorbed by the time one is eighteen or twenty-one, and that all one's future learning needs cannot be forecast so early in life. Learning is a part of living—as is working. It is also a requirement of economic reality that individuals be retooled for changing work needs and that they and their families be supported while doing so. Recessions—such as we have today—are good times for concentrating on such education. The greater flexibility attained through educational sabbaticals can make the labor force more adaptable to economic shifts and facilitate growth and production. The failure of jobs to match and challenge people's skill and education in the last several decades means that people need to find more sustenance from the rest of their life, partially through education. And it is clear that leisure is not an unskilled occupation.

For all of these reasons, continuing educational opportunity for adults is essential. What are the means of bringing it about? The first is surely that of changing attitudes. As long as we are trapped in expectations about what is the right time for education and work, little change of a substantial nature is going to come about. But, given adequate leadership, we ought to be able to recognize the value of educational opportunity extended over time, as well as the need of many young people for relief from overdoses of education in their teenage and early adult years. That leadership must come from three major sources. One is postsecondary education, where already the Carnegie Commission on Higher Education, the Commission on Non-Traditional Study, and the flexible education programs of institutions such as those holding membership in the CAEL Assembly, have begun to affect the picture. Another is employers, where tuition-refund plans continue to grow, and where flexible time arrangements could hasten the opportunity to combine work with education. The third is government, where at the federal level President Ford has asked his agencies to plot a better relationship between work and education, and where the Department of Health, Education, and Welfare includes in the term *career education* the proposition of lifelong learning.

Second, a way must be found to begin to make adult educational opportunity a reality—a way that will have the broadest possible support. The National Manpower Institute has arrived at the conclusion that the place to start with government money is by honoring a social contract already made: namely, that everyone is entitled to twelve years of free education. The fine print now reads that one must obtain this education when young. This should be changed, so that the unused entitlement can be cashed in for a variety of educational pursuits, including attendance at postsecondary institutions, at any age.

Third, as a next step, the educational system needs to undergo changes in traditional practices. For adults long out of school and with a multitude of experiences, the lines between secondary and postsecondary education blur, particularly in community colleges. But higher education should not allow the offerings of adult education to be shaped wholly by past understandings of adult needs. Because of limited opportunities, these needs have been centered on specific occupational preparation and advancement. Institutions of higher education have at least as much obligation to take leadership in what adult education ought to be as they do in defining what youth education is. A thoughtful response on the part of the education community to the content and purpose of adult education is as critical as any of the other variables in the equation.

What of assessment and where it fits in the adult period of life? To repeat a previous statement, the education credentials of youth from high school and college do not always apply in the world of work. Similarly, the experience credentials gained in adulthood are too seldom redeemable in the education world. But does this adequately define the issue? There is, of course, a difference: young people hope to meet job entry requirements with their education credentials, but adults appear to seek experience credentials for more than entry into higher education; they want experience to substitute for formal education and fulfill some part of the requirements for education certification. The desirability of allowing experience to substitute for education is not easily separated from the difficulty of putting this substitution into practice, an issue not easily disposed of.

If the goal of the assessment of experience were to spread education credentials around because they are important and many people do not have them, then, to my way of thinking, the idea would be wanting in content. As Melvin Tumin has noted earlier in this volume, the important issue of equality of access to higher education will not be adequately addressed by a devaluation of the currency. Similarly, if the plan were to shift the responsibility from individual educational institutions to some universal instrument for assessment, then the effort would be misplaced. The problem must be kept clearly identified: it is assessing the degree to which a person, through experience, has achieved some of the educational goals of a particular institution. There is, and should be, great diversity in the content of higher education, and many definitions of what education is.

If the notion behind assessment were that academic credit should be given for whatever it is that comes with experience—for age, skill, maturity (if that is the best word)—then the objectives of educational institutions need serious examination. Academic education has been, by definition, what one learns in a classroom, as compared with what life teaches one. This is not to suggest that the answer must be no to credit for experience alone; only that a yes answer would mean a completely new role for education. That, of course, may be exactly the answer if the currency of experience is to become convertible to content of formal education. What is it that an educational institution expects to happen to people during their enrollment? How can they tell if work experiences produce the same effect unless they know what the desired effect is? This may seem to many to be the wrong end to start with, if the objective is to assess experiential learning, but it may be the only way to find what we are looking for in experience.

What this suggests is that each institution that wants to grant academic credit for experience should state in as precise terms as it can what changes it expects to see in students who have successfully negotiated its processes. Then it will know what to look for in people who have had experience and not instruction. The process would be one of determining what it is students learn through education, and then looking at other individuals to see how much of it they have. Why look at their experiences as such at all? One can no more assume that they have necessarily learned something by having a particular experience than one can assume that students learn something merely by being found in attendance in a class.

If the individual, rather than the experience, becomes the focus of the assessment effort, then assessment can take two quite different directions. The first is to assess how much of what a college expects to have been acquired at a certain state of learning has been acquired without going to college (or to that college), and to award some credit toward a degree, thus reducing the standard amount of time it takes to achieve the degree. The second is to grant a degree when a person has achieved whatever it is that the institution thinks should be achieved in order to be granted its diploma. Then people of any age could draw on their past experience, as well as their classroom effort, to meet the achievement requirements. The quality of their experience (as seen from the standpoint of the academic institution) would be reflected in the lesser time it would take to meet these achievement requirements. No translation of experiential learning into credit hours would be involved.

The goal of giving educational recognition to experiential learning is essential. We must develop means of translating experience if we are to help adults move from work to education. The assessment of experience is equally valid, if it means judging how much of what has been learned from experience is equivalent to what would have been learned in pursuit of the educational objectives of a particular institution.

The movement between education and work is not without friction. New means of assessment can be one of the vehicles for facilitating that movement. The problems of assessment are considerable and no one would be advised to think that they can be easily resolved. But, at the same time, no one should think that such problems are not worth pursuing, for a major advance in the quality of life may well be the reward for the hard work entailed in their resolution.

᠎᠎᠎᠎᠎᠎᠎᠎᠎᠎᠎᠎᠎᠎᠎᠎᠎᠎᠎᠎᠎᠎᠎᠎᠎᠎᠎᠎

Chapter Nine

Cost-Effectiveness of Programs

᠎᠎᠎᠎᠎᠎᠎᠎᠎᠎᠎᠎᠎᠎᠎᠎᠎᠎᠎᠎᠎᠎᠎᠎᠎᠎᠎᠎

George Weathersby and Armand J. Henault, Jr.

We often think of experiential learning as being a new process in higher education. In fact, it is thousands of years older than our current course-oriented process. Plato, Socrates, Aristotle, and other great thinkers of their day embraced a form of experiential learning (notably the dialogic method, with an emphasis on observation and personal discovery by trial and error) as the ideal process for arriving at the truth. It was not until the peak of Roman power that schools as we know them came into being. And it was not until the development of the monastic orders of the Christian church that the lecture-discussion form took shape to become what is currently termed traditional education. Even during this period, however, several forms of experiential education continued to exist in apprenticeships and internships. Today, we can discern the vestiges of these forms in the trades and the professions; for example, in medical and teacher training practicums and internships.

The proliferation of new programs in experiential learning

reflects the greater willingness of faculty, administrators, and students to undertake such programs and to legitimize them. Consequently, policymakers have been forced to deal with the issue of whether or not this new process will substantially augment or burden the financial operations of their colleges and universities. Indeed, in a period of great financial stress, administrators have every incentive to examine the potential benefits and disadvantages of implementing experiential learning programs at their institutions. In addition to the educational and social benefits of experiential learning discussed in the Foreword and in Chapters Three and Four, many educators now see experiential learning as a possible means of relieving colleges and universities of some of their financial distress.

In order to analyze the cost-efficiency of experiential learning programs, we must consider several factors. First, the overall financial condition of an institution is a result of the demand for its services and the cost of supplying that demand. Recently, more attention has been paid to the operating cost of nontraditional programs than to the impacts on demand of an increase in supply of nontraditional opportunities. In a period of declining enrollment demand by traditional college-bound cohorts, the attractiveness of a program and the willingness of students to pay would be two major factors in the income potential of a college or university. The influence of experiential learning on these two factors could be important and would affect the financial feasibility of experiential learning programs.

Second, it is important to understand the meaning of the term *cost-effective*. In general, efficiency is measured as a ratio between two variables: cost of resources used and program output. When outputs quantitatively increase or qualitatively improve while the costs remain constant, efficiency is said to increase. Effectiveness, on the other hand, is the degree to which an objective is accomplished independently of the resources used: individual tutorials may be effective and are expensive. The relative efficiency of tutorial versus self-paced instruction versus contract learning versus large lectures will depend on the effectiveness and cost of each alternative. An option can be very effective and relatively inefficient or vice versa.

Third, in analyzing the cost-effectiveness of experiential programs, the level of decision making should be identified. The chosen measures of costs and effectiveness should be appropriate to the policy makers of interest, whether on the institutional, regional, state, or federal level. A study of the cost-effectiveness of an individual program at one institution would probably be of little use to an administrator at the federal level contemplating an expansion of social security or pension vesting benefits for workers.

For the purpose of this chapter, we have chosen to focus our analysis on teaching institutions that are considering the cost-effectiveness of experiential learning. We use this focus because most of current concern about experiential learning seems to be at the institutional level. Also, the data that are available on the cost-effectiveness of experiential learning programs have been developed by institutions. Organizations dealing on levels other than that of the teaching institution might be able to adapt the format that we have used to meet the needs of their particular decision. Our analysis begins with a look at costs, then turns to the concept of effectiveness, next treats some contextual factors that affect costs and effectiveness, and concludes with some thoughts on an agenda for the future understanding of cost-effectiveness.

Economics of Experiential Learning

As we have noted, it is usually institutions that consider implementing experiential learning programs. Without an external cost standard, we must compare the cost of an experiential program with the cost of the traditional program.

Howard Bowen and Gordon Douglass, in their book *Efficiency in Liberal Education* (1971), have calculated the cost per student of classes in several disciplines, based on a typical traditional liberal arts college with an enrollment of 1,200 students and 100 faculty members, with each student enrolled in four courses of various sizes with an average class size of twenty, which meets two or three times per week for fifty minutes. Their estimates, which now should be increased somewhat to take inflationary increases into account, are shown in Table 1. Costs will vary among institutions depending upon the number of faculty and students, faculty and staff salaries, student enrollment per course, the percentage of fac-

Table 1. INSTRUCTIONAL COSTS FOR TRADITIONAL
LIBERAL ARTS CLASSES

Class	Cost Per Student[a]	Cost Per Class
Laboratory Science Class	$442	$8,843
Other Science Class	334	6,875
Fine Arts Studio Class	228	5,759
Other Fine Arts Class	208	4,167
Language Class	223	4,464
Humanities Class	201	4,017
Social Science Class	216	4,323

[a] Includes staff and faculty salaries, facilities, equipment, supplies and materials, library, computer and other nondirect costs.

Source: Bowen and Douglass (1971).

ulty time spent on a particular course, the cost of facilities, and indirect costs, such as the library, administrative overhead, and other factors. The total operating picture for a typical traditional liberal arts institution might look something like Table 2.

In analyzing the economics of implementing an experiential learning component, it is necessary to look at the interrelationships between various costs and income components. For example, while an experiential learning program might raise the cost of instruction somewhat, it could also substantially decrease the amount of financial aid needed and might increase student demand and, correspondingly, student revenues. General administrative costs might rise to some extent but, correspondingly, recruitment and other admissions activities could become less costly because of increased options and attractiveness to students. In addition, however, the very nature of experiential learning programs will influence the costs of their operations. For example, facilities costs may be limited because students often pursue their interests in the community. Resources might be saved by freeing classroom space that could then be used for other purposes (such as setting up assessment centers) or possibly rented out. On the other hand, other costs will be added,

Table 2. TYPICAL ANNUAL OPERATING COSTS OF
TRADITIONAL LIBERAL ARTS INSTITUTION

Income Component	Amount in Thousands	Percentage
Instruction	2,056	46
Library	224	5
Student Services	313	7
Admissions	134	3
General Administration	447	10
Public Relations/ Development	268	6
Plant Operation and Maintenance	536	12
Student Aid	492	11
	4,470	100

Source: Bowen and Douglass (1971).

such as increased faculty time spent in academic advising, counseling, or academic assessment. What is important is the extent to which these variables influence and affect each other.

In using here particular examples of experiential learning programs and of institutional contexts for them, we aim to clarify their import as models of a particular approach to the control of costs. Whether these institutions thrive or not is not germane to the purpose of this analysis, since many other factors will enter into the determination of their future. Similarly, whether in other respects the institutions and their programs are ideal models is a much more complex issue, the resolution of which turns especially upon the purposes and priorities of those who are judging. Such issues are beyond the scope of this chapter.

Many institutions have implemented experiential learning programs based on the mentor or advisor model: an advisor works with students to develop programs and projects to carry out their studies in the community at large. The role of the advisor can be limited to working with the student to formulate an outline or plan of study, or he or she can also aid the student in intern or job placement, in supervising the student's progress, and in taking part in the assessment process. At the Illinois Board of Governors Bachelor of Arts degree program, faculty (or advisor) supervision is the keystone of the program, as it has been expressed through correspondence with us: "with regard to the evaluation of work experiences this evaluation is done by a faculty member in each of the various areas for which the student requests an evaluation of his nonacademic learning. We deliberately have refrained from developing standard guidelines for this evaluation process. We believe that our faculty members are competent experts in their special areas, and we have entrusted to them the responsibility for giving thousands of hours of credit to thousands of younger students. We pay our faculty members on the expectation that they are highly trained professional people in their field . . . we do not try to second-guess their recommendations for grades and credits."

Another variation on the mentor or advisor theme is the example of Campus-Free College (CFC), a nonprofit, nonresidential college founded in 1971 to award associate, baccalaureate, and master's degrees. CFC does not employ advisors except when they are actually working with students. These advisors usually make their services available to CFC students in addition to their regular professional affiliations, which lie elsewhere. In addition, CFC advisors have no responsibilities to the college other than counseling their CFC students; there are no courses to teach, and they are not expected to produce new research. In this way, CFC has tried to undertake a model that would be self-supporting over the long run. Since CFC is not affiliated with a mother institution, it does not offer courses with an experiential component. The strength of CFC lies in the fact that it is a totally individualized program, where students are not encouraged, but rather expected, to pursue their educational interests in the community.

In its desire not to rely on outside sources of funding, CFC has established student fees that will cover all operating expenses (about $60,000 per year) once the student enrollment reaches about 100 students. Each student pays $1,200 per year to the college, and the college divides this sum evenly between the administration and the program advisors. Thus, an advisor receives $600 per year per student for his or her advising services; moreover, the advisor is only paid if and when he or she contracts to work with a student. Instructional costs (books, workshop fees, or any other costs incurred as a result of helping to establish a student in a community learning project) are paid directly by the student, thus eliminating the cost to CFC of all instruction and the administrative overhead for operating an instructional program. Instructional costs vary greatly depending upon the mix of learning activities undertaken by the student, but the average cost per year has been estimated at from $200 to $500. Thus, the total costs to a CFC student can vary greatly, but average about $1400 to $1700 per year. Furthermore, the fixed operating expenses of CFC remain low because of the lack of facilities (no campus, no library, no dormitories, no health service), and the variable operating expenses of CFC also remain low because of the lack of full-time faculty salaries.

A second type of experiential learning program is one that is partially conventional and partially experiential, either by encouraging experiential learning projects or by crediting life experiences under the aegis of a conventional mother institution. These programs become more difficult to assess in terms of cost-effectiveness because shared costs between the conventional and the nontraditional components are often difficult to identify separately. The Antioch College and the University Without Walls programs are examples of these kinds of mixed options, where students can choose between individualized experiential learning programs or conventional coursework.

A student wishing to pursue two years of experiential learning could undertake such a program through a variety of different models, and the costs to him or her would vary greatly. Table 3 compares some of the financial characteristics of five experiential learning programs or institutions with the national averages of the same characteristics for traditional public or private colleges.

For a more meaningful comparison we can categorize experiential learning programs into components and compare the costs of these components with the costs of courses at more traditional institutions. For example, in a conventional liberal arts institution, a social science class costs the student, on average, about $216 (see

Table 3. COMPARATIVE ANNUAL EXPENDITURES AND
STUDENT COSTS FOR EXPERIENTIAL LEARNING AND
TRADITIONAL LIBERAL ARTS

Type of Experiential Learning Model	Number of Students Enrolled	Expenditures/ Student	Tuition and Student Fees	Expenditures by State or Other Sources
Campus Free College	100ª	$1,200	$1,200ᵇ	—
Empire State College	2,500	3,259.50ᶜ or 3,410.25	649.50 or 800.25	$2,610
USNY	6,000	varies by number and cost of proficiency tests	varies by number and cost of proficiency tests	166ᵈ
Framingham State	no figures available	no figures available	954ᵉ	1,800
Community College of Vermont	2,600	548	240-300	248-308
Traditional Public	9,000ᶠ	1,989ᵍ	380	1,609
Traditional Private	1,234ᶠ	3,906ᵍ	2,500	1,046

ª Projected optimum enrollment, 1975 enrollment approximately 40 full-time equivalents.
ᵇ Does not reflect instructional costs paid directly by students.
ᶜ Depending on student status: upper or lower division.
ᵈ Funding source primarily foundation grants and student fees.
ᵉ Massachusetts residents estimated at $250 fee for 2 years retroactive credit + 32 semester hours (= 1 year academic credit) @ $22/semester hour.
ᶠ National average.
ᵍ Computed from total national expenditures (four-year institutions) divided by total number of students enrolled (FTE in four-year institutions).
Source: Direct contact with indicated institutions and published sources.

Table 1). In comparison, the External Degree Program at Framingham State College grants an average of about two years of credit for life experiences for a one-time fee of $250 (Table 3). For the average student at one of the conventional colleges, the same amount of credit would probably cost the student about $5000 and the instituition about $6000. The Framingham State College crediting fee for two years of credit costs the student only slightly more than a single course offered at a public institution and costs less than a single course offered by a private institution. The crediting fee thus accounts for a great savings on the part of the student, and possibly also on the part of the institution.

Another way of comparing various experiential and traditional programs is to calculate the cost of a bachelor's degree in terms of student costs and government costs. A full-time student with two years of creditable prior learning might pursue an undergraduate degree through several different kinds of institutions with costs that differ greatly. For example, an experiential learner could receive the equivalent of half (two years) of the needed credits at Campus-Free College by paying a one-time retroactive crediting fee of $200. The cost of the other two years of participation in the program would total between $3000 and $3600 (depending on the amount of time needed to complete the program, instructional cost variables, and the like)'. Within the traditional private sector, however, the student could probably not receive two years of experiential learning credit at all, and would thus be forced to attend a college (with a yearly tuition of $2,500) for four years. Contrasted with this $10,000 tuition fee, cfc costs of $3000 to $3600 would appear to be very favorable incentive to enrolling students with some creditable prior learning.

An even lower cost to the student occurs in an institution that does not offer any kind of instruction, but concerns itself solely with the crediting of prior learning, such as the New York Regents External Degree Program and Thomas Edison College of New Jersey. Students in these kinds of programs can complete their undergraduate studies on their own by successfully passing college proficiency tests or other forms of special assessment. Student costs in this kind of program are limited to the charges for taking the tests, which average between $25 to $50 per test and which award an average of six credit hours, and for storing the credits within the Regents External Degree Program. This accounts for the relatively low cost to the undergraduate of $375 to $785 for the entire degree program—a highly desirable attribute to many students who would not normally be able to afford the costs of four years of tuition at a traditional institution. Empire State College and Framingham State College are examples of the kinds of programs that credit prior learning in addition to offering instruction to students. Both institutions award an average of about two years of credit assessed at a set fee ($80 for Empire State and $250 for Framingham) for prior learning and charge their students the tuition equivalent to the rest of the public higher education sector in their states—a total of $730 to $880 for Empire State and $1658 for Framingham for the entire degree program.

Three of the experiential learning institutions mentioned here are state supported. The cost per student to the state government for the various forms of experiential learning and for a traditional undergraduate education subsidized by the state varies enormously. In the case of the USNY External Degree Program, the state does not pay for the subsidy of any student learning since no instruction is offered. Empire State costs New York $5,570 to $5,620—one-third to less than one-half of what New York usually pays to its public sector per degree awarded. A student (with two years prior learning) would cost the Commonwealth of Massachusetts $3,600—one-half of the cost of the state subsidy of instructional costs per degree awarded in the traditional public sector. Thus it seems apparent that some forms of experiential learning can offer a financially attractive option to and within public higher education.

Effectiveness of Experiential Learning

Thus far we have been concerned primarily with the cost of experiential learning programs. Relative cost-effectiveness, as we have said, is a matter of a comparison of ratios of the costs and the effectiveness of two or more programs. To complete consideration of these ratios, we must look at factors in the effectiveness of experiential learning. Effectiveness is a function of objectives: if objectives are fully achieved, a program is of maximum effectiveness. For the degree of effectiveness to be measurable, objectives should be defined in measurable terms. In order to directly compare the effectiveness of experiential learning to that of other modes of learning, the two would need to be assessed with respect to the same objectives.

The analyses in earlier chapters of this book suggest, however, that while experiential and nonexperiential learning sometimes serve the same objectives, more often than not they function as complementary strategies, either serving different aspects of the same objective or serving quite different objectives. For this reason, the most appropriate comparisons of cost-effectiveness might be between different mixes of experiential and nonexperiential learning strategies where each mix is directed toward the same combination of learning objectives. For example, Chickering in Chapter Six discusses objectives in human development, and in a theoretical understanding of it, which might best be served, as far as effectiveness goes, by a combination of classroom or tutorial studies in the theory of human development and a program of action and experiential learning designed to facilitate the student's cognitive development, maturation in ego development, and ethical development. Alternative programs combining work on theory and on personal development might sensibly be compared as to cost and probable effectiveness in order to assist the student to make the most prudent choice of program for this purpose. Similarly, institutions trying to provide cost-effective programs for this purpose might compare alternative mixes of theoretical study and experiential learning in the light of available resources and prospective benefits.

An institution that is considering implementing an experiential learning program will have managerial objectives and social policy objectives that provide context for its educational objectives. Thus it might have in view a number of objectives, such as: increasing enrollment to offset the projected enrollment decline; validating and recognizing learning that takes place outside of the classroom; providing a means of access for the traditionally bypassed (for example, workers, women, minorities, older students); ensuring better job placement results for graduates as a result of actual work experience; and improving student achievement on established or redefined curricular objectives, thereby enhancing the credibility of its credentials.

The preceding discussion of differential costs of different programs also reflects the fact that the purpose of some programs is to insure that the student gains a deserved credential rather than that the student adds new learning or new competences and skills, which in turn would warrant the award of the credential. Naturally a program designed to verify already achieved learning should cost less than a program that both generates new learning and verifies its achievement. An assessment of relative cost-effectiveness of two programs, one of the former type and another of the latter, poses an insoluble problem unless the inquirer specifies a relative weighting to be given to the two objectives. More appropriate would be the assessment of the cost-effectiveness of different approaches to the validation of credentials, taken as a separate objective, and a separate assessment of the cost-effectiveness of different approaches to the achievement of the learning for which these credentials stand. Then, where both purposes pertain and with the outcomes of these two different assessments in hand, it would be possible to examine different combinations of credentialing programs and learning programs to determine which combination would yield the best cost prospects for the dual objectives.

After the objectives of an experiential learning program have been determined, measurable criteria are needed to assess the degree to which the program has accomplished these objectives. For example, an appropriate criterion might be that of increasing enrollment, that is, the extent to which enrollment patterns differ by important student characteristics at similar institutions before and after implementation of an experiential learning program, or the extent to which traditional institutional enrollment patterns differ from those of similar institutions that have implemented an experiential learning program. A second appropriate criterion might be that of insuring better job placement for graduates, that is, the extent to which graduates achieve their job preferences before and after the implementation of an experiential learning program.

A good example of an institutional assessment of objectives is that of Empire State College (1973). Following the progress of 170 graduates in their attempts to secure positions or gain admission to graduate schools, the study reports that of the fifty-seven graduates who applied to graduate schools, 72 percent were accepted, 16 percent were rejected, and 12 percent were pending at the time of the report. These figures, compared with those of a more conventional institution, were slightly lower on average. In addition, the report contains a detailed analysis of the willingness of institutions to accept ESC graduates, and the difficulties encountered by students in applying for admission to graduate schools.

The report also gives substantial information about graduates' work experiences: their successes and disappointments in securing preferred positions, and patterns of change in employment before and after their ESC experience. Results show that 75 percent of the graduates encountered no difficulty in securing positions. Furthermore, 53 percent of the graduates reported an improvement in their employment circumstances after their ESC experience, while 36 percent reported little or no change. When asked about possible other benefits from their Empire State College experience, the graduates overwhelmingly attested to having gained, among other things, a sense of achievement and self-satisfaction.

In addition to defining objectives for themselves and for their students, institutions of postsecondary education have an obligation to society as a whole. Public concern for experiential learning should extend beyond the present programs and clientele of postsecondary education to include groups such as civil service workers, participants in manpower development programs, professional continuing education, or special programs for the elderly. Although these programs need not be administered by the national government (though several of them might appropriately be), the implementing agency needs to be aware of the social objectives for the programs. National objectives for experiential learning might include increasing student access to postsecondary education; increasing student options and choices of programs; increasing student opportunity (through increased academic assistance and counseling or financial aid); and improving the provisions for educational diversity.

Similarly, appropriate quantifiable measures of how well experiential learning programs were accomplishing their objectives might be those that assess student access—the extent to which the student age and the college age populations are similar with respect to age, income, racial composition, ethnic group, sex and family residence; and those that identify student options—the extent to which persons from all income, sex, and age groups are enrolled in institutions with high, medium, and low charges, or the extent to which low-income groups, women, and older students are distributed among the various institutional types.

Institutions or agencies that are concerned with the cost-effectiveness of experiential learning programs could, within the orientation just sketched, begin to understand cost-effectiveness relationships by defining their objectives in terms of measurable criteria. This would allow the accurate reporting of program impacts and of how these are affected by various program activities, which in turn influence program costs. One of the problems confronting administrators on all levels is the dearth of information about the costs and consequences of experiential learning programs. Once accurate data become available, decision-makers will have an easier task of determining whether or not their institution should implement—or the public should support—an experiential learning program, or whether the program they have established is feasible.

Current Concerns and Policies

Several recent developments in the field of higher education may well have considerable influence on the implementation of new experiential programs both on the institutional and regional-federal levels. In some cases, these developments have removed some of the traditional obstacles that have impeded the growth of experiential programs. Other developments have lowered the costs of establishing programs; we include them here for the information of institutions interested in implementing experiential learning programs at reduced costs. Our discussion focuses on three current issues: changes in infrastructures, changes in student demand, and developments in the cost of assessment techniques.

Infrastructures are organizations or programs that support primary educational delivery organizations. Examples of infrastructures are accrediting associations, consortia, external degree programs, life assessment procedures, credit for on-the-job training, and other linking structures. These infrastructures may significantly influence the development of experiential learning programs. For example, the redefinition of regional accrediting board criteria would be one kind of infrastructure change that would be helpful in the establishment of a new program. New accrediting policies could aid fledgling programs in getting off the ground, and without them, many such programs would not be possible (for example, strict enforcement of library requirements would eliminate all purely external degree programs). These policies would also have indirect bearing on student demand for experiential learning programs because of the differential attractiveness of accredited institutional programs.

Another kind of infrastructure that may influence the effectiveness and efficiency of experiential learning programs is the consortium. When institutions share their resources with other institutions, they can often increase their academic programs without substantial cost increases. In some cases, consortia have pooled administration as well as resources, with even greater savings (examples of this kind of consortium, which have made experiential learning programs possible, are the Antioch system and the University Without Walls, each with over twenty member institutions sharing a central administration and offering a great variety of programs). In addition, several institutions exist whose goal is to provide contract services that become experiential learning components of more traditional institutions. Campus-Free College is a good example of this kind of experiential learning program: its services of program coordination, resource recruitment, and academic assessment can be purchased; it has regional offices around the country; and it provides over 250 program advisors selected from various disciplines and geographical areas. This kind of organization might substantially reduce the administrative costs of an institution considering the implementation of its own experiential learning program.

Another example of infrastructure currently in use is the state-sponsored external degree program. This program can greatly facilitate the costly and time-consuming work of crediting nontraditional learning; several other states are considering the establishment of similar external degree programs. Thomas Edison State College is an example of this kind of external degree program; it works in cooperation with the New York Regents External Degree to provide a means of proficiency testing along with storage of degree credits earned. If an institution is considering the implementation of an external degree program and does not wish to get involved in the sometimes costly assessment of experiential learning, it might well utilize an already existing external degree program.

Other infrastructures exist that an institution might utilize. Many are still in the planning stages. Some of the ideas currently being deliberated that would have potential impact on experiential learning programs include credit banks, the development of new instructional media, and new public or private assessment programs. As and when these become available, institutions concerned with experiential learning should examine all possible methods for cooperation and coordination with and through these linking structures.

Another important consideration in the analysis of the cost-effectiveness of experiential learning is the attitudes of those who are going to be participating in the process, including the institutional reaction to these attitudes. Student demand for higher education is one of the best guarantees of institutional stability; nevertheless, enrollment predictions for the coming decade forecast a decline in college attendance of individuals eighteen to twenty-two years of age—a decline that will greatly affect the future of higher education unless steps are taken quickly to insure a greater attractiveness of current programs or to reach a new clientele.

One of the costs of an institution is the financial aid and counseling resources necessary to attract and retain students; consequently, estimating the impact of financial aid and counseling on student demand is critical in assessing the cost-effectiveness of experiential learning programs. If experiential learning is more attractive to potential students, then such programs may be significant in the solution of some of the financial problems of postsecondary education exacerbated by the enrollment decline. Although research on adult demand for nontraditional education is virtually nonexistent (though see Gilford, 1975, and Weathersby, 1974), experiential learning has the potential to make programs more attractive in several ways: it offers a relevant, real-life experience that many students seek; it is often concerned with the affective process in learning; it allows greater freedom and responsibility on the part of the student for his or her own education; it is more flexible and can accommodate a variety of learning styles; and it provides a financial incentive for those students who could not otherwise afford to spend a large amount of time in a traditional institution.

Students involved in many forms of experiential learning are able to take advantage of the wages or stipends paid to them as a part of their work or internship-apprenticeship program. The foregone income of students is a major cost of postsecondary education that has been ignored in past policies supporting postsecondary education. This lost income can be greatly reduced through experiential learning programs. Earning while learning would undoubtedly increase the attractiveness of such programs to potential students, especially if institutions encouraged and aided students in finding positions where they would be able to earn a living as well as a degree. In addition to reaching the traditional student population of white, middle-class people from age eighteen to twenty-two, this process might open the doors to older people, women, low-income groups, and minorities, thereby accomplishing some of the societal objectives of increased access to higher education. This has not been the case in most nontraditional programs developed to date.

On the other hand, experiential learning programs might call for new and improved assessment techniques, which might prove to be costly in both the developmental and the implemental stages. Paper and pencil examination procedures used widely in traditional programs might be adapted to this new format; but if justice is to be done to the spirit of experiential learning, new assessment mechanisms will have to be developed. These will involve great cost for faculty time devoted to the assessment. Highly individualized student assessment, which is time consuming, will cause continuing costs. Difficulties in standardizing assessment techniques for students pursuing a program of experiential learning are great, but some attempts are being made to reduce the costs of assessment.

Tasks for the Future

One of the difficulties encountered in writing this paper has been that of trying to compare the costs and effectiveness of one experiential learning program with those of another. Since there is such a variety of programs that follow radically different models and whose costs and objectives vary greatly, it is difficult to find a common denominator to assess their cost-effectiveness. For example, in trying to determine the institutional cost per student of a program, one should in theory take the operating expenses of the program and allocate them to the number of students enrolled annually. However, in an institution such as the Community College of Vermont, where students may enroll for one or several terms during the year, or at Empire State College, where students are enrolled on a monthly basis, arriving at this figure can become extremely difficult. At times it seems somewhat like trying to compare apples and oranges—they are both fruit, but have little else in common.

Such is the present state of experiential learning research. If this kind of education is to thrive in the future, and if postsecondary education on the whole is to place increased emphasis on experiential learning, we need to develop a common denominator to help determine the solutions to the numerous planning problems (cost-effectiveness being only one of many) that are going to confront experiential learning programs in the future. If comparisons are to be made between the relative costs of various programs, a common language must be developed. Experiential learning is a field with a wide proliferation of terms, argot, and apt colloquialisms; each institution decides what it would like to name its pet program. Researchers will therefore encounter frustration when trying to distinguish between campus-free learning, experiential learning, external degree programs, and open divisions (if such distinctions do indeed exist).

A taxonomy would be helpful for the two major components of experiential programs: the process, or kind of program, and the assessment techniques used. It is perhaps easier to categorize the latter; CAEL has already done a notable job of this in its *Compendium of Assessment Techniques* (Knapp and Sharon, 1974). The greater problem lies with the myriad of programs broadly defined as experiential learning. A recent attempt at developing a taxonomy of experiential or recurrent education learning programs was undertaken by a group of students at the Harvard Graduate School of Education. The task is fraught with enormous difficulties.

If, in order to accurately assess costs of experiential learning programs, we are considering the development of a taxonomy that would reflect the sometimes fine differences between programs, we need to take into consideration the noninstitutionally sponsored programs that exist. Several institutions that would not consider themselves to have experiential learning programs nevertheless allow students to take part in internships and apprenticeships with the approval of their academic advisors.

Furthermore, we need to know more about the numbers and kinds of students who take part in experiential learning programs, and the relative costs of these programs, as determined by faculty salaries and percentage of time spent, cost of administration, cost of materials (if appropriate), and capital costs (where applicable). When and if this information becomes available, policymakers on the institutional, regional, and national levels will be better able to make decisions about the costs of new programs and the variables that will affect those costs. First, we need to determine a common vocabulary applicable to all forms of experiential learning; next, we need to collect the relevant data on these programs and apply them to the taxonomy.

It would seem that some experiential learning programs (such as that of Empire State College) can supplant traditional programs by accomplishing their stated objectives without increasing costs tremendously. Few institutions, however, have taken on the responsibility of assessing themselves and making that data available to others planning to implement similar programs. Increased use of infrastructures will probably help experiential learning programs reduce costs; on the other hand, individualized assessment techniques will probably increase costs. Furthermore, the issue of institutional credibility is bound to have some effect on the acceptance of specific institutional objectives and upon the perception of the effectiveness of that institution in meeting them.

Experiential learning is becoming better-known and better-understood as it merges with the mainstream of postsecondary education. As this happens, one by one the obstacles that increase costs or cause resistance to needed new costs will diminish. Yet experiential learning has itself developed new problems that will take time, energy, and considerable money to resolve. New concepts in educational management are being applied to experiential learning models, such as the CFC self-supporting model. Experiential learning has the potential not only to change the process of postsecondary education, but also to energize the application of new concepts and practices in the management of postsecondary education.

Chapter Ten

Importance
of Assessing Learning

Robert Kirkwood

Many purists bristle at the suggestion of granting credit for anything learned outside the hallowed halls of ivy-covered buildings, despite the fact that field trips, foreign study, internships, practicums, practice teaching, and winter intersessions (to mention a few off-campus learning experiences where some professional supervision is usually involved) are well- and in many cases long-established features of many degree programs. But if one labels such attempts to relate experience to learning *experiential education,* and if one seeks to expand their dimensions to include similar off-campus learning prior to enrollment, then to some the very integrity of the academic degree is suddenly at stake.

In large part I suspect that this attitude reveals the unwillingness or inability of many traditionals to consider outcomes rather than processes as the essence of education—and to define the educated person in terms of demonstrated knowledge rather than of years spent in college. Thus, at a critical point in most arguments about granting credit for experiential learning, attention invariably shifts from the issue of learning itself to that of how the learning was achieved. Nevertheless, it is the advocates of such credit who must accept the burden of proving that learning has in fact been an outcome of experience in order to maintain standards and commonly accepted levels of expectation for postsecondary education. We should all agree that an important distinction exists between experiential learning and mere experience, and that it is the learning that concerns us. Suffice it to say that history is replete with evidence that experience in itself is no guarantor of learning.

Thus when traditionalists argue that experiential learning should be translatable in terms that place it on an exchangeable par with other forms of academic currency, their contention should be respected and the effort made. Innovators in this area must relate new dimensions of educational endeavor to a substantive base that can readily be communicated and understood by other educators and the public.

Most advocates of credit for experiential learning would agree that if such learning is to be creditable in academic terms, it cannot be random. It must be learning that is clearly and demonstrably related to well-defined objectives; the credit granted for it must be proportionate to the total balance of requirements established for the pertinent degree or credential; and it must be neither so esoteric as to defy description nor so mundane as to caricature the academic process. Proponents of experiential learning, in other words, are appropriately and responsibly concerned about the integrity of credits and credentialing as a means for symbolizing learning, not as an end in itself.

A major problem with the traditional academic system for experiential learning, however, is its pretensions to the divinity of the commandments without any of the evidence of revelation. Grades, credits, and credentials form the symbols of this procedural religion with registrars serving as its high priests and computers as their deus ex machina. Creating an accepted system of credit for experiential learning under these conditions, therefore, will require more than effort and imagination: it will require examining the assumptions underlying all practices involved in granting educational credit whether for classroom or off-campus learning. Indeed, we need to achieve a new basis for assessing all learning rather than to create separate procedures and standards for crediting experiential learning.

The issue of crediting such learning is thus timely and directly in line with other challenges confronting higher education. To the extent that we welcome it as an opportunity and relate it to changing concepts of what constitutes legitimate learning and the characteristics of an educated person, to that extent will we further the idea of education as a continuum, embracing rather than excluding the vast potentialities for human development. With proper attention to the assessment of this learning, there need be no dilution or demeaning of the symbols we have traditionally bestowed for educational achievement.

Paul Barton earlier in this volume noted four functions of the assessment of experiential learning. As has long been known, assessment serves several purposes, chief among them education and credentialing. These functions cause some uneasiness among many faculty members largely, I suspect, because of inadequate understanding of how assessment can be used creatively in teaching and learning, but also from an unwillingness or inability to acknowledge credentialing as a professional responsibility.

In its educative role, assessment can be a creative instrument to assist intellectual development rather than a scheme to obstruct development. Examinations, oral reports, term papers, quizzes—virtually every device habitually used to assess student progress suffers unnecessarily from a stigma born of long years of misuse. As higher education has become a mass enterprise, testing has been seen by too many instructors as a service performed primarily to supply the registrar's office with required data at specified intervals in the semester. The more quickly and simply the chore was performed, therefore, the more time professors believed they would have for their true teaching functions, not realizing that the standardization and impersonalization of testing thereby diminished its teaching utility and their own effectiveness.

Few have expressed the positive approach to assessment for learning better than Gilbert Highet in *The Art of Teaching* (1959, p. 125): "There are really two different reasons for asking questions of a class: to find out if each individual has done his work in preparation, and to expose the difficulties they have found collectively in preparing the work. The former is a method of making them learn, the latter helps them to learn. The latter is much more important, but it is sometimes quite forgotten. . . . Teaching is constant expansion and development. The usual way of verifying this development is to question the class on the new work it has done since the last meeting." In other words, without knowing what students have learned, the teacher cannot educate.

Of course the skilled use of testing takes time—time to prepare the kinds of questions designed to stimulate the student and elicit his or her best efforts, time to evaluate the results carefully and constructively, and time to follow up so as to insure the fullest measure of benefit to the student. If coverage of one's subject must be sacrificed in the process, surely the quality of the resulting learning outweighs quantity of coverage in importance.

The second major function of assessment—credentialing—is currently in some disrepute, particularly among egalitarian educators. The assessment process has become so mechanical, so completely detached from teaching and learning, that demands for its abandonment rather than its reform prevail. As a result, a number of institutions have abandoned dean's lists, honors, and indeed most forms of grading. Ironically, the baby is being thrown out with the bath. If other institutions similarly renounce credentialing as a professional responsibility, chaos can only follow.

The fact is that professionalism flourishes only to the extent that informed judgment is exercised. Indeed, what point does any teaching or learning have if it is not intended to cultivate the ability to discriminate? Surely one of the primary functions of intelligence is to be discriminating in the sense of exercising judgment to choose between the lesser of evils or the better of goods on the basis of the soundest evidence we can collect, rather than discriminating on the basis of specious prejudices and ignorance. If egalitarianism is an acceptable rationale for not having to choose among levels of performance, for not having to make judgments about or among people, then any concept of standards would be pointless. But as Orwell so aptly noted in *Animal Farm,* even where all animals are supposed to be equal, some are more equal than others.

The urgency for improved assessment in credentialing is heightened by external pressures for fuller disclosure of what we are about in postsecondary education and how well we are doing. During the 1960s, the historical American faith in education was unchallenged, and administrators of colleges and universities could usually persuade their sponsors to increase annual budgets simply on the evidence of increased enrollments, credits earned, and degrees awarded. That these statistics tell nothing about educational quality has only recently become an issue in legislative debates and trustee meetings. Now, United States senators and state assemblymen vie to ask the hard questions and demand to know what federal or state appropriations are buying in terms of tangible results. Congressmen and state legislators have a right to ask what the public is getting for its tax dollars. But if they are not provided with convincing evidence, they will all too readily succumb to simplistic slogans that may capture the voter's fancy but that terribly distort the purpose and meaning of higher education.

Aside from sound educational reasons for being sensitive to these pressures, there are potential threats to the freedom of educational institutions to be the masters of their own houses. In a July 1975 report, "Toward a Federal Strategy for Protection of the Consumer of Education," issued by the Federal Interagency Committee on Education, the following principle is stated (p. 50): "Consumer concepts, legislation, and mechanisms should be activated in the educational marketplace as is now occurring in the traditional marketplace." No doubt many of us would readily support consumer protection, but the entry of federal regulation into any sphere of activity is always a cause of uneasiness and especially so in higher education. It behooves us, therefore, in the interests of students, sponsors, and other constituencies, to generate and accumulate sufficient information of a kind that presents a convincing picture of institutional achievement. And that achievement, in turn, must increasingly be a reflection of individual achievement.

It is the integrity of the process whereby we determine the value and validity of all learning, not only of experiential learning, that will influence the credibility and public acceptance of postsecondary education. We must find improved means for communicating the essence of our endeavors, and the evidence must be substantial. Unless we honestly try, we shall find increasingly troublesome the task of convincing students and parents and legislators that the educational community deserves their support. Such support will no longer be forthcoming simply on the basis of faith or tradition.

As educators, then, we have a professional responsibility to define and establish measures that are clear, equitable, and relevant to the objectives of the course, curriculum, institution, or framework in which we expect or intend to have learning take place. Few aspects of postsecondary education are in greater need of thoughtful and creative endeavor than the means and methods for assessing results. And I can see no reason why our efforts should be confined to the area of experiential learning. They should apply universally to every facet of teaching and learning. In short, the issues raised in the consideration of credit for experiential learning go to the heart of the current crisis of confidence in the academic enterprise.

Accrediting agencies are under particular pressures from the general public and governmental agencies at both the federal and state levels to insure the quality of institutional achievement and to protect consumer interests. The roles of policemen and regulator, however, run counter to the historic and current posture of the regional accrediting commissions and most of the specialized accrediting agencies. As voluntary organizations, they have defined their role as partners with institutions in the quest for educational excellence. Until recently, they simply assumed that their efforts to improve the quality of higher education by strengthening individual institutions and their professional programs were ipso facto in the public interest. There is abundant evidence that they were, but what was once an article of faith is no longer so. To be cognizant and considerate of legitimate public interests while simultaneously preserving the freedom and integrity of the educational enterprise is thus as much a challenge to the accreditors as to the accredited. Together they must produce the data to demonstrate educational effectiveness and the validity of their credentials.

The regional accrediting commissions have sought to address this issue as it relates to credit for experiential learning in their "Interim Statement on Accreditation and Nontraditional Study," adopted by the Council of the Federation of Regional Accrediting Commissions of Higher Education (FRACHE) in March 1973. Two of the key provisions of that statement read as follows (pp. 1–2): "(1) When degrees based heavily on nontraditional patterns of study are offered, evidence will be required that the degrees are awarded on the basis of definite criteria and demonstrated competency commensurate with the level and nature of the degrees. (2) The appraisal, evaluation, or examination procedures of an institution must be conducted with a high degree of objectivity, with due regard for maintenance of honesty and security, and with explicit statements of criteria and standards for judging satisfactory performance. The learner's self-appraisal of the worth of the learning experience is a valuable, but not sufficient, basis for awarding credit or a degree."

Clearly, these guidelines place the burden of responsibility on institutions to demonstrate the integrity of their credentialing processes. That these guidelines should apply to all assessment of learning, whether experiential or classroom, is obvious. What should also be obvious is the necessity of institutions having sensibly defined policies relating the crediting of experiential learning to their regular educational program. For example, just granting credit in order to attract students is not acceptable. To do so would subvert the integrity of the educational process, cheapen the degree, and establish opportunism as a basis for academic policy. The trouble with assuming that something is obvious, however, is that all too often the assumption is unwarranted.

To help institutions clarify their policies regarding credit for prior learning, one of the regional accrediting commissions—the Accrediting Commission for Senior Colleges and Universities of the Western Association of Schools and Colleges—recently issued guidelines on undergraduate credit for such learning. Recognizing that (1974, pp. 1–2) "demonstrable learning, based on experiences other than those that occur in an academic setting, may be educationally creditable, and any appropriate past learning from experience can be used to undergird or supplement present and future learning beyond the secondary school," the Commission supports awarding credit for prior learning on the basis of eight guidelines. These include: that the student applying for credit at an institution is matriculated at that institution, and that the past learning can be shown to be relevant to the student's stated educational objectives; that the evaluation of such learning is performed by a faculty member at that institution who is competent in the area being evaluated; that the student provides evidence of the prior learning and that the evaluator provides a written evaluation of the evidence (both to be placed in the student's permanent file); that the review and final approval of documentation for credit, as well as the amount of credit given, is performed by a panel of full-time faculty; that the student completes thirty semester units at the institution awarding the credit; that credit for prior learning meets the academic standards of the institution; that fees are charged in accordance with the institution's investment of time and resources; and that all such policies and procedures are described in the official publication of the institution.

The Commission adds, in its definition of terms, that "learning must be demonstrable in the sense that a student can present evidence of learning. The kinds of evidence are numerous and might include written and oral exams, tapes, projects, demonstrations, and performances in a form subject to analysis. The institution has a responsibility to make clear to the student and the accrediting agency the means by which competencies can be acceptably demonstrated" (p. 2).

As with the earlier FRACHE guidelines on nontraditional study, this statement asks the institution to demonstrate the integrity of its processes and the validity of its assessments. One may quarrel with details of the statement, and doubtless it will be improved through time and use. Nevertheless, it reflects the thoughtful efforts of a distinguished and reputable group of educators to insure standards in granting credit for experiential learning.

One thing the statement does not do is specify a single standard of quality for experiential learning. Because of the variety of American higher education institutions, the regional accrediting commissions have found that academic standards vary significantly from one campus to another. The faculty at one institution may be fully as concerned with quality as their counterparts at a more prestigious university, but disparate judgments as to what constitutes quality are as prevalent among institutions as among individuals on the same campus. The regional associations recognize this diversity: rather than establishing universal standards for institutional credit, they are requiring institutional standards to be based on sound educational principles. I agree with them: I confess to a strong skepticism on both the desirability and the attainability of universal standards. What is important is the integrity of the process whereby we establish standards—the extent to which honesty and objectivity, care and thoroughness, equity and due process, characterize the determination of educational objectives and any assessment of their attainment.

A second thing the statement does not do is to tell us how experiential learning can be translated into academic credit. And there is the rub. Frankly stated, there is an appalling ignorance on most campuses about the range of means for measuring the outcomes of the educational process. Despite extensive literature on testing and measurement, it tends to be ignored by academics who not infrequently characterize it with the opprobrium conveyed by the term *educationese*. Consequently, most protagonists of liberal education, and especially the humanists, have treated the concept of outcomes measurement with disdain or diffidence at best, clinging to limited traditional patterns in assessing student performance. On the majority of campuses, assessing outcomes has not been tried and found difficult: rather, it has been found difficult and seldom tried.

We may be further on the way toward coping with this problem of assessing outcomes than we realize. Under the direction of Norman Burns and aided by a grant from the Danforth Foundation, the regional accrediting commissions have a study project in progress designed to shift the practice of institutional accrediting toward a heavier emphasis on the assessment of educational outcomes. In working with institutions on this study, Burns has found that one factor militating against ready acceptance of outcomes data is the lack of information about useful and usable outcomes measures designed to assist both teachers and institutions in their analysis of their work. An unanticipated by-product of the FRACHE study may have great potential here. It is a compendium of information about evaluative instruments suitable for institutional or individual outcomes measurement, containing descriptions of tests, surveys, questionnaires, inventories, scales, and related tools, and including data about costs, administration, and other details. Compiled by Ann Heiss, formerly of the Center for Research and Development in Higher Education at the University of California, Berkeley, the compendium is being field tested prior to publication. When published, it should serve to dispel many of the myths and misunderstandings surrounding educational assessment and outcomes measurement.

Once these misunderstandings are resolved, we may be able to reexamine another problem regarding our credentialing responsibilities: the underlying assumptions about the nature and meaning of academic degrees and diplomas. For example, bachelor of arts degrees awarded to one student who has majored in philosophy and to another who has majored in business administration can hardly be said to represent the same learning, yet the diplomas are identical and one has to read carefully the students' transcripts to discern any differences.

Some have proposed the creation of numerous specially designed degrees to solve this problem—including distinctive degrees to be awarded to graduates whose programs have been based largely on experiential learning. But rather than creating new degrees, perhaps all we need do is to replace the medieval language of most diplomas and the obscure rights and privileges pertaining thereto with a succinct and specific statement about what the degree represents. Where experiential learning has contributed toward the attainment of the degree, let the diploma so note.

What I am suggesting is that diplomas and transcripts be made more integrally related—possibly going so far as to be printed back-to-back, with diplomas containing a substantive statement in plain English of what the degree signifies, and transcripts providing the qualitative and quantitative details, including evidence from outcomes measures, portfolios, and other descriptive arrangements where needed. This change seems relatively simple, and it could result in more effective communication between educational and other social institutions than either diplomas or transcripts currently permit.

Students and faculty have different concerns in using diplomas and transcripts, just as do graduate and professional schools or employers. But the paramount goal of such credentials for all

parties—students, faculty, educational institutions, and employers—
is essentially the same: to maximize the application of learning for
the greatest benefit of all. An undergraduate aiming toward a career
in psychiatric social work, for example, who gains creditable experience through summer employment in the social service department of the local hospital should have this information noted
officially on the transcript, so that on graduation, prospective employers or graduate professional schools can use this information to
determine proper levels of placement. In other words, assessment
records of experiential learning should lead to more informed decisions than are usually possible when undifferentiated diplomas or
transcripts are the only available information.

It is entirely conceivable that, if both the educative and credentialing functions of assessment are kept in mind, the assessment
of experiential learning will contribute new understanding and
validity to the value of all educational assessment as well as to the
teaching process itself. As we endeavor to relate what has been
learned to defined objectives, as we see how certain types of experience develop perceptions and insights, and as we acquire sophistication in distinguishing between substance and superficiality,
we shall extend the dimensions of our professional competence and
enhance the credibility of the total academic enterprise.

Thus those in the vanguard of the movement to gain broad
acceptance for the concept of academic credit for experiential learning should be undeterred in their efforts to expand the parameters
of our educational structure by recognizing the legitimacy and importance of experience as a creditable aspect of personal and intellectual growth. If the current debate brings general agreement that
learning is what matters, and that setting, structure, and process are
the means to that end and not ends in themselves, it will be the best
evidence of all that we do indeed learn greatly from experience.

░░

Chapter Eleven

Tools and Methods of Evaluation

░░

Aubrey Forrest, Joan E. Knapp,
and Judith Pendergrass

The CAEL project and literature have identified six steps in the portfolio assessment process: identification, articulation, documentation, measurement, evaluation, and transcripting. While transcripting is logically placed as the final stage, the development of a transcript for experiential learning actually begins with the first stage of the portfolio assessment process, and potential information for inclusion in the transcript is being generated throughout all of the first five steps. In fact, the narrative transcript can be seen as a logical extension of the portfolio or as a summary of a completed portfolio assessment process.

In this chapter, we describe some of the problems associated with portfolio assessment and the narrative transcript, and recommend some procedures and techniques leading to the solution of these problems. In particular, we suggest that those responsible for choosing methods and instrumentation for experiential learning

161

consider three assessment tools: the use of a portfolio system to support and document a student's claim to learning and to insure adequate communication among those involved in the assessment process, particularly in assessing nonsponsored learning; the embedding of specific measurement techniques in the portfolio process that are selected from the full range of procedures currently available; and the development of a narrative transcript to communicate assessment results more adequately to interested parties, both within and without the institution.

Portfolios

Because effective assessment of experiential learning usually involves several assessors using more than one measurement technique, accurate communication throughout the six steps of assessment can be a problem, especially in assessing nonsponsored learning. Most of the efforts to seek solutions to this problem have centered around the portfolio. A portfolio can be described simply as a file or folder of accumulated information about a student's experiences and accomplishments that can be the vehicle for organizing and distilling raw experiences into a manageable form for assessment. This folder usually contains the following items: a resume listing the student's educational, employment, community, or volunteer experiences, and other pertinent data; a narrative that is usually autobiographical in tone and contains the student's implicit or explicit claim to learning; a statement requesting credit in a specific subject area or recognition of one or several competencies; and a set of documents, such as letters of verification and job descriptions, that provide evidence that the experiences emphasized by the student in the narrative did indeed take place.

Clearly, a portfolio is not only a dossier—it is the result of a process by which experiences can be translated into educational outcomes or competencies, documented, and assessed for academic credit or recognition (Knapp, 1975). In many cases, these procedures are incorporated into the larger effort of formulating and designing an academic program in the form of a contract or degree pact. Rather than emphasizing the tangible portfolio, the process itself, which is open to alternate procedures, should be stressed in discussions concerning this technique.

Because of the significance of the portfolio process in the assessment of experiential learning, both from the standpoint of widespread use and as a communication device, issues and problems concerning portfolio usage have begun to surface. Some of these concern practical matters, such as the amount of documentation required to verify a learning experience; others touch on more conceptual and philosophical problems, such as the value of the portfolio process itself to the student's learning. At the end of this chapter, we make general recommendations for improving the portfolio process so that these issues may be resolved. For now, let us examine some of the problems, beginning with the issue of learning versus experience.

Institutional program literature and brochures repeatedly profess that students undergoing life experience assessment will be evaluated in terms of learning outcomes or competencies rather than in terms of number of years of experience. An examination of student portfolios from various programs, however, shows that many do not contain concise statements of learning outcomes or competencies. An observer is left with time spent in an experience and few notions as to what aspects of a particular student's experiences were indeed measured and evaluated for college credit. One's judgment is naturally colored by years of experience at a job or activity, since time spent has always been a crucial factor when considering job placement and promotion in the world outside academe. Even a well-meaning and objective assessor cannot help being more influenced, for example, by a portfolio that describes a student's twenty-year service in an investment firm for which he now acts as vice-president than by one that describes a student's three-year service as a chief accountant.

The dangers, however, of allowing experience to substitute for outcomes are great and far outweigh the ease of using time spent as a benchmark for assessment. One danger involves the loss to the student of a valuable learning exercise—the translation of past experience into learning, competence, or achievement (Forrest, 1975). Listing years spent in an activity and describing the functions performed in service of that activity is an educationally empty task. One must learn from the past in order to build and plan for a more educationally effective future. Another danger involves fairness and adequacy in assessment. How can an assessor justify his evaluation of the learning outcomes of an experience without any initial evidence, record, or expression of what was learned from an activity or experience?

Another problem that arises in using portfolios is the fact that different standards are used for traditional and experiential learning. In surveying institutions that offer life experience assessment, the problem of a double standard frequently emerges. In some cases, stringent standards are imposed for judging experiential learning, while classroom learning is evaluated as creditable simply because it is offered within the institutional walls of higher learning. In many programs, for example, the following criteria are used to decide whether an experiential learning outcome should be assessed: Does the learning outcome lend itself to measurement and evaluation? Is the learning outcome at the level of undergraduate achievement? Can the learning be applied outside the specific job or context in which it was learned? Does the learning imply a conceptual as well as a practical grasp of the knowledge base? Does the learning show some relationship to degree goals or a lifelong learning goal?

Let us look at these criteria in terms of typical college course offerings. First, are learning outcomes usually stated for courses offered at an institution so that they can be measured specifically? Are all learning outcomes associated with freshman courses at the level of undergraduate achievement? Furthermore, what constitutes undergraduate achievement? Can learning outcomes achieved in the classroom be applied outside the course and classroom? Does classroom learning imply a practical as well as a conceptual grasp of the knowledge base? And for the last criterion, let us ask, for example, how a student's choice of an art history course is related to a degree goal in business administration.

The double standard becomes even more troublesome because the portfolio process, itself a learning experience, may be costly to the student in time and assessment fees. In some situations, the student effort is equivalent to a senior thesis, and yet life experience credits are meted out on a niggardly basis so that many adults feel that their noncollege learning activities are somehow second-rate. The solution to the double standard problem may lie in having higher education in general and individual institutions in particular meet headlong the question of what an educated, intelligent individual is. This question is directly related to the reluctance or inability of individual institutions to define college-level learning.

This leads to the next problem: what constitutes college-level learning? Whether the practice of a college is to award credit for noncollege experience or for the learning outcomes of those experiences, it must determine what it considers to be college-level learning. The institution cannot communicate to a student what should be in a portfolio until the institution sets forth in clear fashion what it is that will be credited and what criteria are considered in judging what will be creditable.

Current practices at institutions that award credit or recognition for experiential learning indicate that satisfactory resolutions of the issue are yet to be found. Particularly unsatisfactory are practices such as the following: requiring students to find course analogs or labels for prior experiential learning; requiring students to relate experiential learning to institutional goals when such goals are vaguely defined; placing responsibility on an individual faculty member or a faculty committee to award a block of credit simply on the basis of the number of years of experience; and placing responsibility on an individual faculty member or a faculty committee to award a block of credit for the total noncollege experience that a student has had without the existence of clear faculty consensus or guidelines. All of these practices tend to focus on the quality and quantity of experiences rather than on the learning outcomes of the experiences. They also tend to ignore the obvious fact that each student's prior experiential learning is unique.

Among those institutions that credit experiential learning, two camps have formed concerning the relative importance of documentation of prior experience—a situation that poses yet another problem in the use of portfolios. One group asserts that documentation is a relatively unimportant and wasteful procedure in the portfolio process because letters and certificates presented by the student merely verify presence during an activity or experience and do not verify that any learning indeed took place. Another group of institutions asserts that verification of the timing and setting of a learning experience is a crucial step in the portfolio process and is somewhat similar to the verification through a transcript as to when a college course took place and how many hours were spent in class and in outside assignments.

The real reasons for the amount of documentation required probably lie between the two extremes. Documentation makes the portfolio look more official than a typical student folder or report, and produces comfortable feelings on the part of faculty and administrators about the legitimacy of the student's experiential learning. Overdocumentation in student folders may be desired by certain administrators so that presentation of nontraditional programs to accrediting agencies appears more official and formal than the presentation of the traditional curricula and programs.

Individuals who prefer underdocumentation are usually assessors focused on the learning outcomes of experience who find rummaging through folders bulging with letters of recommendation and newspaper articles frustrating. But not all types of documentation are equally unimportant. Work samples and products could be, if evaluated by an expert, useful types of documentation in the assessment process, since they substitute for performance testing—a type of assessment that is expensive and, in most cases, impractical.

What about the reliability of faculty decisions? If one assumes that each individual's experiential learning is unique, then faculty decisions as to individual assessment and credit are at best difficult and trying. The typical assessment methodologies do not apply here. Specific paper and pencil tests can be used rarely; normative measurement is not appropriate. Therefore, some quality control mechanism must be devised to assure students that portfolio assessment will be equitable and rigorous. Such assurance cannot be given if faculty are not in agreement as to criterion standards, if they are resistant to learning new measurement techniques, and if they fail to recognize the need for outside experts when their expertise is not at a sufficient level for assessment. Each of these conditions does exist in actual practice at some institutions. In addition, applying a single faculty person's judgment to a student's portfolio (an assessment arrangement in many programs) may not produce reliable or consistent evaluation (a supposition that is confirmed in educational measurement literature).

A similar problem revolves around the issue of the validity of the portfolio process itself. Any discussion of the portfolio as an assessment device provokes a constellation of questions. Is the portfolio an accurate reflection of reality? Should a faculty member or committee believe what is written in a portfolio? If a faculty member or committee has not observed, interviewed, or had any direct contact with a student, can a valid judgment be made about the student's experience and learning on the basis only of a portfolio? How far should a faculty member or committee go in checking the authenticity of a student narrative, letters of verification, records, certificates, or work samples?

All these questions are subsumed under the larger question of what constitutes proof of learning. In many programs, assessors rely heavily on documentation procedures to answer this question. Faculty and administrators are concerned with the validity of the portfolio and with stringent verification of the existence of a learning experience, but the major value of the portfolio as an assessment technique may reside in its educational value and utility to the student. One questions, for example, the utility of a portfolio developed by a student who has had no direct contact with at least one faculty member over a significant period of time.

The development of a portfolio should have value to the student and to the institution beyond being a basis for awarding credit or recognition of prior experiential learning. The process is costly in time and money for both the student and the college; to maximize the benefits to be derived from the process, there should be, but frequently is not, extensive student-faculty contact. Without such contact, many potential benefits will not be realized—benefits such as a realistic understanding of present levels of competence by the student; an effective planning of future learning by the student; student acquisition of knowledge about assessment procedures; possession of a sound, basic document that can be added to and refined throughout the rest of the student's life; feedback to the institution as to student learning needs; and adequate quality control over the portfolio process and the awarding of credit or recognition.

Issues related to the validity and value of the portfolio as an instrument in assessing experiential learning lead naturally to the question of the timing of the portfolio process. Should a portfolio be developed at the beginning of an adult student's entrance or reentrance to college? The answer would appear to be yes for the student who wants to know how much credit or recognition is to be awarded before deciding whether or not to proceed with additional learning at the college. A positive answer would also appear to be appropriate for students who are certain about their educational goals and want to integrate prior learning closely with future learning.

Not all adult students, however, are clear about their educational goals. In fact, an important reason they may be starting or returning to college is to seek assistance in defining educational goals through participating in what may seem to others to be a random series of learning experiences. For these students, waiting until later to begin the portfolio process may be a better idea. Moreover, a student who has had no college work will be handicapped in trying to identify prior college-level learning and in being able to present a case that will maximize the amount of credit or recognition that might be awarded for experiential learning. Where both sets of consideration apply, some institutions give "tentative placement with advanced standing," with performance in the first term or year as a test of the accuracy of the placement.

Specific Measurment Techniques

An adequate introduction to specific measurement techniques has been provided in the CAEL publication, *A Compendium of Assessment Techniques* (Knapp and Sharon, 1974) and the references contained therein. These techniques are described here briefly to emphasize the importance of the use of measurement tools in the portfolio process and to indicate the range of possibilities.

Experiential learning presents unique measurement problems to assessors. Because experiential learning can be highly individualized, frequently associated with an absence of faculty involvement, and usually concerned with student learning by doing—the kind of learning that takes place in a variety of social, artistic, political, work, or cross-cultural activities outside campus environs—its measurement requires the consideration of techniques that have not been widely employed in higher education. It is useful, then, to consider some measurement techniques that have been developed in the fields of psychology, business, industry, and the military. We wish to underscore the point that several measurement techniques can, and indeed probably should, be used to measure a single learning outcome. This is especially true when a great deal of error is associated with each technique or when the measurement procedures are far removed from direct observation of student performance.

Since the portfolio is usually the vehicle by which a student presents a claim to learning, expert judgment must be brought to bear on this evidence to determine the nature and extent of the learning. The techniques described below—product assessment, performance tests, simulations, essay examinations, and interviews— require a holistic judgment stemming from expertise and therefore are not typical psychometric approaches.

Product assessment, as used in the context of experiential learning, pertains mainly to the evaluation of such products as pictures, musical compositions, writing samples, mechanical inventions, and the like. Each product is assumed to represent the skills of the student in a particular activity, with the need to evaluate the product stemming from the evaluator's inability to observe directly the demonstration of the student's skills while the product is being created. For example, an assessor cannot observe a student engaged in creative writing but can observe the written product of that effort.

Performance tests contain a strong element of realism because they resemble the situation in which a specific kind of experiential learning is applied. Frequently, a performance test is nothing but a work sample requiring the accomplishment of specific tasks in a controlled setting, but it may consist of a situational observation of performance in a natural setting. For example, a student's ability to repair electronic equipment could be measured by presenting a piece of faulty equipment that the student would then need to diagnose and correct.

Simulations or situational tests require the student to pretend that he or she is engaged in some realistic task, the nature and content of which are described in some detail before the individual begins to assume an assigned or unassigned role. Often the simulation is less complex and more convenient than the real situation and operates under a compressed time schedule. Such a procedure offers the assessor or assessment team an opportunity to observe and measure the quality of performance in a lifelike setting that often cannot be measured by other means. Simulations are ordinarily used to assess complex qualities such as analytical thinking, goal setting, risk taking, interpersonal competence, decision making, sensitivity to the behavior of others, oral communication, and planning skills.

Essay examinations are characterized by the presentation of questions or tasks to which the student responds by organizing and writing an answer. Some tests are based on the student's giving written responses to situations presented on audio- or videotape.

Interviews are face-to-face interpersonal role situations in which the interviewer asks the student questions designed to obtain answers that will lead to an evaluation of one or more learning outcomes. The interview is the most practical and widely used measurement device in the portfolio process. For this technique to be maximally useful, the assessor should capitalize on the flexibility of this procedure by taking the time to probe for an explanation of the student's perceived learning outcomes, a clarification of learning goals, and an estimate of the limits of knowledge and skills gained from the student's experiential learning. The interview should not be used to test whether the student has acquired discrete knowledge or concepts; objective tests and oral examinations are more suitable for this purpose.

The use of two or more of these techniques in combination and by two or more assessors will usually result in more valid and reliable measurement than the use of a single technique by a single assessor. Consider these examples:

Measuring a student's fluency in a language by use of both an oral interview and an essay examination.

Measuring a student's engineering skill by two experts assessing several products made by the student and by an oral explanation by the student of how the products were designed and made.

Measuring a student's counseling skill by means of a simulated test using three expert observers and by an objective test covering counseling theory.

Measuring a student's competence to operate a small business by having the student demonstrate conduct of a sale, by having three experts assess the business records, and by administering a problem-solving essay examination.

Transcription of Experiential Learning

Once the assessment of what has been learned through experience is completed, there remains the question of how to report this learning and how to translate it into terms that will be accepted by higher education and society in general. This translation can pose problems if the experiential learning transcript is in the traditional format.

Attempts to use course-type labels to identify the subject content of both the learning experience and the resulting outcomes have been called inadequate and lacking in accuracy. The use of credit hours alone in an attempt to quantify the extent of experiential learning has also been judged inadequate because credit hours, as they are currently applied to classroom learning, are determined by time spent in learning activities rather than representing directly the amount of learning that might have taken place. Credit and grades are likewise deemed inadequate as measures of the quality or level of learning achieved, since they do not specify the criterion standards employed (Meyer, 1975, p. 174).

A number of nontraditional programs in higher education have recognized these problems and have been experimenting with alternative forms of experiential learning transcripts (see Forrest, Ferguson, and Cole, 1975, pp. 59–65). Several of these models are examined briefly below.

Forms of alternative transcript models vary according to the degree to which narration is used in presenting the results of the student's learning experiences. In general, institutions list some type of title of the work or experience completed and a description of the activities in which the student participated, particularly since no catalog description of them usually exists. As noted above, many schools convert experiential learning into some measure of time units or credit. The greatest diversity, however, appears to exist in the type and amount of evaluative material included, ranging from standard grades to students' own evaluation of their learning, depending, in some cases, on the student's expected uses of the transcript, the type of experience undertaken by the student, or the amount of experiential learning described in the transcript.　　•

Governors State University in Illinois gives a very specific list of the knowledge or skill demonstrated by the student. (See Exhibit 1 at the end of the chapter.) Where additional information is necessary, a description of the learning process is given. Usually no evaluative material, either grades or narrative, is included.

In contrast to this form, the University of California, Santa Cruz, uses one in which a title and a unit designation are given as well as an indication of whether or not the learning was credited. No letter grades are given, however, and the bulk of the transcript is composed of reproductions of narrative evaluations written by the faculty. (See Exhibit 2.)

Goddard College in Vermont gives, on the transcript, titles of learning experiences and their semester-hour equivalents, determined by the percentage of study time devoted to the experience. The transcript also gives abstracts from evaluations written by both the student and instructors. These abstracts may deal with the affective as well as the cognitive facets of the learning experience. (See Exhibit 3 for samples from one such transcript.)

A more extensive document used by Empire State College includes a narrative summary of the student's accomplishments prepared by the student's advisor, a summary page of titles, list of units completed, supporting materials, the student's graduation contract, and reproductions of evaluations completed by instructors. (See Exhibit 4.) These evaluations describe the learning process as well as the assessment of the outcomes.

A fifth type of transcript from Johnston College, University of Redlands, gives a specific description of the knowledge and skill that the student has demonstrated and of the learning experience that led to the development of those competencies, as well as annotations of evaluations written by the assessors. (See Exhibit 5.) These evaluation sections describe the assessment technique used, the ways in which the student met the criterion standards established to measure competency in each area, the qualifications of the assessor, and the date the evaluation was performed. Johnston College assigns no credits or grades. Though no student assessments are included, students generally aid in the preparation of the transcript.

These models are representative of the types of alternative transcripts, employing varying degrees of narration, currently in use. Though support for them is growing among educational institutions and employers, their adoption has stimulated several concerns peculiar to their preparation and use. One principal concern centers on what should be included in the transcript in order to convey the necessary information. For example, as the models demonstrate, the extent to which the learning experience itself is described varies considerably among institutions. Of course, decisions regarding the use of detail in describing the components of the learning process and its measurement are often influenced by issues of cost of production and interpretation of the transcript by outside agencies.

Perhaps of greater significance is whether or not narrative evaluations of experiential learning should be annotated when evaluative material is placed on a transcript. Certainly a case may be made for the importance of quoting the assessor directly, thus protecting all concerned from the danger of inadvertent distortion or of weakening the evidence of learning the student has presented. On the other hand, factors such as inappropriate length, type of material included in the assessor's statement, and cost factors in producing excessively long transcripts may lead an institution to cull the core elements from evaluations and summarize them on the final transcript in conjunction with the recording of learning outcomes.

Questions about the type of data provided by evaluators of experiential learning arise when the transcript provides a direct quotation, either partial or complete, of the narrative evaluation or of an annotation. In either case, an adequate description of the assessment process and the quality of the student's demonstrated achievement is, of course, necessary. If quotations are to be used, however, or if the narrative evaluation is to be attached to the transcript, the material included must be not only complete but readable and well executed.

In an attempt to alleviate this problem, some institutions that place narrative evaluation material on the transcript have begun training programs for those who serve as their chief evaluators of experiential learning, particularly of nonsponsored learning. Moreover, these institutions have developed written guidelines for evaluators to use in preparing statements that may be used in transcripts, and generally provide continuing consultation and followup services in working with evaluators, particularly when they are external to the main body of college faculty. Certainly such a thorough approach is likely to produce evaluations that are not only appropriate to the transcript model being used but also more complete and precise and, therefore, more useful to both the student and the institution.

But such training efforts are difficult (if not impractical) to implement in working with recognized external experts in a given field, since large numbers and wide geographic distributions are likely to be involved. Difficulties are also likely to arise with both faculty and external evaluators because of the assumption by some subject matter experts that mastery of the subject field is sufficient training for assessing competence in that field. In any case, the role of the institution in training evaluators and thereby strongly influencing assessment procedures and the material included in narrative evaluation is as yet an unresolved issue.

Then, too, students may be asked to aid in determining the use of their transcripts and may take a substantial role in selecting material to be included. Certainly, such a collaboration is likely to make the document particularly useful to each student. In some cases, students prepare a draft of the transcript. Once again, however, we find many institutions concerned about the desirability or practicality of training students to monitor assessment procedures and determine appropriate transcript entries.

If narration is used to substitute for rather than to supplement grades and credits, there is some concern that institutional standards may suffer, assuming that grades and credits are essential motivators of student performance. If students are allowed to set their own criterion standards, they may not be motivated to excel. In a pass-fail grading system, however, the use of narrative evaluations can only enhance efforts to maintain institutional standards.

Since the chief purpose of a transcript is to provide for others an accurate and complete record of learning measured by an institution, the use of a narrative record by agencies such as employers and graduate and professional schools is of considerable concern to schools beginning implementation of narrative transcripts. Certainly one value of such a transcript is that it can provide a complete and precise record of the student's learning activities, particularly those of an experiential nature. This is generally deemed desirable if not essential by most employers and receiving institutions. But these transcripts may pose problems for many receivers.

If, for example, transcripts include no grades and consequently no grade point average is available, they may be viewed as less valuable, particularly when decisions must be made regarding admission to programs or award of honors or financial assistance on the basis of these brief qualitative indices (for a discussion of the problems posed by narrative transcripts from the perspective of graduate school admissions and financial aid officers, see Groesbeck, 1975, pp. 479–82). In some cases, readers of these transcripts are unwilling to sort through narrative evaluations to determine the overall picture of the student's accomplishments. Then, too, as we noted earlier, such narrative evaluations address the individual's experience and are based on criterion standards often specific to that student.

Furthermore, many contend that the interpretation of nontraditional transcripts requires considerable special attention by the reader. If course labels or other standard interpretation devices are not used on the transcript, the reader may find it difficult to relate the outcomes of the student's experience to familiar curricula, and may find it equally difficult to form a general sense of perspective regarding the learning outcomes. To aid the reader, some institutions include a summary page before the main body of the transcript. Such concern regarding the time and energy necessary to interpret a narrative transcript would seem to indicate that special care should be taken to include precise descriptions in a simplified format.

A related question about opening the narrative transcript to external parties involves the legal liability of evaluator and institution for disclosure, or resulting damage of the disclosure to the student. A signed authorization by the student to release the material can alleviate the problem.

Finally, we come to a problem that is closely related to the preceding issues—the potentially high cost of some forms of nontraditional transcripts. One or more of the following factors may contribute to this problem. Increased time is generally involved in the preparation of narrative evaluations; thus, assessor time may increase the overall cost, particularly if additional time has been required to train and provide followup service for those assessors. In addition, the transcript itself must be composed, including collecting the necessary material and placing it in the appropriate style on the document by either faculty members or a special editor or registrar. Typing and duplicating as well as the paper itself increase the overall cost of a transcript. Finally, storing and retrieving these documents, whether through a file or computer system, add to the cost of using a narrative transcript.

Recommendations for Improvements in Developing and Selecting Assessment Tools

Having reviewed some of the problems encountered in the use of the portfolio and the narrative transcript, we have eleven recommendations to offer. It is our belief that application of these proposals would go a long way toward solving such problems.

First, no attempts should be made by an institution to select or design assessment tools until that institution decides specifically what it hopes to assess, what standards will be applied, and who the assessors will be. Such decisions should be communicated to all concerned in clear statements placed in the literature of the institution outlining what will be considered for credit or recognition. The criteria set forth in such statements should present a clear picture of what that institution considers to be college-level learning.

Second, a clear distinction should be drawn among methods of documenting experience, specific techniques designed to measure learning outcomes, and such communication devices or processes as portfolios and narrative transcripts. We further recommend that the mere documentation of the fact that a student participated in a learning activity should not in itself constitute adequate evidence of learning.

Third, to enhance the reliability and validity of the assessment process, we recommend judicious use of multiple assessors and multiple measurement techniques.

Fourth, to achieve all of the potential benefits of a portfolio or narrative transcript process, we recommend frequent student-faculty contact and individualized pacing and sequencing through the steps of the processes.

Fifth, each institution needs constantly to test, analyze, and refine the production and management systems used for portfolios and narrative transcripts. Reference criteria for such systems should include time lines, efficiency, completeness, accuracy, and cost-effectiveness as well as cost control.

Sixth, assessor training workshops and appropriate materials should be developed to stimulate creative thinking in selecting and designing measurement techniques for many types of learning outcomes, to improve the capabilities of assessors in writing concise and appropriate evaluations that speak to specific learning outcomes, and to increase the reliability of the judgment of assessors who must make decisions regarding the actual awarding of credit based on a portfolio process.

Seventh, student training workshops (with appropriate written materials) should be developed to improve the ability of students to participate effectively in all six steps of the assessment process. This would improve the quality and validity of portfolios produced by students and could materially reduce the costs of both the portfolio and the narrative transcript processes.

Eighth, institutions should prepare and distribute publications aimed at explaining the portfolio rationale and process to students, faculty, administrators, and external assessors, and the narrative transcript rationale and language to users, thereby reducing misunderstanding and resistance.

Ninth, institutions using or considering using narrative transcripts should establish user review panels to serve as reactors to the proposed content and format of narrative transcript models. Such panels should consist of employers from both public and private agencies, graduate and professional school admissions personnel, alumni possessing narrative transcripts (where possible), and currently enrolled students. The purposes of such panels would be to determine transcript needs as perceived by users and to clarify areas of misunderstanding.

Tenth, in order to make fair and equitable judgments about students possible within the framework of the policies and procedures of the receiving institution or employer, more information than the simple one-line entry of course label, credit, and grade would seem to be needed on an experiential learning transcript. The transcript designer should consider the following items for inclusion in the narrative transcript: the dates when the experiential learning took place, so that the transcript reader can judge whether the learning outcomes attained years ago are still relevant today or are likely to have suffered from decay; information about each learning activity, including topics investigated, persons providing supervision, location of learning activities, and duration of the learning activity; an indication of how the student documented the learning activities, since it cannot be assumed that someone at the college has personally verified that the student participated in the learning experience; sufficient information about measurement techniques used, so that the transcript reader can estimate the validity and reliability of the evaluation; and an indication of the criterion standards used in arriving at decisions concerning credit or college recognition.

Finally, we recommend that a systematic and continuous exchange of information about current practice and research in the selection and design of assessment tools should take place among all institutions engaged in assessing experiential learning.

Exhibit 1. GOVERNORS STATE UNIVERSITY
Initial Enrollment: September/October 1974
Credit for Experience: 3 Units

Description of Student's Achievements

Local Government and Urban Government: Served as commissioner of public property for eight years; was involved in the day operation of the city of Aurora, Illinois, a city of 85,000 people.

As commissioner, he gained: A knowledge of the impact of unionization on the public sector;

A knowledge of the financial budgeting process for governmental agencies;

A knowledge of hydrology through having responsibility for the production of fifteen million gallons of potable water daily;

A knowledge of engineering and construction through developing a $3,500,000 four-year program for the expansion of the community's water supply and a water billing and collection division;

A knowledge of the existing structure of city governments and improvements on this structure by completely reorganizing the Department of Public Property, the City of Aurora Inspection Division, and the Aurora Civil Service and Personnel Division;

A knowledge of the state laws delegating authority to local governments;

A knowledge of the demands the citizens and special interest groups make upon the public official;

A knowledge of the different institutions that make up a community and the development of various programs within an administrative department;

A knowledge of the effects of growth upon a community and the politics involved in making decisions regarding urban resources;

A knowledge of the election process through having run for public office at the local level;

A knowledge of service clubs and their activities from having participated with the Kiwanis, Rotary, Lions, and Cosmopolitan.

Exhibit 2.   UNIVERSITY OF CALIFORNIA, SANTA CRUZ

Student: T. Y. Jones

Term: Spring 1975

Course: Environmental Studies 183, Planning Internship

Grade: Pass

Instructor: J. B. Pepper

Instructor Evaluation

Enrollment in this course was limited to environmental planning majors of junior standing and was required for the major. The planning internship was a supervised off-campus experience that enabled students to explore and to test the practical applications of planning theory learned in a classroom situation. The internship required twelve to fifteen hours of field work per week in addition to advising time with the faculty sponsor and the program coordinator. Attendance at a weekly seminar was required, as was a written description and evaluation of the internship.

This internship is a continuation of the winter quarter team project preparing the Solid Waste Management Plan for San Benito County (see ES 183 winter 1975 evaluation)'.

During spring quarter, the four team members actually prepared the draft solid waste management plan for the county and presented their report, a 103-page document, to the county steering committee. The report was of very high quality, judged by a county official to be superior to previous professional consultant reports. Since individual contributions are difficult to assess in such a group effort, individual evaluations can only serve to highlight specific aspects of a *very* successful internship.

Mr. Jones was primarily responsible for the section on resource recovery. His contribution tailed off slightly at the end of the quarter, due in part to the fact that he was a graduating senior. Nevertheless, his performance must be evaluated as very good to strong.

Exhibit 3. GODDARD COLLEGE
Permanent Student Record
Student: Joseph B. Berry

1971–72 Spring Trimester

Botany. Semester hour equivalents: 5. The class met twice a week in four-hour blocks, one for lab work and discussion; the other for field work. This student was fully involved in all in- and out-of-class activities, including reading. He kept a useful notebook on wildflowers, trees, shrubs, grasses, sedges, fungi, and so on, which he identified both on field trips and during his climbing expeditions. He also kept a photographic record of much of what he observed. A highly successful study.

Color Photography (independent study). Semester hour equivalents: 5. During the study, the student shot and developed about 260 color slides. He says in his final report, "I tried to inter-twine the photography with my botany study and backpacking. . . . As a result, I have a fairly good collection of spring wildflowers plus pictures that are related to backpacking and climbing. . . . This was the first experience I have had in developing film. Generally, the quality of my slides was rather poor. Although I have a fairly good sense of composition, I have been plagued by faulty, inade-quate equipment from the start. Hopefully I can invest in better equipment this fall. . . . In spite of the problems described, I learned a considerable amount about the medium . . . and am relatively satisfied with the trimester's work." His instructor notes that the student's evaluation of his work is thorough, concrete, and accurate.

1973–74 Winter Trimester

Independent Senior Study Project in Education (culminating in a report of the student's practice teaching). Semester hour equivalents: 15. Mr. Berry's senior study project was in two parts: practice teaching and research in learning disabilities.

Practice teaching: He taught reading, math, science, and spelling to Grade 5 in a nearby school for total of 345 clock hours.

His critic teacher says, "He completed a very successful practice teaching experience. . . . He used source material and various media effectively to develop the work for the class. He was resourceful in finding and making materials for experimentation and arranging bulletin boards and displays. He used both the individual and group approach. He worked particularly well in one-to-one relationships or in small groups. He shows promise of being a very good teacher."

Learning disabilities: The student did a good deal of research on learning disabilities in children. Bibliography: Cohen, *Teach Them All to Read;* Cruickshank, *Psychology of Exceptional Children and Youth;* Goodman, *Children's Rights;* Itard, *The Wild Boy of Aveyron;* Kephart, *The Slow Learner in the Classroom;* Long, Morse, and Newman, *Conflict in the Classroom;* Zuk and Boszormenyi-Nagy, *Family Therapy and Disturbed Families.*

Culminating paper: His culminating paper is a clear and thorough report drawn from the journal he kept on his practice teaching and a long essay on the insights he gained from his study of learning disabilities. His writing flows smoothly. His comments are perceptive and reflect an ability to integrate classroom experience with educational theory.

Exhibit 4. EMPIRE STATE COLLEGE

Student: Ralph J. Brown

Date of Contract: December 9, 1974 to February 3, 1975

Months of Credit Earned: 2

Contract Digest and Evaluation

Purpose of Contract and Specific Topics: Since Mr. Brown's concentration in educational studies was largely completed, this contract in philosophy fulfilled part of the student's degree program in the area of general learning. Through this contract he investigated the writing of Aristotle in order (1) to investigate the major themes treated in the various works and to explore Aristotelian methodology; (2) to explore various theories of knowledge beginning with Aristotle's works and expanding to those of other theorists; (3) to study the *Nichomachean Ethics* and to complement this research with contemporary readings in ethics.

Methods of Evaluation: Because the student worked initially from primary sources suggested by the module on Aristotle, the mentor met with the student on a weekly basis in order to ascertain his grasp of difficult terminology, statements, relationships, and developmental reasoning as well as to suggest interpretations of difficult passages and explanatory secondary sources where appropriate. The student developed his own bibliography of readings and discussed his weekly readings with the mentor. The student exhibited strength in applying the various theories of knowledge to his experiences in teaching and to his personal cognitive development. The student's study of ethics was not restricted to Aristotelian works but was also related to contemporary readings drawn from books, periodicals and newspapers. He chose a contemporary moral problem and wrote a paper concerning it which flowed from criteria gained through his reading, from the facts which he researched, and from his personal philosophical perspective which was further expanded through his study and reflection. The paper was judged on accuracy of interpretation, rational substantiation of positions taken, clarity of expression, logical development of thought, correct grammatical use, and citation of sources.

Mentor's Evaluation: There is no question in the mentor's

mind that the student devoted 36-40 hours a week in fulfilling this contract. This judgment is based on the lengthy feedback which the student supplied at each weekly discussion. Questions for clarification of difficult passages were formulated in advance of the meetings and the student gave ample verbal evidence of having read and comprehended the books on the appended bibliography which he developed during the course of the contract.

The beginning sessions were devoted to an overview of the major Aristotelian works and the student evinced a desire to persevere through difficult passages in primary sources even when secondary sources would have proven less time-consuming. Through this he gained a sincere respect not only for Aristotle's genius but also for the breadth of his intellectual pursuits. He examined major portions of the *De Anima, Posterior Analytics,* the *Physics, Metaphysics* and *Nichomachean Ethics.* He demonstrated ability to do abstract thinking, for example, by his comprehension of Aristotle's differentiation of science, syllogistic reasoning, and a study of human and other animal cognition. His mind was comfortable with and not a stranger to posing philosophical questions and exploring them. As time went on, Mr. Brown began to take exception to passages he read in either primary or secondary sources and to evaluate them critically in relation to other works or experiences. He pointed out fallacious reasoning or incomplete evidence.

His investigations into theories of knowledge and of ethics were equally of interest to him and it almost became difficult for him to choose a topic for his paper because of his many interests in a variety of subjects which had emerged. From among the many possible areas in ethics, he chose to develop a paper on *Ethics and Distribution of Food.*

Mr. Brown is an articulate individual with an openmindedness to a variety of points of view. However, in the past he has had virtually no experience with organizing research into a paper. In many respects, the paper became a vehicle for many learnings. Through it he developed practical skills in organizing his research materials. An initial draft of the paper was reviewed in the presence of the student and the subsequent paper demonstrated a better grasp of logical development of thoughts and the use of transitional phrases. The final paper indicated some need for further practice in these areas and in some of the techniques of citing sources. Often a request for a verbal clarification of the meaning of the student's written text was sufficient to enable him to write a section with greater logical development of thought. In short, Mr. Brown demonstrated fine logical ability which could be verbalized well. Its written formulation required a minimum of refinement—not due to lack of ability but due to some lack of practice.

Mr. Brown was an inquisitive and serious student of philosophy, but perhaps even more importantly, a natural and humane philosopher in his own right.

Exhibit 5. JOHNSTON COLLEGE, UNIVERSITY OF REDLANDS
Student: Ruth Ann White
Term: Spring and Summer 1974
Course Title: Cooperative Education Experience
Instructor: Donald Blatchley, Ph.D.

Permanent Record: Student Evaluation

Course Description: This course was a full-time work experience in the Clinical Pathology Department of Redlands Community Hospital. The student was directly involved in activities that provided practical experience in her chosen career field.

Evaluation: Ms. White is structuring her undergraduate education to prepare for a career in the field of health care. Her co-op experience at Redlands Community Hospital provided both practical on-the-job training in a specific skill area and valuable insights into hospital operation and the medical profession. Her job performance was very good. The evaluation of her work by Dr. Black is attached to this document.

Ms. White utilized various opportunities at the hospital to her advantage. She attended an in-service training class in first aid and a portion of a class on intravenous feeding. She witnessed a live normal birth and also a Cesarean birth in surgery. She became familiar with a number of the procedures used in the pathology laboratory by watching and assisting the laboratory technicians with their work. The varied aspects of this experience have enhanced her personal development. She has significantly increased both her self-confidence and her interpersonal skills.

Ms. White wrote a very substantial evaluation paper that summarized her experience at the hospital. Her paper was both interesting and well-written. The detailed discussion of the technical aspects of her job was especially well done.

Ms. White has completed her contract with distinction.

Employer Evaluation of Cooperative Education Student

Student: Ruth Ann White
Work Period: February 4, 1974 to August 16, 1974

Employer: Redlands Community Hospital
Rated by: K. P. Black, Pathologist, Department of Clinical Pathology

1. Describe the nature of the student's work assignment.

A venipuncture technician obtains specimens for laboratory testing as directed by a licensed physician.

Principal duties: Obtains blood specimens using venipuncture technique and capillary blood technique; receives written requisition from physician for routine or special laboratory tests; distributes laboratory test results by phone, mail, or charting; answers requests and inquiries regarding laboratory procedures; performs clerical duties in cooperation with the office coordinator, such as filing, routine typing, and operation of less complex office machines; responsible for the processing of presurgical patients and outpatients; performs other duties as assigned.

2. Describe the student's overall attitude toward the work assignment.

Ruth's attitude toward the work assignments is positive and happy. She is well-motivated and has good grasp of the total system and contributes to the function of the department by always doing her tasks and making suggestions of how routines might be improved. Her initiative is expressed in proceeding without excessive supervision.

3. Describe the student's ability to communicate with others. Assess both verbal and writing skills, if possible.

Ruth is eager to communicate and work with others. She always takes time to communicate fully by working problems through to the best solution. Her verbal communication is clear and to the point. She organized both her verbal and written communication quite concisely. Her written project work on Sickle Cell Disease was extremely well done.

4. Describe the student's ability to make decisions.

Ruth has good decision-making ability that will get even better with her will to meet challenges. She takes all responsibilities quite seriously and may, occasionally, be doing too many heavy projects at one time. This may exhibit itself in her being physically fatigued.

5. How has the student responded to constructive criticism?

Ruth responds well to constructive criticism. She is eager to learn and to benefit from others' knowledge.

6. Describe any specific skills the student has acquired or improved.

Ruth has learned to communicate with patients and co-workers. She has acquired the skills of skin- and venipuncture. The importance of accurate test results with efficient turn-around time has become paramount in her thoughts.

7. What suggestions do you have to further the student's career development?

Johnston College is ideal for Ruth for she needs quality guidance for her abundance of drive. The work-study program is ideal in the field of medical technology.

8. Additional comments or suggestions.

It has been a pleasure to work with Ruth. She will continue to work in the Department of Pathology on weekends through the school year.

Chapter Twelve

𝖲𝖲𝖲

Assessors and Their Qualifications

𝖲𝖲𝖲

Urban G. Whitaker

While a great deal has been written about the techniques of assessment, and quite a bit of research has been done about the purposes and uses of assessment, relatively little work has been done to answer the questions: Who are the assessors? Who should be the assessors? How can they be trained for excellence in performing various assessment functions? In this chapter, we develop an analytical framework for answering these questions in a variety of situations.

One of the toughest problems in the selection of good assessors is the fact that, too often, it is not considered to be a problem

Bernice Biggs (San Francisco State University), Paul Breen (San Francisco State University), Jan Hagberg (Metropolitan State University) and Myrna Miller (then of Empire State College; now at the Community College of Vermont) collaborated in the research and conceptualization on which this chapter is based. They have not, however, had the opportunity to participate in writing the final draft, and I must take full responsibility for errors and other weaknesses.

189

at all. The implicit assumption seems to be that the teacher is, and should be, the assessor. Even when that assumption is questioned it is in support of another assumption: that experts ought to be the assessors.

All assessors should be experts, but not all experts, including teachers, necessarily make good assessors. Choosing effective assessors and training them to do the job well are difficult assignments. The most basic improvement needed in this process is the development of a model that identifies the key questions, such as the kinds of training needed by various potential assessors, and facilitates the explanation of relationships among them. This chapter is devoted primarily to that endeavor, but we have tried to go further, to actually use the model as a device for raising questions and making recommendations as to who should be the assessors.

Six steps are suggested below as the model. (Richard Heydinger, 1975, has sketched out an assessment model that identifies four dimensions: purposes, criteria, techniques, and uses. While we found his model helpful, we have necessarily taken a somewhat different approach because our focus is on the question of selecting assessors.) The first three steps of the model involve the identification and analysis of three vital variables in the process of selecting assessors. Step one involves identifying and categorizing all of the potential participants in the assessment process. Step two consists of identifying all of the components of the assessment process and determining the order and relationship of these functions. Step three involves listing and analyzing the basic, general characteristics or qualifications that assessors ought to possess. These three variables are referred to throughout the paper as *assessors, functions,* and *characteristics,* respectively.

The next three steps of the model involve analysis and commentary on the critical relationships among the three vital variables. Thus, in step four, one makes judgments about which of the assessor characteristics are most important to which of the assessment functions. In step five, one makes judgments about the degree to which each of the potential assessors possesses each of the required characteristics. In step six, one utilizes the conclusions of steps four and five, matches potential assessors with assessment functions, and determines who should be the assessors.

The model is not value free. From the beginning it requires the user's judgments and conclusions, and the effects of these early conclusions are cumulative. What comes out at steps four, five, and six reflects the value orientations and other assumptions that influence what goes in at steps one, two, and three. This is not necessarily a weakness, provided that it is understood and accounted for. In fact, one of the strengths of this approach is that it allows for local variations in educational philosophy, policies, and procedures.

In order to provide a complete description of the model, and to demonstrate how it works, we carry it to its terminal point with examples that reflect our values and assumptions. The reader should be particularly wary of the numerical ratings that are entered in the boxes of the tables used to illustrate steps four, five, and six. While the conclusions of this chapter are necessarily related to the assumptions reflected in those ratings, it is the model itself rather than this particular application that is presented as a proposal for the improvement of assessment practices in postsecondary education. Before turning to the six steps, it may help to list the most important assumptions that have influenced our own conclusions about the model.

First, various types of postsecondary education, including traditional classroom learning and both sponsored and unsponsored experiential learning, are necessary to serve the diverse needs of learners.

Second, some balance between theoretical and applied learning is appropriate for all well-educated people, and the proper balance cannot usually be achieved within the traditional classroom.

Third, self-direction (including both learning how to learn and learning how to assess) is a vital objective for all postsecondary students.

Fourth, assessment has important, and generally neglected, formative uses as well as its more commonly assumed summative uses.

Fifth, more effective learning occurs when learning objectives are specified—thus, sponsored programs of experiential learning are more effective than unsponsored (prior) learning.

Sixth, learning is more effective when the learner understands and accepts its objectives—thus, it is important for learners to set their own objectives.

Seventh, it is easier to see and to set objectives in an experiential context than in a theoretical context.

Eighth, competency-based, criterion-referenced educational programs are desirable, but it is not realistic to believe that they are norm free, or that they will eliminate the need for comparative judgments about levels of competence (for example, grading).

And ninth, in making comparative judgments about the measurement of competency levels (such as assigning grades and credits), ideally neither the learner nor the teacher should be involved except as sources of information for the assessor.

Just as our beliefs have influenced the illustration of this model, each reader will bring an individual set of values to the consideration of assessor characteristics and qualifications for the various assessment functions. All of us, without necessarily changing our values and beliefs, will also vary in our application of the model as the time, place, personnel, and other circumstances change.

Step One: Identifying Potential Assessors

In the simplest analysis there are only three categories of potential assessors: the learners, their teachers, and observers. Except for the collective observers category, this parallels the assessors identified by Trask (1975, p. 3): "Thus while the emphasis will vary with the program, all these entities—student, program staff, agency supervisors, and faculty—may participate legitimately in the evaluation process." In the most complex analysis there are endless possible variations in each category. For our purposes, it is important to make formal recognition of two types within each category for a total of six groups of potential assessors: student learners, prior learners, faculty teachers, agency teachers or trainers, participant observers, and outcome observers.

Within the CAEL context of experiential learning, student learners are those in sponsored programs, as distinguished from those who are seeking credit for prior learning. Such programs include fieldwork, internships, cooperative education, and similar arrangements that are undertaken as part of a formal postsecondary program.

Prior learners are those who, whether or not they were enrolled as students at the time of the experience, seek credit for learning acquired in experiential situations not sponsored by a postsecondary institution.

Faculty teachers are those who formally assist in the development of the learner's education. They may perform their instructional functions as faculty members in postsecondary institutions or in some other capacity, such as work supervisor or technical training expert. Faculty teachers are identified as a separate category because of their special relationship to some components of the assessment process that are not familiar to instructional personnel in other professions. Some faculty members may be involved in the assessment process not as teachers but as expert judges or outcome observers.

In some sponsored programs (and, by definition, in prior learning), the teacher is not a faculty member but a supervisor or training instructor in an outside agency. These nonfaculty teachers fall into the category of agency teachers or trainers, but may also be included in one of the other two categories defined below as observers.

Participant observers are those persons, such as supervisors, clients and coworkers, who have the opportunity to observe the learners during the learning experience.

Outcome observers are persons who have not participated in the learning process in any way, but are called upon to participate in the assessment of the learning outcomes. They may observe a product (such as a paper, report, written examination, work of art) or a performance (such as oral examination, dance, role playing). This category may be labeled *expert judges,* though that term is sometimes used to include anyone with special qualifications whether or not the expert is also a participant in the learning process—in CAEL Working Paper No. 10 (Reilly and others, 1975, p. 1) for example, an expert is defined as "an individual having special skill or knowledge derived from experience, education, or training."

In some assessment situations, as many as five of these six categories will be available as a pool of potential assessors. (One of the two learner categories will always be missing since one refers to student learners in sponsored programs, and the other refers to those seeking assessment of prior learning acquired in nonstudent status.) But there are various circumstances in which the pool shrinks to as few as two. For example, in the assessment of possible learning outcomes from an unsponsored, solo trip around the world, there may be only the prior learner and the outcome observer as expert judge (probably a faculty member, but not the teacher in this case since there was none).

In situations where multiple potential assessors are available, it may be helpful to distinguish between primary and secondary assessors, depending on the degree to which they possess the appropriate qualifications. For example, in step six, some of the more peripheral observers in the participant observer category could be considered as secondary assessors who serve as information sources for primary assessors (such as teachers, supervisors, expert judges, or the learners)'.

Step Two: Identifying Assessment Functions

Six assessment functions have been identified for study in the CAEL project: identification of college-creditable competencies; their articulation to student goals; documentation; measurement; evaluation; and transcripting (Willingham, Burns, and Donlon, 1974, pp. 41–43). Before trying to set up a matrix—with these six functions along the top and the six categories of potential assessors along the side—it will be useful to consider whether the list of six assessment functions can be used as it is, or whether it should be revised in order to fit this specific purpose.

The CAEL assessment functions are related to the evaluation of the student. It is clear, however, that the evaluation of programs, including their objectives and methods, is also a vital aspect of the total assessment picture. In fact, it is not possible to fully assess learning outcomes without assessing at least some aspects of the programs in which the learning takes place. For example, in determining whether, when, and how a particular student should undertake field studies, it is necessary to know whether the field study program effectively provides the types of training and supervision that the student's goals and other characteristics require. In program evaluation, the role of the student as assessor may be significantly more important than in the evaluation of learning outcomes—although the two are necessarily closely related (for an excellent example of student participation in program evaluation see Duley, 1974, p. 20).

Program evaluation is important to the purposes of this chapter primarily because of its relationship to the formative aspects of assessment. These are reflected in the first two of the CAEL assessment stages, identification and articulation, and are related to the fourth, measurement. It is tempting to drop documentation out of the list and to arrange the remaining five items as a continuum from the formative end (identifying what is college-creditable, deciding what each individual student needs to learn, measuring what level of competence has been achieved) to the summative end of the list (what grade to assign, what credit to give, what to put on the transcript). In the assessment of prior learning, however, documentation not only has some formative results, but is central to the entire process. And in sponsored learning programs, even in the traditional classroom, documentation may play some formative role, and may even be the essence of the summative evaluation. Rather than eliminate it, therefore, we decided to enlarge it to include a feedback role for sponsored programs, and to move it forward in the lineup for the assessment of prior learning. The functions are presented in Table 1.

These six basic functions (or seven, if feedback is considered separately) are not equal, and their relative importance may vary from one assessment situation to another. Because of this fluctuation factor it is not possible to weight them easily—making some primary and some secondary—as we suggested with the assessors. It is important, however, to realize when considering any individual assessment problem that some of the basic decisions have been predetermined. This is particularly true of part of the first function— the determination of what is and is not college-creditable learning. It is also often true of the sixth function, transcripting, in the majority of cases where traditional methods are used. In the following paragraphs, the basic assessment functions are defined as they are used in the rest of the model.

Table 1. ASSESSMENT FUNCTIONS

Sponsored Programs	Prior Learning
1. Identification of Competencies	1. and 2. Documentation and Identification of College-creditable Competencies
2. Articulation to Student Goals	
3. Documentation and Feedback	3. and 4. Measurement for Competence and Articulation to Student Goals
4. Measurement for Competency	
5. Evaluation for Credit	5. Evaluation for Credit
6. Transcripting	6. Transcripting

Identification may be defined as the answer to two questions: What competencies are college-creditable? Which of the college-creditable competencies are to be assessed in a particular case? The first part of this definition is central in the assumptions of this chapter. In some cases, as suggested above, this decision is predefined in the policies of the institution. The first step then becomes the identification of the particular competencies that are the target for the assessors in an individual case. This is partly an identification problem and partly a problem of the next function, articulation.

Which college-creditable competencies are appropriately included in each student's educational program? This is a vital consideration early in the assessment process for students in sponsored programs. It sets the objectives of the learning experience and thus projects standards against which the learning outcomes are to be measured. For prior learning, articulation is more difficult because it seeks to relate learning outcomes to student goals that may or may not have been set at the time of the learning experience. Since some further learning may take place in the process of documentation and measurement, it may be important to consider goals throughout the process. In any case, goals should be reviewed before evaluating prior learning for assignment of credit.

Documentation (that is, preparation of the portfolio) and identification of college-level competencies are central activities occurring simultaneously in the assessment of prior learning. For sponsored programs, documentation is shown as the third function —although the first two should be completed before the program in the field begins. Documentation not only sets the summative stage for measuring levels of competence and evaluating the amount of credit earned, but also plays a formative role through feedback about both student performance and program effectiveness.

Measurement is the process of determining the learner's level of competence. It is, therefore, the largest part of the process of determining grades in cases where they are assigned. (The grading process is, in some respects, also related to evaluation for credit as, for example, in credit-no credit systems. For sponsored programs, measurement can and should overlap with documentation, although written forms of documentation are not necessarily required where performance can be judged from direct observation (a helpful distinction between direct and indirect evaluation is described by Breen, Donlon, and Whitaker, 1975, p. 52). Even in these cases, however, the measurement and feedback processes should be closely coordinated, for prior learning measurement is combined with articulation. Except for learning that occurs from the assessment itself, the major value of feedback to the student is in the clarification of goals and the planning of continued educational activities to complement, supplement, and extend the prior learning.

Evaluation for either sponsored or prior learning is the penultimate component of the process by which the assignment of credit is determined. Evaluation should be based on definitive prior decisions about what is college-creditable, what is relevant to a particular student's overall educational program, and what level of competence has been acquired.

Transcripting is the final component in the assessment process. It may, in some institutions and for some types of learning, be predetermined and require no substantive consideration once the evaluation has been completed (for example, in a sponsored program, "three units of credit for completing Sociology 698, Field Studies in Juvenile Delinquency"). For prior learning it may be slightly more difficult. When it is clear, however, that the learning corresponds with that expected from a particular course the result may be entered, for example, as "credit by examination for Accounting 317."

When the learning being credited does not correspond with what is expected in an existing course, the transcript entry may simply read "undistributed units in natural science" or, as is common in many institutions, "six units credit for military service." Narrative transcripts require some substantive considerations that have a substantial effect on the selection of appropriate assessors. Narrative transcripting is not exclusively summative, and should begin early, along with documentation—of which all transcripting is, in fact, a part.

Step Three: Identifying Essential Assessor Characteristics

Before we begin to match up the potential assessors identified in step one with the assessment functions identified in step two, it is important to determine the general characteristics of effective assessors. We identify five essential assessor characteristics: subject matter expertise, psychometric expertise, familiarity with the data in a particular case, objectivity, and motivation.

Assessors should be experts in the subject area being assessed. In some ways this seems so obvious as to require no further comment. But, as pointed out in CAEL Working Paper No. 10 (Reilly and others, 1975), there are many kinds of experts and many ways of defining and measuring expertise. For our purposes, it is most important to note simply that there are different kinds of expertise (for example, theoretical knowledge versus practical skills, generalist orientation versus narrow specialization, and so forth) and that the assessor's expertise should parallel as closely as possible that which is being assessed.

Similarly, there are various kinds of psychometric expertise, and it is important for assessors to be reasonably expert about particular techniques appropriate to each function. But not all experts are always expert in all assessment techniques. *Reasonably* is not a very exact term, but it seems appropriately descriptive of a characteristic that is both important and rare. The characteristic referred to in this paper as *psychometric expertise* is defined as secondary knowledge of the assessment process that is sufficient to enable one to select and adapt techniques and instruments that others have developed and perfected. At the very least, assessors must know how to recognize when they need psychometric help in the assessment process.

The third characteristic of effective assessors is familiarity with case data. Assessors should be familiar with all aspects of the case being assessed, including the learner, the teacher and other persons involved in the learning process, the learning objectives, the learning environment and methods, the documentation, and all other sources of information about learning outcomes.

The fourth characteristic is objectivity. Assessors should be unbiased judges who can weigh the evidence without prejudice and who can reach conclusions based on the evidence rather than on whatever personal preference they may feel about the results. This does not necessarily mean that anyone with a personal or professional stake in the outcome is automatically disqualified from playing any role in assessment. But it does mean that there must be compensation for the influence of any vested interest that may skew the assessor's judgment.

The final important characteristic is motivation. Assessment is obviously an impossible task—how to find the perfect assessor? Where can we find anyone, or even a team, to reflect such a virtuous combination of expertise, familiarity, and objectivity? Of course, it cannot be done. The best possible assessors will not be perfect, but will be those who come closest to such standards of perfection as multiple expertise, omniscient presence, and total objectivity.

We make two assumptions as we approach the task of conducting perfect assessments with imperfect (human) assessors. First, we assume that the best assessment occurs when there is more than one assessor. Bloom, Hastings, and Madaus (1971, p. 26), for example, surveyed the kinds of evaluation techniques needed by educators and concluded that, "in an ever-increasing number of instances . . . evaluation demands the expertise of several different types of specialists working together." Second, we assume that it will always be important for assessors to be motivated to overcome their assessment handicaps. Good assessment is likely to be hard work.

Perhaps the most important characteristic for assessors is the motivation to maximize their qualifications—as experts in subject matter and in assessment, as close observers of all the essential facts, and as objective judges of the learning outcomes.

There are, of course, incompatibilities among the characteristics listed here. Familiarity with the data (as, for example, when one is the teacher or the learner) is likely to militate against objectivity about the outcome. Similarly, some of the strongest sources of motivation may be grounded in a biased interest about the results. Recognizing these basic difficulties in the selection of assessors, we reiterate the importance of using multiple assessors and we add the conclusion that there should also be multiple assessments. The essential characteristics of good assessors are so elusive that assessment should never be a one-time process.

Step Four: Matching Qualifications and Functions

In Table 2 the six assessment functions are matched with the five essential assessor characteristics. While the Xs placed in some of the columns represent our estimate of the most significant relationships between qualifications and functions, it is the process represented by the columns, not the opinions represented by the Xs, that we want to emphasize. In fact, the placement of the Xs will vary not only from person to person, but for the same person from one assessment situation to another. Similarly, the relative weighting, both of functions and of characteristics, may vary considerably from case to case. And, finally, both of the lists themselves are subject to revision.

With all disclaimers entered, we may note that Table 2 suggests some provisional conclusions that will be pertinent in the discussion of the next two steps in the application of the model. The fourth column contains twice as many Xs as any other—is measurement of competency perhaps the heart of the assessment process, as well as the one component function that requires the most highly qualified assessors? Are identification of college-creditable competencies and transcripting such technical functions that they might require the services of only one category of assessors? Is subject

Table 2. ASSESSOR CHARACTERISTICS ESSENTIAL FOR VARIOUS ASSESSMENT FUNCTIONS

Assessor Characteristics	ASSESSMENT FUNCTIONS					
	Identification of College-Creditable Competencies	Articulation to Individual Student Goals	Documentation and Feedback	Measurement of Competency Levels	Evaluation for Credit	Transcripting
Subject Matter Expertise				X		
Assessment Expertise				X	X	
Familiarity with Relevant Case Data	X	X	X			X
Objectivity				X	X	
Motivation		X	X	X		

Note: Each of the five characteristics may be important, in some way, for each of the six functions. However, for purposes of identifying major strengths and weaknesses of various potential assessors, only the most critical are marked.

matter expertise a vital characteristic in only one of the six assessment functions?

While we do not urge these conclusions, we must reiterate
that, as our own tentative conclusions, they necessarily influence the
way in which the final two steps of the model are presented. It is
essential to note that the utility of the model depends on its being
adapted to reflect all of the elements of the assessment situation in
which it is applied—including wide variations in individual conclusions about which characteristics are important to which functions.

Step Five: Judging Assessor Strengths and Weaknesses

We have identified six categories of potential assessors and
five characteristics essential to various assessment functions. Before
we can match up the assessors and the functions we need to get
a better idea of the strengths and weaknesses of the potential assessors. Which of them possess which of the characteristics essential
to effective assessment? For the purposes of the CAEL project, it is
particularly important to note the significant differences in the answers to this question when it is applied to the assessment of prior
learning and when it is applied to sponsored learning. It is also
important to recognize the ways in which the answers differ within
the sponsored learning continuum, which ranges from the traditional classroom program on one end to field study programs on the
other.

The three matrices reproduced as Tables 3, 4, and 5 illustrate
how the qualifications of each class of potential assessors vary in accordance with the type of learning being assessed. These matrices
are presented both to bring the question of assessor qualifications
into full focus by forcing a consideration of each potential assessor's
qualities in each essential area and to stimulate progress toward answers to the question of essential qualities or characteristics. Again
we want to emphasize that we are not urging particular answers as
much as demonstrating what we believe to be an effective way of
seeking answers. Nevertheless, the best way to demonstrate the
model is to apply it. In the experiential spirit of the CAEL project,
we would urge one go through the process oneself, putting in one's

Table 3. General Qualifications of Potential Assessors in Traditional Classroom Learning Situations

| | ASSESSOR CHARACTERISTICS | | | | | |
Potential Assessors	Subject Matter Expertise	Assessment Expertise	Familiarity with Relevant Case Data	Objectivity	Motivation	Average (Percent)
Sponsored Student Learner	1	4	4	1	4	28
Prior (Non-student) Learner		NOT APPLICABLE				
Faculty Teacher	10	7	10	7	7	82
Agency Teacher or Trainer		NOT APPLICABLE				
Participant Observer	1	1	4	1	1	16
Expert Judge	10	4	1	7	1	46
						Overall: 43

10 = Fully Qualified with respect to this characteristic.
7 = Qualified, but with reservations about deficiency that may be correctable.
4 = Not Qualified as primary assessor; possible secondary role; may be trainable.
1 = Disqualified for any role with respect to this characteristic.

Table 4. GENERAL QUALIFICATIONS OF POTENTIAL ASSESSORS IN SPONSORED PROGRAMS OF EXPERIENTIAL LEARNING

Potential Assessors	ASSESSOR CHARACTERISTICS					
	Subject Matter Expertise	Assessment Expertise	Familiarity with Relevant Case Data	Objectivity	Motivation	Average (Percent)
Sponsored Student Learner	1	4	7	1	7	40
Prior (Non-student) Learner	NOT APPLICABLE					
Faculty Teacher	7	7	4	7	4	58
Agency Teacher or Trainer	10	4	7	7	4	64
Participant Observer	4	4	4	7	4	46
Expert Judge	10	4	1	10	1	52
						Overall: 52

10 = Fully Qualified with respect to this characteristic.

7 = Qualified, but with reservations about deficiency that may be correctable.

4 = Not Qualified as primary assessor; possible secondary role; may be trainable.

1 = Disqualified for any role with respect to this characteristic.

Table 5. GENERAL QUALIFICATIONS OF POTENTIAL ASSESSORS OF PRIOR LEARNING

| Potential Assessors | ASSESSOR CHARACTERISTICS | | | | | |
	Subject Matter Expertise	Assessment Expertise	Familiarity with Relevant Case Data	Objectivity	Motivation	Average (Percent)
Sponsored Student Learner	NOT APPLICABLE					
Prior (Non-student) Learner	4	4	7	1	10	52
Faculty Teacher	10	7	1	7	1	52
Agency Teacher or Trainer	10	4	7	7	1	58
Participant Observer	4	4	4	7	1	40
Expert Judge	10	4	1	10	1	52
						Overall: 50.8

10 = Fully Qualified with respect to this characteristic.

7 = Qualified, but with reservations about deficiency that may be correctable.

4 = Not Qualified as primary assessor; possible secondary role; may be trainable.

1 = Disqualified for any role with respect to this characteristic.

own numbers, stimulating one's own questions and answers, and developing one's own conclusions about the relative qualifications of the various potential assessors.

Necessarily, the selection of a scoring system for such an exercise involves some arbitrary decisions. One need go no further in a search for the ultimate in difficult assessment problems than the attempt to give numerical grades for characteristics such as expertise, motivation, and objectivity to assessors like learners, teachers, and observers. Clearly it is a formidable task. But the effort is worthwhile, provided that we treat the results as suggestive rather than as conclusive.

The assignment of specific scores to categories of unknown people for hazily defined strengths and weaknesses requires the setting of some substantial ground rules. We have tried where possible to be specific about the assumptions on which assigned scores are based, and to note some of the variable factors that might dictate very different scoring if different assumptions were made. Even with these precautions, however, it is still somewhat hazardous to assign numerical ratings as shown in Tables 3, 4, and 5. We have done so only for the heuristic value of the exercise, and to illustrate the application of our model. We have chosen a four-point scale: 10, 7, 4, and 1, which translates roughly into fully qualified, qualified, not qualified, and disqualified.

Fully Qualified (10) means that most of the potential assessors in this category possess the specified characteristic or qualification to such a degree that they could perform functions that depend exclusively on that characteristic. A score of 10 means that generally, no further training is necessary to insure fully effective performance. This category denotes a condition of not perfect, but not requiring improvement.

Qualified (7) means that most of the potential assessors in in this category could satisfactorily perform assessment functions requiring this particular characteristic. A score of 7 means that, generally, the persons in this category could improve the quality of their performance with further training.

Not Qualified (4) means that most of the potential assessors in this category could not, without further extensive training, satisfactorily perform assessment functions requiring this qualification.

A score of 4 means that, generally, unless the deficiency is inherent in the role, these persons could become qualified through further training.

Disqualified (1) means that most of the persons in this category could not, even with further training, satisfactorily perform assessment functions requiring this characteristic.

Those in the Fully Qualified and Qualified categories can be considered as potential primary assessors, to be assigned as the persons responsible for completing particular assessment functions. Those in the Not Qualified category should be considered as available secondary assessors, useful informants or associates in the assessment process by assisting a primary assessor. Conceivably, after being qualified by further training, persons in this category could play some role as primary assessors. Disqualified persons should be considered as ineligible by reason of nonremediable deficiencies to perform any assessment function without further training. Even with further training, it is assumed that the role deficiency would permit such persons to serve only in a secondary capacity.

To focus the selection problem more sharply, we will analyze Tables 3, 4, and 5 in three ways: first, looking at each table as a whole; second, looking at each characteristic column for all three tables as a group; and finally, looking at each potential assessor for all three situations (traditional, sponsored, and prior learning).

For classroom learning (Table 3), there are fewer qualified potential assessors than is the case for field studies (Table 4) or prior learning (Table 5). Yet the only well-qualified assessor, across the board, to show up in any of the three learning situations is the classroom teacher. Among the possible conclusions that might be drawn from this arrangement of data are the following: that the source of learning is narrow, that is, primarily one person, a teacher; that single-source learning is best evaluated by that source; and that any change in this traditional arrangement would require some efforts in training the other potential assessors—in this case, the student learner, his or her peers, and outside experts. Bloom, Hastings, and Madaus (1971), while recognizing that new ways of looking at education may mean that more evaluators will be required, are firm in their conclusion that the "educational measurement person" will continue to be an important assessor. It may further be suggested that training the learner or peers in assessment would improve both the learning and the assessment process through the beneficial aspects of evaluative feedback (see, for example, Van Aalst, 1974).

In the field studies learning category (Table 4), perhaps the most significant overall message we get is that there are many variables that can have strong influence on assessment. It is tempting to conclude that careful matching of individual student characteristics and field learning opportunity can facilitate learning and assessment far superior to that available in the classroom, and that, conversely, careless selection of the experiential learning situation can virtually eliminate the possibility of meaningful learning and assessment.

For the evaluation of prior learning (Table 5), the pool of potential assessors is large, and almost evenly qualified. Given a greater degree of motivation, across the board, and some training in assessment techniques, the evaluation outlook could be excellent. The time lapse between the learning and the assessment is a source both of strength and of weakness. For some types of learning, and for purposes of comparison with other learners, the passage of considerable time may add a helpful perspective for several of the potential assessors. On the other hand, too much of a time gap may dull both memory and motivation.

Of all the potential assessors we have identified, only participant observers (in this case, other students in the class) rate lower than student learners (Table 3). The major weaknesses of the student as assessor are bias and lack of expertise—both in subject matter and in the assessment process. Bias is a significant factor when the purpose of assessment is competitive, such as assignment of grades or credits. It may, however, actually be helpful when the purpose is diagnostic or developmental. Lack of subject matter expertise is an unavoidable weakness for self-assessment since student status itself is grounded in the assumption of significant need for learning. Still it is possible, particularly for advanced students, to know enough about the specific outlines of their educational needs to be able to recognize progress clearly enough to make accurate assessments. Some field studies provide prerequisite training, which helps to surmount the problem of subject matter deficiency. In any case, one of the weaknesses of assessment in traditional education is that the student has not been told (and too often the instructor has not even determined) what criteria are to be used. If teachers were more specific about assessment criteria, it might not qualify learners to determine their own grades or credit, but it would make the learner a better partner in the assessment process.

In addition, there are important formative reasons to train students in assessment techniques. Competence is, in fact, often defined to include an evaluative component. Thus it is not enough for students simply to acquire knowledge, or even to acquire and to be able to apply it; competence also includes the habit and the ability to judge the results of knowledge applied in a particular situation. While evaluation does not mean precisely the same thing in this context as it does in the assessment process, the essential intellectual skills are similar.

Bloom, who believes that it is one of the most important of all educational objectives, defines evaluation as "the making of judgments about the value, for some purpose, of ideas, works, solutions, methods, material. . . . It involves the use of criteria as well as standards for appraising the extent to which particulars are accurate, effective, economical, or satisfying. The judgments may be either quantitative or qualitative, and the criteria may be either those determined by the student or those which are given to him" (Bloom and others, 1956, p. 185). Bloom's frame of reference for these remarks is not evaluation for the purposes of determining levels of competence but for the more general intellectual purposes of understanding issues and making choices. There is a close relationship, however, among three important ways in which evaluation is useful to the learner: for formative purposes (evaluative feedback can improve the learning process), for summative purposes (self-evaluation skills can facilitate the learner's contributions to the assessment process), and for general educational purposes (evaluation skills can become a vital component of the learner's intellectual strength). There is more than ample evidence that both learning and assessment could be improved significantly if greater attention were given to training students in various aspects of the measurement and evaluation of their educational progress.

The category of nonstudent learners as potential assessors is relevant only for prior learning. In some ways they are the best, perhaps the only, assessors because the sources of prior learning are so numerous, various, and complex. The worst problem is the learner's bias, since the assessment question usually arises in the context of a request for credits or a waiver of requirements. There is also a weakness in knowledge of assessment techniques, but this is, to some degree, correctable. Since the learning situation is in the past, however, some of the developmental advantages of assessment expertise cannot be recovered. On the other hand, the assessment process itself is a potential learning opportunity that is often underrated. Experiential learning may form an educational foundation, the careful exploration of which facilitates and accelerates additional learning.

Overall, faculty teachers rate the highest of all potential assessors. They are assumed to be subject matter experts. Whether or not they have received formal training in assessment, they usually have had experience as assessors, and are motivated to succeed at it not only because it is part of their assigned duties, but also because of its formative value as an element of the teaching process. Faculty teachers are better assessors of classroom learning than of field study or prior learning. Their problems with field study are with data (here, their contact is indirect and not continuous as in the classroom) and with the subject matter (to the degree that the field learning situation may involve types and aspects of material outside the teacher's own discipline and concentration). The worst problem for faculty teachers as potential assessors is their negative motivation with respect to the assessment of prior learning. Part of the problem is economic: in a time of declining enrollments faculty members—whose support resources are tied to some measure of credit production—oppose the awarding of credit by examination or evaluation that does not show as part of their workload. This problem can and should be partially resolved by blending the prior learning evaluation into the campus academic program. As noted above, there is also great learning potential in the assessment process, which itself is often creditable.

The more difficult part of the problem is faculty concern about the academic validity of experiential learning that takes place incidentally, without benefit of planned objectives, methods, and evaluation procedures. It has to be conceded that the amount and quality of learning are correlated positively to the amount and quality of advance planning. That is not to say, however, that no college-creditable learning can occur without it. Unsponsored and unplanned learning may be inferior but it does occur, and is sometimes the only substantial learning that an individual has acquired. Without shaving academic standards, faculty members can strengthen their teaching and counseling services to students by developing a greater willingness to evaluate prior learning. Administrators, in turn, can encourage more effective faculty participation by developing accounting procedures that more adequately reflect faculty workloads in this vital aspect of academic evaluation.

Nonfaculty teachers rate second highest, overall, as potential assessors. They share the faculty reluctance to participate in the evaluation of prior learning, though it does not pose any economic threat to them; it is simply a bother for which there is no particular reward. In sponsored field studies, nonfaculty teachers have an advantage over faculty teachers because they are on the learning site and presumably are fully qualified as subject experts. Nonfaculty teachers are likely to lack assessment skills so far as grading and credits are concerned, but may be superior to faculty members in the evaluation of competence and evaluation for diagnostic purposes. Motivation may vary depending on the type and purpose of the field arrangement. Again, the elasticity of sponsored field studies is apparent. A well-chosen field site in which the interests of the student and agency are complementary may result in high motivation for both (as, for example, when the student is interested in apprenticeship for career purposes, and the agency is interested in recruiting and training prospective employees). If, however, the agency has agreed to accept a student intern primarily because it wants free labor for performing menial activities, the motivations of both may be so low as to destroy the possibility for any significant learning.

Participant observers. Overall, the participant observer is the least qualified of the potential assessors. Motivation is low both in sponsored and prior learning assessment, and bias is high—particularly in traditional classroom settings where the observer is a fellow student competing for grades. The strong point for this category of assessor is high opportunity to observe, particularly in a sponsored learning situation in which supervisors, clients, and coworkers may be included in an evaluation plan and perhaps instructed in some relevant aspects of assessment.

Subject matter experts, faculty or others, who have not participated in the learning process with the student being evaluated are potentially the most effective assessors. Since nonparticipant expert judges are chosen for their expertise, they are assumed to know the subject well. They may also be chosen for assessment expertise, or they may be trained in assessment techniques. Expert judges are subject to some of the same biases as other potential assessors, but are less likely than any of the others to have developed conclusions about the person being assessed.

Motivation is likely to be a problem in most current academic environments because resources are not provided for paying expert judges. But the problem is not insurmountable. One of the possibilities is restructuring the academy to separate the teaching and assessment functions, theoretically improving both by making the student and the teacher partners in the learning process. Faculty workloads would increase, however, because it would take time for the faculty assessor to become familiar enough with the data to perform the measurement and evaluation functions. There would not be any significant compensatory savings for the faculty teacher, who would still have to assess learner progress for formative reasons. The greatest weakness of nonparticipant expert judges, even if they are faculty members, is the low level of their prior acquaintance with the individual learning situation that produced the outcomes being assessed. What is a strength with respect to bias is a weakness with respect to data.

Looking at the three tables together, there is a significant variation in the overall averages, which reflect all characteristics for all potential assessors. What is suggested by the overall averages is that the total pool of qualifying characteristics is at its highest in sponsored programs and at its lowest in traditional classroom programs. The potential assessment strengths in sponsored programs of experiential learning are considerably more than those of traditional programs for two major reasons: more potential assessors are available, and more of the available potential assessors are either already qualified or are qualifiable. Serious sustained efforts to improve the assessment of learning outcomes would pay high dividends in all three of the learning situations represented in Tables 3, 4, and 5. Clearly, however, sponsored programs of experiential learning offer superior opportunities for effective assessment of learning outcomes.

Finally, there may be some limited advantage in comparing the two classes of learners, of teachers, and of observers as composite groups. If we total the scores for these three groups in the final columns of Tables 3, 4, and 5, the average obtained for each is as follows: teachers, 63 percent; observers, 42 percent; and learners, 40 percent. The reader must determine whether this is a fair indication of real strengths and weaknesses or whether it overly reflects our biases. In any case, it is necessary for all of us to consider the question of the basic strengths and weaknesses of teachers, learners, and observers as potential assessors of learning outcomes and program objectives. To the degree that subject matter expertise and objectivity are vital characteristics for assessors (especially when the purpose of assessment includes the assignment of grades and credits), learners start with two strikes against them: their status as learners and as those to be assessed seriously weakens their potential as subject matter experts and as objective judges.

There are compensatory strengths in other areas, however, that justify giving serious consideration to learners as assessors. Of all possible assessors, learners are potentially most motivated to develop relevant expertise and most familiar with the data in their own cases. This raises a significant question with relation to the third column in Table 3 for the student learner: a score of 4, not qualified, was entered with respect to the learner's familiarity with the relevant case data. Why? The score is low because the assumption was made that assessment requires a judgment of relative performance or competency in comparison with other students. To some degree, this consideration changes when the measurement or evaluation functions are competency-based rather than norm-based. Certainly, if the purposes of assessment were to become more associated with the learner's personal achievement of individually specified objectives and less associated with societal labeling of the learner's relative competence, then the learner's qualifications as assessor would rise significantly.

It is our conclusion that much of the current popularity of

competency-based learning is grounded in a serious misconception. Yes, competency ought to be defined whenever possible in absolute terms (for example, typing at seventy-eight words per minute) rather than exclusively in relative terms (for example, the best typist in the class). The absolutely defined competency, however, gains much of its relevance only when viewed relatively and comparatively. To express a learning outcome in competency-based or criterion-referenced terms like *seventy-eight words per minute* or *skill at counseling troubled teenagers* is not to avoid norm-based assessment altogether, but only to provide a more specific and objective norm-referenced assessment.

We strongly favor the movement toward competency-based education but cannot share the expectation of some that it will eliminate the need for comparative judgments. Learners can and should be taught to measure their own competency. But employers and others will, understandably, continue to compare competence levels and to prefer the best. When the results of assessment are ultimately used for comparative purposes, the learner's qualifications for making the assessment diminish. While this is true even for such quantifiable skills as typing speed, it is much more marked with respect to such skills as creative writing, statistical analysis, problem solving, interpretation of history, leadership, ethics, and musical composition. In all of these subjects, competency-based education may introduce major improvements in the identification of objectives and in the instructional process, but it will remain limited as a source of objectified judgments about levels of learning outcomes.

Step Six: Selecting the Right Assessors

Having considered which assessor characteristics are essential to which assessment functions (step four), and which of the potential assessors possess which of the essential characteristics (step five), we are now prepared for the final step: deciding which of the potential assessors is best qualified to undertake which of the assessment functions. We will consider this final question in two ways: first, by briefly looking at the overall picture for sponsored programs and for prior learning (Tables 6 and 7, respectively); and second, by considering each group of potential assessors, across the board, for all functions in both prior and sponsored learning situations.

Table 6 presents the picture for assessment in sponsored programs. As a whole—if all of the potential assessors participated equally in the process at every stage—the outlook would not be good. The overall score of 39 percent is a point below the level we have identified as qualifiable. In other words, either a great deal of training to improve assessors' performance, or a careful selection of particular assessors for particular functions, is necessary to insure adequate results.

Table 7 presents the picture for assessment of prior learning. The overall outlook appears to be almost identical, but there are two major differences. First, because of the necessary combining of functions in the assessment of prior learning, there is less opportunity to strengthen the assessment program through use of different assessors for different functions. Second, because the learning is in the past, the opportunity to train potential assessors is severely restricted, and the opportunity to alter the learning methods by feedback from the assessment process is already lost.

Turning to groups of potential assessors, we begin with learners. Across the board, learners are second best (to teachers) as assessors. The functions for which they are least qualified are the identification of college-creditable competencies and the evaluation of competencies for crediting purposes. They are not qualified, in technical respects, to perform the transcripting function except in the case of narrative transcripts. Their strongest qualifications are in documentation of learning and in providing formative feedback to themselves and to their teachers. The primary source of the learner's strength as an assessor is familiarity with the individual case. The sources of the learner's weaknesses are subjectivity and lack of expertise, both in the subject matter and in the assessment process.

Motivation to overcome the three weaknesses is not high in most cases because the student does not have a substantial role in those assessment functions which require objectivity and expertise. It is assumed that learners have some motivation to overcome subject matter deficiencies, particularly in experiential learning situations, especially if they are not required courses. Motivation to acquire assessment expertise can be stimulated if learners are given a

Table 6. OVERALL ELIGIBILITY OF POTENTIAL ASSESSORS IN SPONSORED PROGRAMS

Potential Assessors	Identification of College-Creditable Competencies	Articulation to Individual Student Goals	Documentation and Feedback	Measurement of Competency Levels	Evaluation for Credit	Transcripting	Average (Percent)
	ASSESSMENT FUNCTIONS						
Student Learners	1	4	7	4	1	1	30
Prior (Non-student) Learner	NOT APPLICABLE						
Faculty Teacher	10	7	7	7	7	10	80
Agency Teacher	1	4	7	7	1	1	35
Participant Observer	1	4	4	4	1	1	25
Expert Judge	1	4	1	7	1	1	25
							Overall: 39

10 = Fully Qualified with respect to this characteristic.
7 = Qualified, but with reservations about deficiency that may be correctable.
4 = Not Qualified as primary assessor; possible secondary role; may be trainable.
1 = Disqualified for any role with respect to this characteristic.

Table 7. OVERALL ELIGIBILITY OF POTENTIAL ASSESSORS OF PRIOR LEARNING

	Columns 1 and 2. Documentation and Identification of College-creditable Competencies			ASSESSMENT FUNCTIONS *Columns 3 and 4.* Measurement of Competency Levels and Articulation to Student Goals			*Column 5.* Evaluation for Credit	*Column 6.* Transcript-ing	*Column 7.* Average (Percent)
Potential Assessors	Documen-tation	Combined	Identifi-cation	Measure-ment	Combined	Articulation			
Student Learners				NOT APPLICABLE					
Prior (Non-student) Learner	7	4	1	4	4	4	1	1	30
Faculty Teacher	4	7	10	7	7	7	10	10	80
Agency Teacher	4	2.5	1	7	5.5	4	1	1	30
Participant Observer	4	2.5	1	4	4	4	1	1	25
Expert Judge	1	1	1	7	5.5	4	1	1	25
									Overall: 38

10 = Fully Qualified with respect to this characteristic.
7 = Qualified, but with reservations about deficiency that may be correctable.
4 = Not Qualified as primary assessor; possible secondary role; may be trainable.
1 = Disqualified for any role with respect to this characteristic.

greater role in the process, and if the formative values of assessment are stressed. Postsecondary education in general and experiential education in particular can be substantially improved, both in the development of learning and in its assessment, by training students in assessment techniques as part of the learning program.

Teachers are the best assessors when all characteristics and all functions are considered as a package. If only one assessor is to be used, it should be the teacher. The functions for which teachers are most qualified are the identification of college-creditable competencies, evaluation for credit, and transcripting. The function they are least qualified to perform is the documentation of prior learning. The source of their strength is their familiarity with the data in identifying and crediting their subject matter expertise. The sources of their weaknesses are their lack of familiarity with the data in prior learning and their negative motivations about prior learning. As with learners, what is most needed to improve teachers as assessors is training in the assessment process. Faculty development programs for the improvement of teaching should emphasize assessment training for its formative as well as its summative values.

Participant observers—clients, coworkers, supervisors (except those who function primarily as teachers or trainers), fellow students—do not, in general, make good assessors. Because they lack familiarity with the data on what is creditable, they cannot perform and cannot realistically be expected to learn three of the assessment functions: identification, evaluation, and transcripting. In the other three functions—documentation, measurement, and articulation—some training would be necessary before the observer could play a substantial role as assessor. The potential value of parcipant observers as assessors is their familiarity with the learning situation and the subject matter, but they lack both the motivation and the training to overcome their deficiencies. They should be utilized in the assessment process only as secondary assessors providing information for primary assessors who have the necessary expertise. While it is not worthwhile, in general, to try to train these observers in order to improve their performance as assessors, it is important to develop effective communication with them as information sources.

Subject matter experts who have not participated in the learning process may be useful assessors with respect to the measurement function. Such nonparticipant observers are not likely to be helpful with the other assessment functions unless they happen to be faculty members acquainted with the academic profession. They may, as subject matter experts, be qualifiable with respect to the articulation function. The source of their strength is, of course, their subject matter expertise. The sources of their weaknesses are their lack of familiarity with the data and their lack of assessment expertise. The latter can be developed by training, and is well worth it, provided there is sufficient motivation for the expert to perform the measurement function. Nevertheless, it must be noted that the nonfaculty expert judge, even when trained in assessment as well as subject matter, can be useful in only one of the six assessment functions, measurement. And even then the expert's value is likely to be restricted to the summative aspects of measurement. It is difficult to imagine a situation in which postsecondary educators might have access to sufficient resources to utilize the continuing services of nonfaculty expert judges for formative purposes. One might argue, however, that even though their services are restricted to just one of the six assessment functions, it is the most vital one and therefore worth any extra effort or expense necessary.

Recommendations for Improvements in Selecting and Training Assessors

First, requirements for postsecondary degrees should be stated in terms of competences or other well-defined educational outcomes. To require students to complete a specific number of courses or a specific number of units is not sufficient to insure that they receive an appropriate education. Students individually and society generally are better served when the goal is, for example, exhibiting a specified level of literacy rather than passing a specified English course, or when the depth requirement is stated as a set of competencies, such as the ability to analyze a political problem, identify alternatives, and recommend a solution, rather than the passing of a specified number of units in political science.

The advantages of competency- or outcome-based learning programs are not exclusively, or even primarily, related to assessment. To treat courses and other learning experiences as means rather than ends improves the learning process and facilitates assessment—provided that institutional procedures encourage explicit identification of learning goals, procedures, and evaluative techniques.

Second, all students should be required to develop affective and applicative competence in addition to cognitive competence. Field experience learning may be the best (and in some cases the only) way to develop affective and applicative competence. Adequate assessment of these kinds of learning outcomes necessarily begins with individualized advising and counseling. The selection and training of appropriate assessors, and the selection of appropriate assessment techniques, depend on the particular configuration of each student's learning objectives. The assessment of experiential learning can be more effective if it is clear why, when, and how much experiential learning should be included in a student's educational plan.

Third, a statement of the learning objectives and methods of instruction, and a detailed proposal for evaluation, should be standard requirements for all courses. All parties to the learning process, including outside agency personnel in the case of field experience education, should be participants in the application of these conditions to the specific learning situation. Even in a well-administered program, learning objectives are too often stated in general terms and evaluation is too often treated as a purely summative process. A more serious problem, compounding the others, is that the learner is often excused from coresponsibility for determining objectives and excluded from participation in the process of assessing the outcome.

For experiential learning programs, all three elements—objectives, methods, assessment—present more difficult problems. At worst, it is experience itself (rather than learning) that is credited. And even in the best programs it is more difficult to specify and to implement instructional and evaluative methods in the field than it is on the campus. For experiential learning programs, it is particularly important for students and outside agency supervisors to participate in identifying objectives, planning the learning methods, and performing both formative and summative evaluation functions. Field personnel cannot be expected to serve as effective assessors of academically creditable learning unless they are aware of student educational objectives as well as agency purposes. Thus it is strongly recommended that learning experiences that involve an outside agency be supported by an agreement that specifies the agency role in achieving and assessing educational outcomes.

Fourth, the training of assessors and the development of effective assessment techniques should be given as high a priority as the training of teachers and the development of instructional methods. The best road to progress in the selection and training of more effective assessors is more conscious attention to the problem. The model presented and illustrated in this chapter could serve as a starting point for focusing attention on problems that require more research, for identifying ideas for experimentation, and for developing more effective models to facilitate the selection and training of assessors.

For its formative as well as its summative advantages, the training of assessors should be a continuing aspect of the educational program of all postsecondary institutions. Bloom, Hastings, and Madaus (1971) concur that "in spite of its complexity, evaluation appears to be one of the most important categories of education objectives in our society" (p. 205). What is needed is an assessment of assessment practices and then an effort to respond to weaknesses with appropriate training.

Faculty members of postsecondary institutions are key persons in the assessment process. Not only are they important as assessors, but their own performance is one of the important functions to be assessed, and they are in the best position to act as trainers of other potential assessors. Faculty development programs should include both training in self-assessment and training in the assessment training of others, including learners, nonfaculty teachers, and subject matter experts.

The problem of training assessors should be attacked simultaneously on several fronts. A comprehensive faculty development program and the training of learners by their teachers have already been mentioned. How can these programs be encouraged, and what else ought to be done? At the minimum, both for prior learning and for sponsored field programs, the training of assessors ought to be considered a joint responsibility approached both individually and collectively by postsecondary education, foundations, governments at all levels, business, and community agencies. In addition, training in all aspects of the assessment process ought to become a standard part of graduate training programs that produce either future postsecondary faculty members or supervisory and management personnel. Moreover, training materials should be produced to facilitate either individual or group development in all aspects of assessment. The CAEL Working Papers, the Assembly workshops, and the faculty development project are major contributions toward the achievement of this goal.

Fifth, it should be standard institutional policy and practice to avoid assessment error by utilizing multiple assessors and multiple assessments. The ingredients of perfect assessment can seldom be found in a single assessor or blended properly in a single technique. Baines (1974), for example, concludes that "the faculty supervisor should take the initiative in evaluation. The assessment should seek wide participation by faculty members, student and agency staff. There is no one best method of evaluating field experience" (p. 44). Because teachers, learners, observers, and outside experts all have unique contributions to make to effective assessment, after careful review of the conditions of each case (a step-by-step model is recommended), a team of assessors should be chosen to insure that all essential strengths are adequately represented. And because it is rare to find all of the essential assessment strengths even in a carefully chosen team of assessors, and because it is difficult to find a single assessment technique that can cover every important aspect of the learning outcomes in a particular case, it is always desirable to have more than one assessment whenever possible. (For an analysis of the need for a core of assessment techniques, see Breen, Donlon, and Whitaker, 1975, p. 55.) In addition, a distinction should be made between those participants in the assessment process who are qualified to conduct it—the primary assessors—and secondary assessors, whose role should be limited to providing information for the use of the primary assessors.

Finally, the assessment contributions of learners should be enhanced and utilized. Careful attention should be given to the determination of those assessment functions that learners themselves can and cannot perform effectively. Training provisions for learners should be built into educational programs for both formative and summative purposes. In sponsored programs, assessment should be a formal part of both the preparatory course or orientation program and the followup seminar.

For prior learning, a formal assessment course is strongly recommended. The faculty members and students should both be given credit for what they teach and learn about the process of evaluation. For example, a variable unit course entitled "Assessment of Experiential Learning" might be taken for one, two, three, or four units by students seeking credit for learning in military service, Peace Corps, Vista, intercultural travel and residence, work experience, or volunteer activities. The units would be awarded as credit in education for learning, during the course, about evaluation and assessment. At the conclusion of the course, additional units could be recorded as credit by evaluation (the course is the evaluation) in whatever fields and whatever amounts the instructor believes to be appropriate. Such an arrangement has the dual advantage of providing excellent training for both teacher and learner and of incorporating the payment for faculty assessment directly into the regular instructional program.

༚༚

Chapter Thirteen

Critical Issues and Basic Requirements for Assessment

༚༚

Warren W. Willingham

Throughout higher education, as earlier chapters in this book have elaborated, there is marked interest in experiential learning as an important element in nontraditional education. This interest is partly directed to the extension of educational opportunity, enhancement of lifelong learning, and improvement in the relationship between education and work. Experiential learning has also captured the imagination of many educators as a means of basic reform—to improve the value of the educational experience for students with respect to content as well as process and with respect to old as well as new objectives of higher education. Finally, many institutions are interested in experiential education as a means of improving the attractiveness of their programs in order to recruit additional students.

For whatever reasons, large numbers of institutions are placing increasing emphasis on crediting experiential learning that is relevant to student and institutional objectives. The definition of experiential learning is a matter of no small importance. As used here, the term refers to two types of learning. One is called variously *learning through life experience, prior learning,* or *nonsponsored learning.* It includes any type of creditable learning—through work, travel, volunteer service—that a student may have acquired independent of an educational institution and, typically, prior to matriculation. A second broad category of experiential learning, generally called *sponsored learning,* is that incorporated in institutionally sponsored programs that are designed to give students more direct experience in integrating and applying knowledge—especially off-campus internships, service activities, work programs, and the like. In both instances, it is important to understand that the learning or competence that is acquired must be relevant to student and institutional objectives.

It is widely recognized that there is critical need for improved means of assessing such learning. The reasons are obvious. Experiential learning tends to be highly individualistic; that is, the conditions under which competency has been acquired vary widely. The potential range of relevant learning experiences is wide-ranging and not well-defined. By its nature, experiential learning is often not subject to close faculty supervision, and assessment may come after the fact with little or no opportunity to structure the learning experience. These are not minor complications; they often tend to preclude traditional procedures of examining students on their understanding of a body of knowledge defined by a course syllabus. Thus sound new methods of assessment are needed not only to benefit students but also to support the development of nontraditional programs and to assure the credibility of credit awarded in those programs.

Critical Issues

The purpose of this concluding chapter is to identify important issues and suggest improvements in the development of such assessment procedures. In order to deal effectively with the subject, it is necessary to approach it from three points of view or frames of reference: practical—the important stages of assessment as they are carried out in actual programs; technical—the fundamental psycho-metric principles that should characterize good assessment; and philosophical—the broad educational issues that provide the rationale for experiential learning. One objective of this discussion is to show the relationship among these three frames of reference. They can be described briefly as follows.

The first or practical frame of reference deals with identifying the steps and procedures actually involved in assessment. As the word *assessment* is normally used in reference to experiential learning—particularly to learning prior to enrollment—the term has a broader meaning than might ordinarily be appreciated. As Urban Whitaker noted in the preceding chapter and as indicated in Table 1, it is useful to distinguish six stages of assessment: defining the learning; articulating it to an educational goal; documenting the learning; measuring its nature and extent; evaluating whether the learning meets an acceptable standard for a given amount of credit; and transcribing that credit in a suitable record system. Each of these stages represents an important aspect of the assessment problem; each engages the student and a number of other individuals on and off the campus. These stages involve a host of pragmatic questions concerning desirable practice, and superficially at least, are far removed from the administration of a traditional examination.

From a second and technical frame of reference, it is useful to consider the assessment of experiential learning as a traditional measurement problem. There is, of course, a seventy-five-year history of theoretical and applied research and development concerning the general problem of measuring individual ability and accomplishment. Psychometric literature, though often technical and specialized, concerns such basic issues as what a measurement really means and how much error it includes. Such issues appear in Table 1 as technical terms that will be clarified somewhat by discussion. Measurement issues apply to any application of assessment, so it is important to look at the assessment of experiential learning not only from the eyes of an educational practitioner but also as a measurement specialist might view the problem.

From a third and philosophical frame of reference, a number of basic educational issues come up repeatedly in discussions con-

Table 1. CRITICAL ASSESSMENT ISSUES FROM THREE FRAMES OF REFERENCE

FRAME OF REFERENCE

Issue	Practical (Stage of Assessment)	Technical (Psychometric Topic)	Philosophical (Educational Question)
1. What is creditable?	IDENTIFY the learning acquired through life experience or learning incorporated in a sponsored program	Content Validity	What types of experiential learning justify college-level credit; and to what extent must learning be specified?
2. What does experiential learning mean?	ARTICULATE such learning to the educational goals or academic degree of the student	Construct Validity	Does crediting experiential learning change the meaning of the B.A. degree?
3. What constitutes evidence of learning?	DOCUMENT the fact that the student has participated in the learning experience	Intrinsic Validity	Should credit be based upon experience or learning?
4. How to insure equity?	MEASURE the extent and character of the learning acquired	Reliability	When learning experiences differ widely, how can assessment be consistent and equitable without being standardized?
5. How to define standards?	EVALUATE whether the learning meets an acceptable standard and determine its credit equivalence	Scaling	When learning experiences differ widely, how can educational standards be publicly understood and maintained?
6. What are adequate records?	TRANSCRIBE the credit or recognition of learning	Score Interpretation	How should the qualitative value of learning achievements be communicated to the student and to third parties?

cerning the basic rationale of experiential learning and how its assessment may ultimately affect higher education and the role it serves. All three frames of reference are represented in the three columns of Table 1.

The principal implication of Table 1 is that the critical issues in the assessment of experiential learning have parallels in day-to-day assessment practice, in psychometric literature, and in the broad educational issues of ultimate concern. This is no great surprise. If the six stages of assessment are in fact issues of practical significance, then they may be traced to larger, philosophical educational issues of current concern. Furthermore, if these stages of assessment are important in dealing with experiential learning, they probably represent fundamental technical issues in measurement that have not escaped the attention of specialists over the years. While Table 1 includes a number of problem areas, it may be viewed most simply as six issues from three vantage points. In the following paragraphs, each issue is discussed in turn.

The first issue concerns the question of what is creditable. The first practical step in assessing experiential learning is to determine what learning has taken place or is intended to take place. This turns out to be a good deal more complicated than it sounds. Frequently, the learning objectives of sponsored off-campus experiential programs are poorly defined. Perhaps it is assumed that a particular experiential activity has such obvious educational value that there is no need to specify intended learning outcomes in detail. There is merit in this argument and there are those who speak strongly against the trivialization of education through excessive preoccupation with detailed objectives (see Ebel, 1972, and Epperson and Schmuck, 1969). But the lack of clear learning objectives in an internship, for example, makes it difficult for students to channel their energies and difficult for faculty to know whether the experience was successful or not. Such lack of clarification is especially troublesome if learning involves limited faculty contact.

A much more difficult problem is faced by an adult reentering higher education who has the opportunity to petition for recognition of significant learning in work or other life experiences. This turns out to be an exceptionally difficult task for the individual but also one that can be uncommonly rewarding from an educational standpoint.

The main question at this stage of assessment is what does the learning actually consist of—what skills, knowledge, competencies? To measurement specialists, it is a problem of content validity: does the assessment focus upon appropriate substance? Whether the substance is appropriate frequently involves the question of whether a particular type of learning is creditable. There are many examples that are highly debated: dressmaking skill acquired at home, art appreciation based upon museum visits abroad, personnel management learned on the job, and so on. The same question applies to much learning in higher education. Whether such learning is creditable depends both on the depth of the learning and on the particular institutional program. Even though similar learning is included in the curriculum of hundreds of institutions, there seems to be a natural inclination to question whether learning is worthy of college credit when it is based on independent experience. Thus, on this point, assessment of experiential learning does not raise a new educational issue but rather dramatizes an old one—what is college-level credit?

The second issue involves the meaning of experiential learning. Even though student learning may be judged to be of college-level in character, most institutions would not regard that as a sufficient basis for awarding credit. Thus a second problem in this stage of assessment is to articulate such learning to the educational goals or academic degree of the student. This step is especially critical to individualized degree programs and in the conception of institutionally sponsored off-campus programs. From a practical standpoint, does prior learning based on life experience have to be identical to or merely equal to usual degree requirements in order to justify an award of credit? But the question of how closely experiential learning must match degree requirements is not simply a matter of reaching equitable decisions in individual cases. The larger educational issue at stake is whether crediting experiential learning and fostering such programs have the ultimate effect of changing the meaning of a B.A. degree.

It seems likely that different colleges line up differently on this issue. Some are interested in experiential learning primarily as an alternate means of recognizing competence in a traditional degree program; others wish to change the nature of the competence expected in students, and see the practical, goal-directed forms of learning common to independent activities and off-campus learning situations as means of effecting such change. The important point is that assessment should have the effect of emphasizing what the institution wants to emphasize. In measurement language, this corresponds partly to what is meant by construct validity—in this case, taking care that the procedures and underlying assumptions of the assessment are consistent with the objectives and philosophy of the institution.

The third issue focuses on adequate evidence of learning. Documenting the fact that the student has actually participated in a learning experience is a routine and frequently trivial step in assessment. In most instances where credit is awarded—when a passing grade is turned in to the registrar—we assume, among other things, that the student has participated in the course to the instructor's satisfaction. But in the case of awarding credit for independent learning prior to matriculation, documentation is an interesting and highly significant step in the assessment process. The basic issue centers on what constitutes satisfactory evidence of learning.

In presenting a petition for credit for learning prior to matriculation, the student is expected to document that petition with evidence of the learning claimed. There are many forms of documentation: some simply verify that the student has participated in a learning experience—for example, passport entries attesting to visits to countries in the Far East; other forms of documentation provide direct evidence of competence without revealing the experience that led to that competence—for example, a reprint of a published article; some documents do both—for example, a professional certificate may guarantee that the individual has participated in a particular training program and developed specific competencies.

The larger educational issue is whether credit should be based on experience or learning. The quick response from most quarters is that credit definitely should be based on evidence of learning, but the matter is ambiguous. Many colleges do in fact award credit for certain types of life experience per se. When they do, it is usually based on the assumption that there is an underlying surrogate variable that implies particular creditable learning outcomes. For example, some institutions give a certain amount of credit toward a particular degree for so much experience in a particular civil service position; additional credit might be awarded for having been promoted to a higher position. The surrogate variable here is the list of competencies assumed for those positions and the assessment process that presumably took place in making the original appointment and the subsequent promotion. Furthermore, as in traditional academic settings, it is frequently assumed that students acquire desirable learning outcomes when exposed to rich learning situations.

The problem, of course, is that the assumptions may not hold true. When one measure (experience) is used as a surrogate for another (learning), the critical measurement question is whether the surrogate really measures what one wants it to measure or only appears to do so. This is another aspect of construct validity that has been discussed in the psychometric literature as the problem of intrinsic validity (Gulliksen, 1950). From a practical standpoint, we need a much better basis for understanding the character of different types of documentation so that we can determine which types are more likely to have intrinsic validity. From a broader view, there is the question of the extent to which education should allow itself to depart from direct measures of learning. The competency-based educational movement is a major effort to focus both instruction and assessment on demonstrable skill and understanding rather than on accumulation of the credit hour which, as a surrogate variable, may represent timeserving more than acquisition.

The fourth issue concerns the problem of how to insure equity. In a practical program context, the next stage of assessment is that of measuring the actual extent of learning or level of competence for the various types of learning an experience may involve. Having already considered the appropriateness of the learning and the validity of the assessment process, we are here concerned primarily with the accuracy of measurement. This is the only stage of assessment that actually involves quantification, but quantification may ultimately amount to qualitative judgments of competence.

Since the measurement stage of assessing experiential learning is most often a matter of applying expert judgment, accuracy of assessment boils down to consistency of judgment—consistency from one judge to another, from time to time, or from department to department. When such judgments are inconsistent to an unacceptable degree, the assessment process is unfair to individual students. It is in this sense that the basic issue is one of equity. Of course, the measurement specialist calls it reliability, and there is a rich literature on the technology of estimating reliability and the techniques of improving the consistency of judgments (see, for example, Stanley, 1971).

Herein may lie the strategy for dealing with a puzzling broader issue. Many educators interested in the assessment of experiential learning are perplexed by the problem of improving the consistency of assessment without at the same time applying standardized methods of assessment. Diversity of experiential learning often precludes standardized instruments or approaches. There seems no alternative but to undertake a substantial effort to make the basic principles of applying expert judgment better known and to develop illustrative procedures and instruments that can be adapted to local circumstances and needs.

The fifth issue centers on the definition of standards. Evaluation is an especially important procedural step in assessing experiential learning—the term itself implies judging whether knowledge or skill meets an acceptable standard by determining how much credit or recognition is awarded. Evaluation is often intertwined with measuring, since measuring may simply involve comparing a student's accomplishment with previously determined standards; but measuring and evaluating are distinct stages in the sense that evaluation implies some judgment as to how much the learning is worth in academic currency.

Definition of standards is a key issue in reaching individual credit decisions, and there is a corresponding larger issue. When learning experiences differ widely, how can educational standards be publicly understood and maintained? In such circumstances, normative standards are obviously inappropriate; it is necessary to define criterion standards that describe individuals of different levels of accomplishment in different areas of competency. In a very general technical sense, this corresponds to the scaling problem in psychometric literature. In the actual application of assessing experiential learning, it is likely to be a matter of developing model procedures for reaching local consensus regarding the definition of levels of competence. Depending on the program and the context, such standards may be defined in reference to individual educational goals, institutional degree requirements, or standards imposed by an external agent such as an employer. Levels of competency thus defined become powerful instruments in helping students understand their learning goals and their own development and in determining whether diverse educational programs actually succeed in meeting intended objectives.

Finally, the sixth issue confronts the question of adequate records. The final stage in assessing experiential learning is to transcribe the credit or other appropriate description of the learning. Credit must be described to the student and on the student's permanent record in a way that communicates what it represents. Since experiential learning does not come with course labels, transcription becomes an important and unavoidable aspect of assessment.

There is also a very practical problem of efficiency. While each case may be unique in certain types of experiential learning, the transcription problem is not solved simply by depositing a unique case history in the student's folder. This is to ignore the transcription problem rather than deal with it. Such case histories become voluminous and thus may not be read. In routine circumstances, some form of narrative transcript is required, but how it can incorporate the substance of the learning within a reasonable format is not a simple problem to solve.

If we place this issue in a broader context and ask how such records are to be used, other problems become apparent. Third parties (for example, graduate and professional schools) are concerned not only with the nature of the learning and the fact that credit has been granted but also with the qualitative value of the learning achievement. Traditionally, this problem would fall in the general area of score interpretation. The narrative transcript is unlikely to provide scores, though it is very likely to be interpreted. The real problem is how to prepare the transcript so that it is a fair and usable record that minimizes the possibility of gross errors of interpretation.

These six issues are represented in Table 1 because each is especially connected with a particular stage in assessment. Two additional issues of great importance cut across all of the six steps previously described: those of cost and of the function of assessment.

As already noted, the highly individual character of much experiential learning often necessitates assessment tailored to the specific learning experience. As a consequence, a particular assessment technique may appear desirable from a technical and educational standpoint but may be quite unreasonable with respect to cost. Assessment needs to be cost-effective in its direct benefit to students, in its efficiency in institutional operation, and in its integrity and value for education generally. An added problem is the fact that cost realities are easy to overlook in experimental educational programs—either because special funds are available for initial support or because the enthusiasm of a new activity insures special faculty time commitments that are not likely to endure in routine programs involving large numbers of students.

Consequently, it is especially important to study carefully the cost implications of new methods of assessment lest developmental effort be expended needlessly on methods that prove unfeasible because of their expense. Such study should involve systematic identification of the basic parameters that differentiate assessment methods, the educational and psychometric strengths of each, the direct and indirect cost of each, the reasonable range of alternatives for approaching the assessment of various types of learning, and the most likely conditions under which different assessment methods might prove economically feasible. One should also consider practical cost analysis models that can be applied to operating assessment programs as one criterion for selecting assessment methods and as a basis for justifying the cost of assessment.

An even broader issue that bears upon all of those discussed thus far is the question of what values one wishes to emphasize in improving assessment. In this connection it is useful to distinguish two functions of assessment: the certifying function and the educative function. Improvement in both functions is badly needed. With respect to the certifying function, for example, there is a widely recognized need to support nontraditional education through encouragement and development of systematic and equitable means of determining what students know. This need is associated with such familiar problems as establishing credibility of programs, minimizing abuse of flexible credit policies, and insuring public recognition of credit granted. With respect to the educative function of assessment, there is the equally important problem of improving the value of assessment to the individual. From this perspective, self-assessment takes on special significance in helping to foster individual learning and aspiration, and in reinforcing individual acceptance of responsibility for learning. For these purposes, the results of assessment must give substantive information about personal development.

These two functions are to some extent in conflict. In the extreme case, for example, it is not possible to tailor assessment exclusively to the needs and characteristics of the individual student and at the same time to follow assessment procedures that are generally comparable across groups of students. Of course, insofar as possible, it is desirable to develop assessment approaches that serve both ends. Since a major goal of experiential learning is to improve the value of education for the individual, its assessment obviously must further that goal and at the same time develop confidence in the legitimacy of the learning. On the other hand, it is useful to distinguish which of these two functions one wishes to emphasize. Note, for example, that the cost of assessment takes on a different perspective if the primary emphasis is on enhancing the educative value of assessment. Thus, as assessment becomes more an inherent part of the instructional strategy, its cost is more properly viewed as an instructional cost.

This discussion of critical issues tends to leave a strong impression that assessment of experiential learning is much more an educational than a measurement process. This impression may result partly from the common misapprehension that traditional measurement of achievement is somehow not an educational process. Generally, however, assessing experiential learning does join assessment and learning in more fundamental ways than in traditional assessment practices. This educative emphasis is especially apparent in the extent to which assessment of experiential learning engages the student in the assessment process and forces examination of individual learning experiences.

Clearly, experiential learning involves an endless proliferation of different learning situations and combinations of content and educational goals. It is not feasible to consider developing specific instruments or techniques to fit an endless number of situations. By the same token, however, it is hardly warranted to throw up one's hands and say that educational diversity is inherently beyond the pale of generalizable good practice. While we cannot deal with these problems by developing routine measurement procedures and carrying out routine reliability and validity studies, other solutions are possible: we can develop prototypes and model procedures, suggest principles and desirable practices, systematically foster local applications and adaptations, provide demonstration studies, and encourage broad efforts in faculty development concerning these problems. These are some of the things that the CAEL Project is attempting to do through the development of a variety of experimental materials and the participation of a large number of institutions of higher education.

Details of the work done by CAEL are available in the substantial number of CAEL publications listed in Appendix A. The discussion of major issues in the assessment of experiential learning suggested that there is a parallel between practical steps in assessment and well-known principles in formal measurement literature. Consequently, the following discussion of basic requirements of sound assessment draws on both practice and theory. While the suggested requirements are directed to the problem of assessing experiential learning, they apply with almost equal force to assessment in the traditional classroom.

Basic Requirements

In considering sound assessment practices, it is useful first to consider briefly the general nature of the situation with which an educator is faced in assessing experiential learning. Whether through prior learning or learning in an institutionally sponsored program, the specific learning outcomes are likely to be quite diverse from student to student. Because of this diversity, by far the most common type of assessment is a flexible procedure that employs some form of holistic expert judgment, as is characteristic of interviews, supervisory ratings, or evaluation of essays and reports.

Such modes of assessment have the great advantage of readily tuning the assessment to the content of the learning, but the trade-off is an inherent subjectivity in assessment that can be hazardous. The problem is not with subjectivity per se, but rather with inconsistencies that may unconsciously enter in when judgments are based on a private process that is not easily communicated or trained. To the extent that there is looseness or ambiguity, assessment may lack equity from student to student, may lack educational benefit to the learner, and may lack ultimate educational value for all parties owing to eventual erosion in the credibility of the process.

Sound assessment depends, of course, on the professional expertise and judgment of individual faculty members. It may be useful, however, to outline some basic requirements in assessing experiential learning that are suggested by current good practice and by relevant principles that have developed in the measurement field over the years. These requirements are offered not as prescriptions, certainly, but as possibly useful ways of orienting oneself toward the problem of assessing experiential learning. The following suggestions concentrate on the measurement aspects of the problem rather than on such administrative questions as who should assess, how policy should be decided, or how programs ought to be organized.

1. Institutions should develop a policy that states the philosophical rationale for crediting experiential learning. One institution may be primarily interested in attracting older students by reducing artificial space and time barriers to education; another institution may wish to alter fundamentally the type of learning emphasized in a degree program. It is important to be clear about the rationale of such a basic orientation because it both determines and justifies much of what follows. If, for example, the institutional purpose is primarily to reduce space and time barriers, its credit policies might stress the need to identify learning comparable to specific traditional courses. If, on the other hand, the institutional purpose is to use

experiential learning in order to enhance the value of the learning experience to the individual, then comparability to existing courses may actually be an inhibiting requirement.

2. Institutions should develop a policy that states what general types of experiential learning are creditable. Individual institutions may or may not be willing to credit learning based on work experience, travel, volunteer activity, and the like. In fact, however, it is often more a matter of defining the conditions and restrictions under which such learning may be credited. Policy on this matter is much dependent on the basic orientation of an institution; policy needs to be stated here as well because the question of what is creditable is especially subject to confusion and controversy. Many institutions use an inductive approach to this problem, developing an informal set of guidelines of what the faculty considers creditable on the basis of experience. A deductive effort to identify the classes of knowledge and competence that ought to be creditable is perhaps more rational but undoubtedly a more imposing task.

3. Students should be required to differentiate clearly between learning and experience in requesting credit. Particularly in seeking credit for prior learning, the individual is prone to think of experiences and to have difficulty in identifying the actual competences acquired. It is one thing to seek credit for having done a lot of work for the League of Women Voters; it is another matter to have learned how to employ moderately sophisticated accounting methods in handling extensive financial dealings of a local chapter. Identifying the learning content is important because experience does not necessarily equal learning; furthermore, such identification is itself an important learning experience for the student.

4. Learning outcomes should be identified with enough specificity that they can be readily communicated. Broad learning skills like communication, analysis, or management are frequently useful in classifying learning outcomes but are not especially helpful in making clear what learning was accomplished. To say that a person has learned to communicate may mean many different things at different levels of competence. More specific description of learning is necessary if faculty and student are to know clearly what is to be learned and to recognize when learning has in fact taken place. Use-

ful descriptions of learning should make obvious what the student is able to do or how deeply her or his knowledge extends.

5. Institutions should develop policy concerning what types of experiential learning are creditable to what limits and in what programs. Institutions may adopt a variety of administratively inspired credit policies that are intended to put a premium on certain programs or to attract certain types of students. Such policies should also reflect an educational rationale concerning the substance of the learning and how it contributes to a properly balanced curriculum. For example, a specific number of hours of automatic credit for managing a business may attract older students, but if such learning makes a greater contribution to a management curriculum than to a liberal arts program, the credit policy should reflect that fact.

6. Institutions should require individuals petitioning for degree credit to specify satisfactorily how experiential learning contributes to the individual's degree program. It is commonly acknowledged that most people acquire a great deal of useful learning through life experience, but that learning is not necessarily relevant to a college degree—nor do most institutions recognize a responsibility to credit learning simply because it has occurred. Put more bluntly, critics argue that institutions are sometimes too inclined to credit learning that has little relevance to proper goals of higher education.

7. Institutions should develop routine procedures for determining periodically whether there is adequate agreement within the faculty as to what experiential learning is creditable. The only objective basis for evaluating whether assessment practices are following institutional policy is to determine whether faculty agree in the actual interpretation and implementation of that policy. It is one thing to agree verbally on a principle; it is another matter to show that two informed faculty members independently make similar judgments in evaluating learning for credit.

8. Institutions should develop general guidelines of what constitutes adequate documentation of learning. Some learning may require direct evidence such as an examination or actual observation of performance; in other instances, it may suffice to use indirect

methods like the testimony of a supervisor or verification that the individual has achieved some recognized status that ordinarily demands a given level of competence. Since not all documentation necessarily provides direct evidence of learning, documentation of different types of learning helps to insure quality control.

9. If indirect evidence of learning is accepted, periodic checks of the authenticity of such evidence should be made. For example, self-reports of occupational competences, while ordinarily quite accurate, are subject to careless reporting unless there is a periodic check to see that they are accurately matched by actual capability. If certificates or similar documentation are taken as evidence of specific competence, periodic checks should be undertaken to insure that the meaning of the certificate has not changed.

10. Assessment of experiential learning should be based on techniques that fit the character of the learning, especially its individuality. Some learning experiences are designed to develop specific competences, in which case a standard appraisal technique like an objective test is appropriate and desirable. Much experiential learning, however, is characterized by different learning outcomes for different individuals. In this case, more holistic methods of expert judgment are required to determine the value of individual learning outcomes. In either instance, assessments are not likely to be effective unless the degree of specificity of the assessment technique is tuned to the degree of specificity in the intended learning outcomes.

11. In evaluating an individual's learning, assessors should use techniques that are appropriate to the background and characteristics of the learner. For example, individuals from some subcultures may be handicapped by oral examination in a group situation; procedures that seem routine to an eighteen-year-old may put off a person who has run a business for thirty years. In part, achieving a valid assessment means avoiding methods that involve inherent biases against any particular individual.

12. The assessment process should be an integral part of the learning process. What a person gains from a learning situation is much dependent upon individual initiative, especially in the case of experiential learning. It is important that assessment goals be reflected in the learning activity and that learners understand the nature of the assessment process and what function it serves. An ap-

preciation of the purpose of assessment helps to reinforce a sense of the individual's responsibility for her or his own learning and a sense of mutual accountability with the faculty.

13. Experiential learning should be assessed with reference to criterion standards of what the individual should be able to do. For pedagogical as well as practical reasons, students involved in individualized experiential learning programs should be evaluated in terms of expected learning outcomes rather than purely on a competitive basis. In experiential learning, a clear statement of expected learning outcomes necessarily becomes the primary means of motivating learning and maintaining appropriate standards.

14. Whenever possible, criterion standards for particular learning outcomes should be stated at several levels of competence. In a pluralistic educational system, different individuals in different programs or institutions might quite rightly place their learning goals at different levels of competence. Thus, clearly specifying different levels of competence for a particular learning outcome serves not to standardize educational practice but to foster diverse standards that fit diverse educational objectives.

15. Where applicable, levels of competence required for awarding credit should be clearly defined. The standard of accomplishment necessary for credit is ordinarily defined by the institution, though in actual fact it may be determined largely by a third party such as an employer or by the student in an individualized program. In any event, the standard of performance expected should be understood by all parties in order to provide a valid basis for assessment. Furthermore, in sponsored experiential learning programs, it is important to clarify performance standards before the fact so that the student knows what is expected and so that the learning is guided accordingly.

16. The basis for translating learning outcomes into credit hours should be specified. There is a variety of approaches: credit hour equivalencies can be established for particular accomplishments, learning outcomes can be matched with existing courses, equivalent academic hours required to achieve the learning can be estimated, and so on. Formal guidelines are especially desirable in order to insure equity in awards. Another reason that these practices deserve close attention is the fact that the amount of credit

awarded becomes connected eventually with faculty compensation and institutional financing, both extremely important issues in the long-term viability of a program.

17. A complete description of institutional practices concerning assessment of experiential learning should be readily available. This document should include policies (for example, a description of the types of experiential learning that are creditable and how learning must be articulated with the student's degree program), as well as procedures (for example, how such learning is assessed and how credit is awarded). The purpose of such a document is not only to inform but also to foster consistency and to reassure all concerned that the process is rational and regulated.

18. Insofar as possible, the results of individual assessment should be objectively stated. Even though the assessment process may emphasize a subjective, holistic judgment, the outcome of the assessment should be as explicit as possible in identifying what specific learning outcomes were involved, what levels of competence were reached, what standards were employed, and what basis was used to award credit. Even the simplest forms of measurement (categorization, rank ordering) can be extremely useful in making assessment a more objective process. Objectivity not only fosters accurate assessment and minimizes misinterpretation, it also facilitates quality control of the assessment process itself by making it possible to compare assessments and to determine how they were reached.

19. The results of assessment should be sufficiently consistent to insure equity to individual students. Institutions should insure that generally comparable assessment procedures are employed, that assessors are properly trained, and that the faculty is sensitive to the need for consistent judgments concerning levels of competence displayed and amount of credit awarded. Institutions must guard against the tendency to allow assessment to be inconsistent in policy or practice or to award the amount of credit on the basis of the disposition of the assessor rather than on the competence of the student.

20. Institutions should establish routine procedures for monitoring the consistency of assessment outcomes. Periodically, repeated independent assessments of the same records can identify undesir-

able discrepancies from one assessor to another or imperceptible drift in the way learning is evaluated. It is only through such routine checks that an institution can adequately guard against unconscious but systematic bias from assessor to assessor, department to department, or term to term.

21. Feedback to students concerning the outcome of assessment should foster learning and personal development. If assessment is to help the individual, it needs to be tied to his or her learning, both backward and forward in time—backward to the prior learning objectives and forward to new learning possibilities. An important outcome of assessment should be increased student awareness of the implications of new competencies and new options that may consequently be available. Assessment should facilitate a sense of personal progress and contribute in its own right to the learning experience.

22. The permanent record of the student should communicate effectively to third parties. Employers and graduate and professional schools must be able to understand the content of learning (what competence or knowledge was involved) and to judge reliably the level of learning credited. Understanding content of learning suggests a need for narration on the transcript; understanding the level or depth of learning suggests a need for some appropriate form of quantification or categorization. Well-defined criterion standards of performance can help to serve both ends if levels of competence are differentiated clearly.

23. Finally, basic requirements of sound practice in assessing experiential learning should not be sacrificed merely because they seem superficially more expensive than traditional assessment procedures. This is not to say that cost considerations should be ignored, but rather that cost-benefit should be emphasized. Frequently, good practice in assessing experiential learning is costly because it overlaps considerably with the learning or instructional process. Rather than separating assessment and instruction artificially, institutions might better seek ways to integrate the two, both with respect to substance and cost allocation.

Perhaps it is unnecessary at this point to reemphasize that experiential learning is an integral part of higher education, not an appendage or a transitory interest. Most of the issues raised in this volume apply equally well to classroom learning and off-campus learning. The experiential learning movement can and should have significant impact on traditional pedagogy. Similarly, while the assessment issues addressed in this chapter are dramatized by the advent of new external forms of learning, they also apply to much traditional assessment both in and outside the classroom. While it is legitimate to expect that credit awarded through experimental programs should be carefully justified, that is no excuse for a double standard either in the learning expected of students or in the rigor of the assessment process.

Indeed, the issues addressed here represent a challenge to higher education generally. Most institutions are much in need of improved methods of assessing student achievement that take fully into account the individual character of students and their learning experiences. It is reasonable to expect that development of improved means of assessing experiential learning will have corresponding benefit for all higher education, and that requirements such as those suggested here have their corollary, if not direct application, in the traditional classroom.

░░

Current CAEL Publications

░░

CAEL Working Paper No. 1 *Current Practices in the Assessment of Experiential Learning* is a paper which reports on the survey and site visits conducted by the CAEL project in the Spring of 1974. Prepared by Warren W. Willingham, Richard Burns, and Thomas Donlon.

A Compendium of Assessment Techniques brings your attention to various techniques and methods that have potential for assessing experiential learning. The paper was originally produced as CAEL Working Paper No. 2 and has now been reprinted as a final publication. Prepared by Joan E. Knapp and Amiel Sharon.

CAEL Working Paper No. 3 *"Reflections on Experiential Learning and Its Uses"* is a collection of selected papers from the first CAEL Assembly Meeting including a commentary by the chairman of the CAEL Steering Committee, first versions of the chapters by Melvin Tumin and James S. Coleman in the present book, and

245

comments by Virginia B. Smith from which the Foreword to this book was adapted.

CAEL Working Paper No. 4 *The Learning and Assessment of Interpersonal Skills: Guidelines for Administrators and Faculty* suggests procedures for (1) identifying and categorizing interpersonal skills, (2) articulating them to student's goals, (3) discovering and utilizing experiential situations in which interpersonal skills can be acquired and sharpened, and (4) assessing the learning of interpersonal skills for purposes of granting academic credit. Prepared by Paul Breen, Thomas Donlon, and Urban G. Whitaker.

CAEL Working Paper No. 5 *The Learning and Assessment of Interpersonal Skills: Guidelines for Students* is the student version of Working Paper No. 4. Prepared by Paul Breen, Thomas Donlon, and Urban G. Whitaker.

CAEL Working Paper No. 6 *A Guide for Assessing Prior Experience Through Portfolios* presents an eight-stage framework for portfolio assessment and describes practical procedural alternatives for each stage. Sample institutional materials are included in the Appendix. Prepared by Joan E. Knapp.

CAEL Working Paper No. 7 *A Student Handbook for Preparing a Portfolio for the Assessment of Prior Experiential Learning* takes the reader step-by-step through the process of identifying learning outcomes, relating them to educational goals, documenting experience, measuring learning outcomes, and requesting credit or recognition. Prepared by Aubrey Forrest.

CAEL Working Paper No. 8 *A Task-Based Model for Assessing Work Experience* presents a generalizable model for assessing and crediting specific competencies acquired in occupational fields. The paper describes the application of the model to three very different fields (data processing, law enforcement, and secretarial science) and includes a section on how to apply the model to other occupations. Prepared by Amiel Sharon.

CAEL Working Paper No. 9 *A Student Guide to Learning Through College-Sponsored Work Experience* is designed to help students plan and integrate the learning derived from college-sponsored work programs into their ongoing academic programs. It is organized around eleven basic steps and includes useful checklists and worksheets. Prepared by Hadley Nesbitt.

CAEL Working Paper No. 10 *The Use of Expert Judgment in the Assessment of Experiential Learning* discusses problems, principles, and procedures in using expert judgment in interviewing, product assessment, performance assessment, and the assessment of free-response written materials. Alternative approaches and models are described. Prepared by Richard Reilly.

Institutional Report No. 1 *The Use of Expert Judgment in the Assessment of Demonstrated Learning in the Antioch College Yellow Springs Adult Degree Completion Program* is a report prepared at Antioch College in Yellow Springs with major emphasis on faculty workshops on evaluation of demonstrated learning. Prepared by Robert Lewis.

Institutional Report No. 2 *Interpersonal Learning in an Academic Setting: Theory and Practice* is a report prepared at Empire State College with major emphasis on the incorporation of interpersonal learning into the formal educative process. Prepared by Lois Lamdin and Miriam Tatzel.

Institutional Report No. 3 *Evaluation and Expert Judgment* is a report prepared at the University of California at Los Angeles with major emphasis on the identification of competencies, identification of expert judges, assessment procedures, development of guidelines. Prepared by Jane Permaul.

Institutional Report No. 4 *The Refinement and Modification of an Instrument for Assessing the Achievement of Interpersonal Skills of Social Work Students* is a report prepared at Wayne State University with major emphasis being the application of a checklist for assessing performance in field work practicum. Prepared by Kurt Spitzer.

Institutional Report No. 5 *Guidelines and Procedures for the Assessment of Experiential Learning and for the Selection of Training of Field Experts* describes how William Rainey Harper College established tentative procedures for assessing the non-sponsored experiential learning of students applying to the Associate in Liberal Studies Program. Prepared by Frank Christensen.

Contents of CAEL *Resource Book-Volume I* includes Institutional Annotations, Agency Annotations, and Literary Annotations;

loose-leaf, three-hole punched for convenient housing in a binder. Includes *Assembly Directory*.

CAEL *Assembly Directory* is a list of current members including official representatives and addresses.

Interpersonal Skills: An Analytical Framework (Tape/Slide Presentation #IPS-1) An adaptation of Sidney Fine's theory of human performance applied to the learning and assessment of interpersonal skills by Paul Breen and Urban G. Whitaker at San Francisco State University. Includes charts, diagrams, case studies and examples both for prior learning and sponsored experiential learning. This *tape/slide presentation* is useful either as an introduction to CAEL Working Papers 4 and 5 or independently for classes and in-service programs in the human services or other areas concerned about concepts in the interpersonal domain. Especially helpful in curriculum planning, faculty development programs, advising and counseling, career education, and as background for the development of assessment techniques. 160 color slides, 32 minute audio tape synchronized for use with Wollensak Cassette system and slide projector. Instructions included.

Interpersonal Literacy (Tape/Slide Presentation #IPS-2) Identifies and illustrates the role of sociocultural variables and affective qualities which influence choices of communicative behavior. Develops the concept of interpersonal literacy as "knowing when and how to communicate what to whom in order to achieve specified goals." Developed by Paul Breen and Urban G. Whitaker at San Francisco State University as a special project for CAEL. Useful either with Working Papers 4 and 5 or independently for students, faculty, or others interested in basic concepts of interpersonal communication. 90 color slides, 14 minute audio tape synchronized for use with Wollensak Cassette system and slide projector. Instructions included.

These materials are available at cost from CAEL Publications, Educational Testing Service, Princeton, New Jersey 08540.

~~~~~~

CAEL Committees

~~~~~~

Executive Committee

George Ayers, vice president and dean for academic affairs, Metropolitan State University (since September 1975)

Barbara A. Barbato, director, Contract Center, Webster College (since September 1975)

Sheila C. Gordon, associate dean, Division of Cooperative Education, LaGuardia Community College (since September 1975)

Morris T. Keeton, acting president and provost, Antioch College (since November 1975), *Chairperson*

Jules Pagano, dean, Community Affairs Area, Florida International University, *Vice Chairperson*

Peter Smith, president, Community College of Vermont, *Secretary*

Steering Committee

Richard J. Allen, director, Division of Arts and Sciences, The Johns Hopkins University Evening Campus (since September 1975)

249

George Ayers, vice president and dean for academic affairs, Metropolitan State University

Barbara A. Barbato, director, Contract Center, Webster College

Neal A. Berte, vice president for educational development, and dean, New College, University of Alabama (through January 1976); president, Birmingham Southern University (since February 1976)

James D. Brown, Jr., president, Thomas A. Edison College

Anne-Marie Carroll, staff associate, Massachusetts State College System (through September 1975)

Arthur W. Chickering, vice president, Empire State College

Hortense Dixon, vice president for urban programming, Texas Southern University

John S. Duley, director, Field Experience Program, Justin Morrill College, Michigan State University (since September 1975)

Shelia C. Gordon, associate dean, Division of Cooperative Education, LaGuardia Community College (since September 1975)

Cyril O. Houle, professor of education, The University of Chicago

Morris T. Keeton, acting president and provost, Antioch College, *Chairperson*

Winton H. Manning, vice president, development, Educational Testing Service

Jules O. Pagano, dean, Community Affairs Area, Florida International University, *Vice Chairperson*

Jean M. Pennington, director, Continuing Education for Women, Washington University

David H. Provost, state university dean, New Program Development and Evaluation, California State University and Colleges

Gilberto de los Santos, dean of instructional development, El Paso Community College

Herman B. Smith, Office for Advancement of Public Negro Colleges, National Association of State Universities and Land-Grant Colleges (1974)

Peter B. Smith, president, Community College of Vermont, *Secretary*

David Sweet, president, Metropolitan State University (1974)

William G. Thomas, chancellor, Johnston College, University of Redlands

Implementation Committee

Richard L. Burns, director, college and university programs, Educational Testing Service

Ruth D. Churchill, dean for educational evaluation, Antioch College

Laurent Daloz, director of learning services, Community College of Vermont

Arnold Fletcher, vice president for academic affairs, Thomas A. Edison College

Aubrey Forrest, dean of assessment, Metropolitan State University, *Chairperson*

Myrna R. Miller, assessment specialist, Community College of Vermont

Joseph R. Palladino, dean, Continuing Education, and director, external degree program, Framingham State College

Dabney Park, Jr., director, external degree program, Florida International University

Jose R. Rivera, director, University Year for Action, El Paso Community College

Bernard J. Sloan, associate dean, New College, The University of Alabama

Urban G. Whitaker, dean, undergraduate studies, San Francisco State University, *Vice Chairperson*

Warren W. Willingham, executive director, program research, Educational Testing Service, *Project Director*

Bibliography

Accrediting Commission for Senior Colleges and Universities of the Western Association of Schools and Colleges. *Guidelines on Undergraduate Credit*. Oakland, Ca.: Accrediting Commission, 1974.

Accrediting Commission for Senior Colleges and Universities of the Western Association of Schools and Colleges. *Interim Statement on Credit for Prior Learning Experience*. Oakland, Ca.: Accrediting Commission, 1974.

ADLER, A., *Understanding Human Nature*. Philadelphia: Chilton, 1927.

ALLPORT, G. W. *Pattern and Growth in Personality*. New York: Holt, Rinehart and Winston, 1961.

An Early View of the Land-Grant Colleges. Urbana: University of Illinois Press, 1967.

ANGYAL, A. *Foundations for a Science of Personality*. New York: The Commonwealth Fund, 1941.

253

ANSBACHER, H. L., AND ANSBACHER, R. R. *The Individual Psychology of Alfred Adler.* New York: Basic Books, 1956.

ARGYRIS, C., AND SCHON, D. A. *Theory in Practice: Increasing Professional Effectiveness.* San Francisco: Jossey-Bass, 1974.

BAILEY, S. "Flexible Time-Space Programs: A Plea for Caution." In D. Vermilye (Ed.), *The Expanded Campus.* San Francisco: Jossey-Bass, 1972.

BAINES, T. R. "The Faculty Supervisor." In J. Duley (Ed.), *New Directions for Higher Education: Implementing Field Experience Education,* no. 6. San Francisco: Jossey-Bass, 1974.

BERG, I. *Education and Jobs: The Great Training Robbery.* New York: Praeger, 1970.

BLOOM, B. S., AND OTHERS. *Taxonomy of Educational Objectives, Handbook I: Cognitive Domain.* New York: Longmans Green, 1956.

BLOOM, B. S., HASTINGS, J. T., MADAUS, G. F. *Handbook on Formative and Summative Evaluation of Student Learning.* New York: McGraw-Hill, 1971.

BOWEN, H., AND DOUGLASS, G. *Efficiency in Liberal Education.* Berkeley, Ca.: Carnegie Commission on Higher Education, 1971.

BREEN, P., DONLON, T., AND WHITAKER, U. *The Learning and Assessment of Interpersonal Skills: Guidelines for Administrators and Faculty.* CAEL Working Paper No. 4. Princeton, N.J.: Educational Testing Service, 1975.

BRUNER, J. S. *The Process of Education.* Cambridge: Harvard University Press, 1961.

BRUNER, J. S. *Toward a Theory of Instruction.* New York: Norton, 1966.

Carnegie Commission on Higher Education. *Higher Education: Who Pays? Who Benefits? Who Should Pay?* Berkeley, Ca.: Carnegie Commission on Higher Education, 1973.

CHICKERING, A. W. "Institutional Differences and Student Characteristics." *Journal of the American College Health Association,* Dec. 1966, *15,* 168–181.

CHICKERING, A. W. *Education and Identity.* San Francisco: Jossey-Bass, 1969.

CHICKERING, A. W., AND MC CORMICK, J. "Personality Development and the College Experience." *Research in Higher Education,* 1973, *1,* 43–70.

CHICKERING, A. W., MC DOWELL, J., AND CAMPAGNA, D. "Institutional

Differences and Student Development." *Journal of Educational Psychology,* 1969, *60,* 315–326.

COLEMAN, J. S., AND OTHERS. "The Hopkins Games Program: Conclusions from Seven Years of Research." *Educational Researcher,* Aug. 1973, *2,* 3–7.

COLLIER, G., WILSON, J., AND TOMLINSON, P. *Values and Moral Development in Higher Education.* New York: Wiley, 1974.

CROSS, K. P., VALLEY, J. P., AND ASSOCIATES. *Planning Non-Traditional Programs: An Analysis of the Issues for Postsecondary Education.* San Francisco: Jossey-Bass, 1974.

DEWEY, J. *The School and Society.* Chicago: The University of Chicago Press, 1902.

DEWEY, J. *Interest and Effort in Education.* Boston: Houghton Mifflin, 1913.

DEWEY, J. *Human Nature and Conduct.* New York: Modern Library, 1957.

DEWEY, J. *The Child and the Curriculum.* Chicago: The University of Chicago Press, 1958.

DEWEY, J. *Democracy and Education.* New York: Macmillan, 1961.

DULEY, J. "Cross-cultural Field Study." In J. Duley (Ed.), *New Directions for Higher Education: Implementing Field Experience Education,* No. 6. San Francisco: Jossey-Bass, 1974.

EBEL, R. L. *Evaluation and Educational Objectives—Behavioral and Otherwise.* Paper presented at the annual convention of the American Psychological Association. Honolulu, Hawaii, Sept. 5, 1972.

EISENDRATH, C., AND COTTLE, T. *Out of Discontent: Visions of the Contemporary University.* Cambridge, Mass.: Schenkman, 1972.

Empire State College. *Ten Out of Thirty.* Saratoga Springs, N.Y.: ESC, 1973.

EPPERSON, D. C., AND SCHMUCK, R. A. "A Critique of Programmed Instruction." In D. Vandenberg (Ed.), *Teaching and Learning.* Urbana: University of Illinois Press, 1969.

ERIKSON, E. *Childhood and Society.* New York: Norton, 1950.

ERIKSON, E. "Identity and the Life Cycle." In G. S. Klein (Ed.), *Psychological Issues.* New York: International University Press, 1959.

ERIKSON, E. *Insight and Responsibility.* New York: Norton, 1964.

Federation of Regional Accrediting Commissions of Higher Education. *Interim Statement on Accreditation and Non-Traditional Study.* Washington, D.C.: FRACHE, 1973.

FELDMAN, K. A., AND NEWCOMB, T. M. *The Impact of College on Students.* San Francisco: Jossey-Bass, 1969.

FINE, S. A. *Nature of Skill: Implications for Education and Training.* Washington, D.C.: W. E. Upjohn Institute for Employment Research, 1970.

FOOTE, N. N., AND COTTRELL, L. S., JR. *Identity and Interpersonal Competence.* Chicago: The University of Chicago Press, 1955.

FORREST, A. *A Student Handbook for Preparing a Portfolio for the Assessment of Prior Experiential Learning.* CAEL Working Paper No. 7. Princeton, N.J.: Educational Testing Service, 1975.

FORREST, A., FERGUSON, R. J., AND COLE, N. S. "The Narrative Transcript: An Overview." *Educational Record,* Winter 1975, *56,* 59–65.

GILFORD, D. "Statistical Snapshot of Adult Continuing Education." *Journal of Higher Education,* July/Aug. 1975. *XLVI,* 409–426.

GOFFMAN, E. *Asylums.* Garden City, New York: Anchor, 1961.

GOULD, R. L. "The Phases of Adult Life: A Study in Developmental Psychology. *The American Journal of Psychiatry,* Nov. 1972, *129,* 521–531.

GREER, C. *The Great School Legend.* New York: Basic Books, 1973.

GROESBECK, B. "Admissions from Non-Traditional Colleges." *College and University,* 1975 *50*(4), 479–482.

GULLIKSEN, H. "Intrinsic Validity." *American Psychologist,* Oct. 1950, *5,* 511–517.

HALL, J. C. "A History of Special Baccalaureate Programs for Adults, 1945–1970." Mimeographed. Chicago: Roosevelt University, 1975.

HARVEY, O. J., HUNT, D., AND SCHROEDER, D. *Conceptual Systems.* New York: Wiley, 1961.

HEATH, D. H. *Growing Up in College: Liberal Education and Maturity.* San Francisco: Jossey-Bass, 1968.

HERSEY, P., AND BLANCHARD, K. *Management of Organizational Behavior.* Englewood Cliffs, N.J.: Prentice-Hall, 1972.

HESBURGH, T. M., AND OTHERS. *Patterns for Lifelong Learning.* San Francisco: Jossey-Bass, 1973.

HEYDINGER, R. *The Assessment of Student Performance: A Model and the Reforms.* Report to 30th National Conference on Higher Education. Chicago, Mar. 25, 1975.

HIGHET, G. *The Art of Teaching.* New York: Knopf, 1950.

HOULE, C. O. *The External Degree.* San Francisco: Jossey-Bass, 1973.

JENCKS, C., AND OTHERS. *Inequality: A Reassessment of the Effects of Family and Schooling in America.* New York: Basic Books, 1972.

KATZ, J., AND OTHERS. *No Time for Youth: Growth and Constraint in College Students.* San Francisco: Jossey-Bass, 1968.

KEETON, M. (Ed.) *Reflections on Experiential Learning and Its Uses.* CAEL Working Paper No. 3. Princeton, N.J.: Educational Testing Service, 1974.

KIDDER, S. J. *Instruction-Learning-Gaming: Theory.* Paper presented at the annual meeting of the American Sociological Association. Montreal, Aug. 1974.

KLUTZNICK, P. M. *The Management and Financing of Colleges.* New York: Committee for Economic Development, 1973.

KNAPP, J. *A Guide for Assessing Prior Experience Through Portfolios.* CAEL Working Paper No. 6. Princeton, N. J.: Educational Testing Service, 1975.

KNAPP, J., AND SHARON, A. *A Compendium of Assessment Techniques.* CAEL Working Paper No. 2. Princeton, N.J.: Educational Testing Service, 1974.

KOHLBERG, L. "Stages of Moral Development as a Basis for Moral Education." In C. Beck and E. Sullivan (Eds.), *Moral Education.* Toronto: University of Toronto Press, 1970.

KOHLBERG, L. "The Concepts of Developmental Psychology as the Central Guide to Education: Examples from Cognitive, Moral, and Psychological Education." In M. C. Reynolds (Ed.), *Proceedings of the Conference on Psychology and the Process of Schooling in the Next Decade: Alternative Conceptions.* Washington, D.C.: Bureau for Educational Personnel Development, U.S. Office of Education, 1973.

KOHLBERG, L., AND MAYER, R. "Development as the Aim of Education." *Harvard Educational Review,* Nov. 1972, *42,* 449–496.

KRACKE, E. *Encyclopaedia Britannica,* XXI (1972), 425.

LASKER, H. M. "Stage and Style: Developmental Perspective on Learning Environments." Mimeographed. Cambridge, Mass.: Harvard Graduate School of Education, 1975.

LEVINSON, D. J., AND OTHERS. "The Psychosocial Development of Men in Early Adulthood and the Mid-life Transition." In D. Ricks, A. Thomas, and M. Rooff (Eds.), *Life History Research in Psychopathology.* Minneapolis: University of Minnesota Press, 1974.

LOEVINGER, J., AND WESSLER, R. *Measuring Ego Development: Con-*

struction and Use of a Sentence Completion Test. Vol. 1. San Francisco: Jossey-Bass, 1970.

LORD, R. *The Agrarian Revival.* New York: American Association for Adult Education, 1939.

MAEROFF, G. "More in High School Doing College Work." *New York Times,* June 1, 1975, *1*, 36.

MEDSKER, L., AND OTHERS. *Extending Opportunities for a College Degree: Practices, Problems, and Potentials.* Berkeley, Ca.: Center for Research and Development in Higher Education, 1975.

MEYER, P. *Awarding College Credit for Non-College Learning: A Guide to Current Practices.* San Francisco: Jossey-Bass, 1975.

MICKEY, B. "Designing the External Degree Program." *Journal of Higher Education,* June 1973, *44*, 453–461.

MILL, J. S. *Dissertations and Discussions.* Vol. IV. New York: Henry Holt, 1874.

MILLER, G. A., GALANTER, E., AND PRIBRAM, K. H. *Plans and the Structure of Behavior.* New York: Holt, Rinehart and Winston, 1960.

MILLER, J. W., AND SULLIVAN, E. J. *Guide to the Evaluation of Educational Experiences in the Armed Services.* 1974 Edition. Washington, D.C.: American Council on Education, 1975.

MUSHKIN, S. J. *Recurrent Education.* Washington, D.C.: National Institute of Education, 1973.

National Commission on the Financing of Postsecondary Education, D. E. Leonard, Chrm. *Financing Postsecondary Education in the United States.* Washington, D.C.: U.S. Government Printing Office, 1973.

National Commission on the Financing of Postsecondary Education, D. Carlson, Chrm. *A Framework for Analyzing Postsecondary Education Financing Policies.* Washington, D.C.: U.S. Government Printing Office, 1974.

NEUGARTEN, B. L. "A Developmental View of Adult Personality." In J. Birren (Ed.), *Relations of Development and Aging.* Springfield, Ill.: Thomas, 1963.

NEUGARTEN, B. L. *Dynamics of Transition of Middle Age to Old Age, Adaptation and the Life Cycle.* Presented at an interdisciplinary meeting of the Boston Society for Gerontologic Psychiatry, Dec. 6, 1969.

NEWMAN, F., AND OTHERS. *The Second Newman Report: National Policy and Higher Education.* Cambridge, Mass.: M.I.T. Press, 1973.

OSLER, W. *Aequanimitas,* London: Lewis, 1906.

PECK, R. F., AND HAVIGHURST, R. J. *The Psychology of Character Development.* New York: Wiley, 1960.

PERRY, W. G. *Forms of Intellectual and Ethical Development in the College Years.* New York: Holt, Rinehart and Winston, 1970.

REILLY, R., AND OTHERS. *The Use of Expert Judgment in the Assessment of Experiential Learning.* CAEL Working Paper No. 10. Princeton, N.J.: Educational Testing Service, 1975.

RIESSMAN, F. "The Strategy of Style." In F. Riessman (Ed.), *Strategies Against Poverty.* New York: Random House, 1969.

ROGERS, C. R. *On Becoming a Person.* Boston: Houghton Mifflin, 1961.

RUYLE, J., AND GEISELMAN, L. A. "Non-Traditional Opportunities and Programs." In K. P. Cross and J. R. Valley (Eds.), *Planning Non-Traditional Programs: An Analysis of the Issues for Postsecondary Education.* San Francisco: Jossey-Bass, 1974.

SANSBURY, D. L., AND OTHERS. "Evaluation of University Year for ACTION." Duplicated report. Washington, D.C.: School of Education, American University, 1975.

SCARNE, J. *Complete Guide to Gambling.* New York: Simon and Schuster, 1961.

SCOTT, W. "Chivalry." *Encyclopaedia Britannica,* Supplement, IV, (1824), 129.

SHEEHY, G. "Catch-30." *New York Magazine,* 1974, *7,* 30–44.

STANLEY, J. C. "Reliability." In R. L. Thorndike (Ed.), *Educational Measurement* (2nd Ed.). Washington, D.C.: American Council on Education, 1971.

STERN, G. G. *People in Context: Measuring Person-Environment Congruence in Education and Industry.* New York: Wiley, 1970.

STEVENSON, A. E. "Our Ramparts Are . . . Here." *Syracuse University Alumni News,* 1963, *45,* 24.

SULLIVAN, C., GRANT, M. Q., AND GRANT, J. D. "The Development of Interpersonal Maturity: Application to Delinquency." In O. S. English, *Introduction to Psychiatry,* 2nd ed. New York: Norton, 1957.

SUSSMAN, MARVIN, B. "Family Systems in the 1970's: Analysis, Policies, and Programs." *Annals of the American Academy of Political and Social Science,* July 1971, *396,* 40–56.

SZASZ, T. S. "Some Observations on the Relationship Between Psychiatry and the Law." *A.M.A. Archives of Neurology and Psychiatry,* 1956, *75,* 297–315.

"Toward a Federal Strategy for Protection of the Consumer of Education." Washington, D.C.: Federal Interagency Committee on Education, 1975.

TRASK, A. E. "Academic Credit for Community Service Learning." *Findings,* Nov. 1975, *11,* 3.

TRIVETT, D. A. *Academic Credit for Prior Off-Campus Learning.* Report to American Association for Higher Education, Washington, D.C.: 1975.

TRUE, A. C. *A History of Agricultural Education in the United States.* U.S. Department of Agriculture Miscellaneous Publication No. 36. Washington, D.C.: Government Printing Office, 1929.

VAN AALST, F. D. "Program Design." *New Direction for Higher Education,* Summer 1974, *6,* 69.

VANDEN DAELE, L. "A Developmental Study of the Ego-ideal." *Genetic Psychology Monographs,* 1968, *78,* 191–256.

WARREN, J. "External Degrees: Coping with the Problems of Credit." *Journal of Higher Education,* June 1973, *44,* 466.

WEATHERSBY, G. "A Broad View of Individual Demand for Postsecondary Education, Major Policy Issues." In *Postsecondary Educational Issues: Visible Question, Invisible Answers.* Boulder, Colo.: WICHE/NCHEMS, 1974a.

WEATHERSBY, G. *The New Learners.* Paper presented at the Kansas State University Conference on the New Learners: Challenge to Higher Education, Dec. 1974b.

WHITE, R. W. "Sense of Interpersonal Competence: Two Case Studies and Some Reflections on Origins." In R. W. White (Ed.), *The Study of Lives.* New York: Atherton Press, 1963.

WHITE, R. W. *Lives in Progress.* New York: Holt, Rinehart and Winston, 1966.

WILLINGHAM, W., BURNS, R., AND DONLON, T. *Current Practices in the Assessment of Experiential Learning.* CAEL Working Paper No. 1. Princeton, N.J.: Educational Testing Service, 1974.

WITKIN, H. A. *The Role of Cognitive Style in Academic Performance and in Teacher-Student Relations.* Paper presented at the Graduate Records Examinations Board Invitational Conference on Cognitive Styles on Creativity in Higher Education, Montreal, 1972.

Index

261